MARX'S PROLETARIAT:
THE MAKING OF A MYTH

MARX'S PROLETARIAT
THE MAKING OF A MYTH

DAVID W. LOVELL

ROUTLEDGE
London and New York

First published in 1988 by
Routledge
a division of Routledge, Chapman and Hall
11 New Fetter Lane, London EC4P 4EE

Published in the USA by
Routledge
a division of Routledge, Chapman and Hall, Inc.
29 West 35th Street, New York NY 10001

© 1988 David W. Lovell

Printed in Great Britain by
Billing & Sons Ltd, Worcester

British Library Cataloguing in Publication Data

Lovell, David W.
    Marx's proletariat: the making of a myth.
    1. Economics. Marx, Karl, 1818-1883 —
    Critical studies
    I. Title
    335.4'092'4
    ISBN 0-415-00116-1

Library of Congress Cataloging-in-Publication Data
ISBN 0-415-00116-1

Contents

for Christopher

Preface

George Orwell wrote in his *Nineteen Eighty-Four* that 'If there is hope, it lies in the proles'. A century earlier, Marx was unequivocal: the future belonged to the proletariat. Today we might wonder at such confidence. The proletariat has yet to fulfil Marx's expectations, and seems unlikely ever to do so. Parties acting in its name, however, have helped to dim our hopes and to debase his theory. In the work before you, I have explored the origins of what Raymond Aron, in his *The Opium of the Intellectuals*, appropriately called 'the myth of the proletariat'.

How could Marx have entertained the notion that the proletariat would emancipate humanity from capitalism and from class rule itself? By examining the sources and development of his concept of the proletariat, I contend that it was a significant departure in socialist thought—which had generally relied on class unity as the solution to the 'social problem'—and a crucial element in the elaboration of Marx's theory. I also suggest that not only may Marx have been mistaken in attributing to the nineteenth century proletariat qualities and actions which betokened the momentous role he assigned to it, but that his vision of communism may be compromised for more fundamental reasons. Although there are hints in his work of a positive conception, Marx's proletariat is chiefly the class of suffering, not of freedom; historically, the proletariat has often preferred security to enterprise.

Built into the structure of this inquiry is the assumption that there was a progression in Marx's work from conceptual to political to economic categories; I document this progression in relation to his proletariat. In the continuing debate over 'How many Marxes?' this notion posits a basic continuity while not neglecting the importance of change. Another feature of the work is its discussion of Marx's conception of universality, which I contrast with Hegel's. Both Marx and Hegel, it seems to me, attempted to understand the conditions in which man can feel himself to be part of one community rather than an isolated individual. Hegel believed that particularity and universality must coexist and be mediated to provide for man's self-identity as well as his need for community. Marx's concept of universality, as the transcendence of particularity, does not allow for the conflicting demands of self-definition and belonging. It means not just a simplified theoretical solution to a complex problem, but an inability on his part to recognize and value man's attempts at self-definition in spiritual, national, occupational or other terms. I find Marx's vision of the universal man neither attractive nor desirable.

This work began as a Doctoral Dissertation in the History of Ideas Unit of the Institute of Advanced Studies in the Australian National University. I learned a great deal from, and owe an especial debt to Professor Eugene Kamenka and Dr Bob Brown, who impressed upon me the virtues of clear thinking and lucid writing about even the most difficult concepts. May they judge their efforts not to have been in vain. The influence of Professor Kamenka will no doubt be apparent; I hope that he will not be blamed too much for the result, for which I alone am responsible. I also wish to acknowledge a Special Research Grant from the Faculty of Military Studies of the University of New South Wales (now the University College of the UNSW), which enabled me to work in France during part of 1985 gathering information on early French socialism to supplement the analysis I had begun in Chapter Three. I am happy to acknowledge a subsidy from the Australian National University towards publication of this book. Thanks must also go to Brett Lodge and Alvaro Ascui, for help with the basic and sometimes finer points of word processing.

The constant support of my wife Sue, made the writing of this work a less lonely task; I dedicate it to my son Christopher.

DAVID W. LOVELL

Canberra,
October 1987

Citations and Abbreviations

The *Bibliography of Works Cited*, at the end of the text, indicates the editions used; page references are to these editions. Note numbers in the text are raised; the *Notes* are also to be found at the end of the text.

I have used the following abbreviations for works frequently cited in the text:

C—Marx: *Capital*, vols. I–III, Progress Publishers, Moscow, 1954–59

CW—Marx and Engels: *Collected Works*, Lawrence and Wishart, London, 1975

FIA—Marx: *The First International and After*, edited by D. Fernbach for the Pelican Marx Library, Penguin, Harmondsworth, 1974

G—Marx: *Grundrisse der Kritik der Politischen Ökonomie (Rohentwurf)*, translated into English by M. Nicolaus for the Pelican Marx Library, Penguin, Harmondsworth, 1973

OFI—Marx: *On the First International*, edited and translated by S.K. Padover for the Karl Marx Library, McGraw-Hill, NY, 1973

SW—Marx and Engels: *Selected Works* (in three volumes), Progress Publishers, Moscow, 1976

In citations from *Capital* and *Selected Works*, the abbreviation will be followed by a Roman numeral to indicate the volume number, and then by an Arabic numeral to indicate the page number. Thus C I,715 refers to page 715 of Volume I of *Capital*.

In citations from *Collected Works*, CW will be followed by two sets of Arabic numerals separated by a comma. The first set will indicate volume number, the second page number. Thus CW 3,168 refers to page 168 of Volume 3 of the *Collected Works*.

All other citations in the text consist simply of the appropriate abbreviation followed by one set of Arabic numerals.

1

Introduction

Marx's theory is the most cogent, and has been the most influential in the socialist tradition. So dominant has it become that it frequently obscures other strands of socialist thought: strands which were prior to, and coexist with, Marxism. Many histories of socialism tend to treat Marx's theory as the combination, culling and culmination of the welter of confused and partial theories that preceded it; and socialism after Marx—to borrow an expression—as a series of footnotes to Marx. Thus early socialism becomes simply an anticipation of Marx, an artist's palette of raw colours used by Marx to create a masterpiece of subtlety and strength. Such an approach is apparent not just in those tendentious Marxist accounts which enshrine Marx's own (although rather more limited) distinction between 'utopian' and 'scientific' socialism, and which apportion praise or blame to particular socialisms depending on the relations of each to Marx's theory; but also in many standard treatments of socialism. It occurs in part because concepts which were central to Marx's thought are sometimes assumed to have been central to the socialist tradition Marx found and remoulded. This work explores a concept which played a crucial role in the distinctive development of Marx's thought, as well as contributing to the transformation of socialism from an ambiguously all-class, to an unashamedly working class project: Marx's concept of the proletariat. To recover the history of early socialism, and properly to appreciate Marx's contribution to the socialist tradition, we must clear away the received opinions that socialism was a product of the working class, that it was formulated solely in the interests of the working class, and that it was founded on the notion of class struggle.

Early socialism, that is, socialism in France between 1830 and 1848, was a diverse and catholic doctrine in many respects, not least in having religious currents. Theoretically, it is perhaps the most interesting period in the history of socialism: indeed, it is proper to talk of *socialisms*. It was a period of self-clarification. Socialists sought to define their goals more precisely, to locate their proper audience and to settle upon their methods. Marx made an impact because he had definite and strong views on these issues. Furthermore, he expressed them with considerable intellectual and polemical vigour.

Despite these strengths, however, Marx's theory became the paradigmatic socialist theory largely by default and historical accident, and only many years after the halcyon days of French socialism. Having moved to Paris in 1843, Marx continued to publish in German for Germans, and his passionate discussions with other socialists confined his influence to small circles. He later judged the effect that these discussions had had on Pierre-Joseph Proudhon as unfortunate.[1] In 1847, Marx's *The Poverty of Philosophy*, written and first published in French, failed in its aim to destroy, or even to stem, the growing reputation of Proudhon as France's foremost socialist. Instead, the Revolutions of 1848 gave Marx the opportunity to become known more widely. Their generally anticipated outbreak spurred him to write the *Communist Manifesto*, one of the great revolutionary documents. With its appearance, revolutionary catechism became obsolete. The Revolutions of 1848 were decisive in the survival and ascendancy of Marx's theory because many of the socialisms that Marx had excoriated in the *Manifesto* soon lost their appeal and their most prominent leaders.

It is a testament to the essential link between early French socialism and the French Revolution of 1789 that the major strands of French socialism all but collapsed in 1848. Socialism was an attempt to fulfil the ideals of the French Revolution, particularly the radical egalitarian ideal of the 'little people', the *menu peuple*. But more complex social divisions, which the socialists themselves had helped to identify, jeopardized this goal; and the democratic republic in which they had placed so much hope turned out, in 1848, to be an unwilling inheritor of the goals of 1789. Only determined revolutionaries, chiefly Blanquists of one sort or another, and theorists of *la longue durée*, notably Marx, weathered the general disillusionment among socialists in the years immediately following 1848. The history of socialism at least until the formation of the Second International in 1889 is largely a story of the now amicable, now hostile relations between these two hardy currents. If Marx's theory survived 1848 and prospered, because it took a critical stance toward the French Revolution and because it relied on the social division between bourgeoisie and proletariat which most other socialists considered a hindrance, the sentiments which pervaded early socialism reappeared to bedevil Marx and Marxism. The anti-political programme of Bakunin and the Proudhonists; the ethical strain and class conciliation of Revisionism, and of democratic socialism in general: these had their counterparts in early socialism. Above all, Marx's theory survived because Marx turned the defeats of 1848 into a victory of sorts, the victory of his analysis. The theory of class struggle triumphed over the theory of class reconciliation because it seemed as if a class struggle had taken place: unsuccessful, to be sure, but class struggle nevertheless. In his articles, later collected as *The Class Struggles in France, 1848-1850*, and in *The Eighteenth Brumaire of Louis Bonaparte*, he explained why socialism had not been realized in the same terms with which he maintained its ultimate triumph. Marx's theory did not hinge on a victory in 1848, but 1848 sustained it. Socialism was henceforth freed from its dependence on the model and the spirit of the French Revolution. Tocqueville had asked: 'Will Socialism remain buried in the disdain with which the Socialists of 1848 are so justly covered?'[2] Early socialism was finished, as Tocqueville hinted, but Marx's theory had just begun its career.

Nineteenth century socialism might be divided conveniently into three major periods: 1830-1848, the period of formation, diversity and experiment; 1850-1872, the period when Marx established his intellectual and political credentials—in *Capital* and in the First International—as the foremost theorist of socialism; and 1889-1914, when Marx was generally, but posthumously, acknowledged as the foremost representative of socialism, even as his grand theoretical synthesis was disintegrating. When Marx's theory was most compelling, that is, during his adult lifetime, his authority as a socialist was never unchallenged; in death, with his theories becoming less and less convincing, and much more dogmatically held,

Marx achieved an authority he might scarcely have believed. He contributed to socialism by taking elements from existing theories and elsewhere, imaginatively refashioning them, and through sheer force of personality and intellect, as well as historical accident, outlasting early socialisms to make his the chief imprint on our conception of socialism. Berki declares that 'For socialism itself Marx's appearance is the greatest, and perhaps the only, [intellectual] watershed'.[3] If Marx was to an important extent a child, and inheritor, of early socialism, he found it difficult to gain the same mastery over the new elements attracted to socialism in its second period. The German workers' movement owed its origins and theoretical allegiance primarily to Ferdinand Lassalle; the English workers' movement was trade-unionized, and was satisfied with legal recognition and with increasing political influence; and revolutionaries in the Latin countries of Europe, especially, looked for leadership to Mikhail Bakunin, Marx's arch-rival. Marx persisted and overcame his opponents; but his was a Pyrrhic victory. He effectively destroyed the First International to save it from heterodox contamination. The elevation of Marx to the theoretical head of the Second International, through his friend, collaborator and interpreter, Engels, also had its price. Self-proclaimed Marxist parties honoured Marx more in the breach than in the observance.

To admit that Marx has an enormous influence over the way we think about socialism, and particularly its origins and history, is also to suggest that some aspects of socialism that we may take for granted are properly contributions by Marx. One such aspect is the relation between socialism and the working class. That socialism is a theory of the working class and its role in history, and that socialism will be the product of working class power, are peculiarly Marxian notions, even if they are accepted as more generally socialist. They go to the very heart of our conception of the socialist idea. If they strengthen the popular identification of Marx with socialism, they obscure the significance and novelty of Marx's concept of the proletariat. Identifying Marx and socialism does a disservice to the diversity of socialism and to the achievement of Marx. His concept of the proletariat, it seems to me, was one of Marx's signal intellectual contributions to socialism, as well as being one of the keys to our understanding the failure of his theory adequately to explain, and beneficially to change the world.

There can be little doubt about the importance of Marx as the finest mind in the socialist tradition, and as a figure of continuing political significance, or about the importance of his concept of the proletariat as a linchpin in his theory. It is therefore somewhat surprising that more attention has not been devoted to it.[4] Two studies, however, deserve special note here. The first is an undeservedly neglected, early work by Goetz Briefs, *The Proletariat: A Challenge to Western Civilization* (1934). Briefs examined the origins of the term 'proletariat', its use in the social and economic thought of the nineteenth century, and the modern reality of the proletariat. The proletarian, according to Briefs, is not just a worker, and not just poor; he is an industrial worker who lives by the sale of his labour power in the market, and whose condition is effectively hereditary. By this account, wage earners are not necessarily proletarians. Proletarianism is rebelliousness born of the despair of the worker ever to improve his lot. Briefs sensed a 'contradiction between the proletariat and Western civilization',[5] a contradiction between a system of values which serves as the handmaiden to individual personality and a position which threatens to deprive the worker of his personality. The 'challenge' of Briefs' title, in more popular terms, is to remove alienation from labour, to integrate the worker into Western civilization. The danger of not responding to this challenge, Briefs argued, is to succumb to the proletarian value—security—and thus ultimately to totalitarianism.[6] Briefs' is a sympathetic, but perceptive treatment of the proletarian condition.

The second study which must be mentioned is a recent book by Timothy McCarthy, *Marx and the Proletariat. A Study in Social Theory* (1978). It is more an essay than a book, perhaps, but McCarthy rightly emphasized in it the abstract nature of Marx's concept of the proletariat, and Marx's later attempts to fill the abstraction with empirical, social and economic, content. But the two basic antinomies which McCarthy claimed to have found in Marx's work to explain the inherent implausibility of Marx's concept of the revolutionary proletariat are themselves unconvincing. One stems from a misunderstanding of the use Marx made of the speculative philosophical notions of particularity and universality in relation to social classes. McCarthy declared that

The fundamental ambiguity in Marx's thinking about the revolutionary proletariat. . . was expressed in terms of a tension between the universalism of ends (human emancipation) and the particularity of means (the emancipation of a class).[7]

The other is McCarthy's view that Marx's political and economic work does not support his abstract, or a priori, conception of the proletariat. Both views rely on a sharp separation of abstract and concrete, theory and practice. The attempt to overcome such separation is not just a central feature of Marx's project, but a dynamic factor in Marx's developing conception of the proletariat. Marx introduced the proletariat as an intensionally universal concept. The actual proletariat, whatever its extent, still represented the universal interest; and, for Marx, the pursuit by the proletariat of its material interests was the means by which it would come to the realization of its mission. The proletariat, by pursuing its own emancipation, must necessarily pursue human emancipation. Whatever its present limitations, Marx believed that the proletariat would, through class struggle, become one with its concept. He was not theoretically inconsistent, even if he assigned to the working class imperatives it could not fulfil. McCarthy's essay is not without its merits, but as an explanation of the problems of Marx's concept of the proletariat it is limited.

I do not mean to suggest that no attempts have been made to elucidate Marx's concept of the proletariat, or that these attempts are not of significance. In general, there is little in Marx's thought that has not been subjected to intense, and often intelligent, scrutiny. Since the late 1950s, when Marx's early manuscripts became more accessible to English-speaking scholars and Stalinized Marxism began to lose any intellectual appeal in the West, Marx scholarship has produced some of its best (and some of its worst) works. To indicate the advances that have been made, it is enough to mention George Lichtheim's *Marxism, An Historical and Critical Study*,[8] Robert Tucker's *Philosophy and Myth in Karl Marx*,[9] Eugene Kamenka's *The Ethical Foundations of Marxism*,[10] Shlomo Avineri's *The Social and Political Thought of Karl Marx*,[11] and Leszek Kolakowski's *Main Currents of Marxism*.[12] Each has added to our understanding of Marx's concept of the proletariat, since each has drawn upon the more complex Marx revealed by his manuscripts. Each has carefully charted the early intellectual and political development of Marx, in which the concept 'proletariat' figured so large. No competent study of Marx can ignore their discussions.

It is from such foundations that I propose to examine the formative and enduring role of the concept of the proletariat in Marx's theory, as well as how Marx conceived of the proletariat. This work, therefore, has two characteristics which must be mentioned here. It is, first of all, a work of exposition rather than exposure. The recent scholarly fashion to 'unmask' subjects, while sometimes producing insights, has a destructive tendency which is not to my taste and does not suit my purpose. Marx wrote surprisingly little about the proletariat as such, so my duty is to present his conception of the proletariat as coherently and fairly as possible. Nevertheless, my study is based on the belief, which I think it substantiates, that Marx was fundamentally wrong and, in an important sense, self-deceiving, in his views on the nature and the potential of the proletariat. Secondly, my work largely confirms much that has been written in the recent past about Marx's concept of the proletariat. But by focusing on Marx's notion, or notions, of universality—which were central to his concept 'proletariat'—and by treating them as a theme of Marx's *oeuvre*, we have a new way to understand the basic continuity of his work, as well as a means to illuminate issues such as those surrounding his intellectual development, his revolutionary strategy and his economic doctrine. In particular, my results corroborate those of Avineri, who devoted an important section of *The Social and Political Thought of Karl Marx* to a discussion of the 'universal class', although they were arrived at in a qualifiedly independent manner. I chose to base my account and analysis of Marx's concept of the proletariat on a close examination and working through of Marx's texts. Kamenka has written to the effect that it is the fate of the amateur to relive the various stages in the development of his subject of inquiry.[13] Because I chose to be an 'amateur', to be schooled in Marx by Marx, I learned that there is truth in Kamenka's warning. But having relived, I hope I have also learnt and found illumination in the process, for myself and others.

Until now, there have been two major scholarly interests in Marx's concept of the proletariat, and one more general interest. Recent scholars, notably Tucker and Avineri, have contributed to a debate about the source, or sources, of Marx's concept—a debate which began around the end of last century. The strongest contender for the title of Marx's direct inspirer, it is usually agreed, is Lorenz von Stein. His *Socialism and Communism in Contemporary France,* first published in 1842,[14] was written for the information of the Prussian government as part of its effort to prevent the proletarian disease from reaching Germany. The other scholarly interest, fuelled particularly by Avineri, is in Marx's 'proletariat' as a universal class, as a concept with Hegelian resonances. The influence of Hegel's works upon the development of Marx's theory is by now well known, and the speculative origins of Marx's 'proletariat' provide conclusive evidence of the importance of that influence. The more general interest—shared by scholars and others—is perhaps best summed up by the title of a recent article by Seymour Martin Lipset: 'Whatever Happened to the Proletariat?'[15] That the proletariat has not fulfilled Marx's expectations is clear even to the most committed Marxists, who now rely on the 'oppressed'—racial minorities, sexual minorities, women, students or even 'third world' countries—to release the potential energy they still maintain resides with the working class. The expression 'revolutionary proletariat' has become an oxymoron. But is it necessarily so; is there some fundamental flaw in Marx's theorizing about the proletariat which vitiates his vision of the proletariat's revolutionary potential? Marx would admit no imperfection in the basic analysis he set down in his twenty-sixth year. As he wrote twenty one years later, 'The working class is revolutionary or it is nothing' (FIA,148). Marx made substantial additions to the concept he outlined in the 1844 'Introduction' to the *Contribution to the Critique of Hegel's Philosophy of Law*, or his 'proletarian manifesto', as Rubel has described it.[16] He 'filled' his concept of the proletariat with empirical content. He was too honest and intelligent to ignore evidence of the proletariat's passivity and susceptibility to 'bourgeois prejudices' such as racial intolerance; but when he discussed these characteristics he considered them transient, isolated and inessential. However he added to it, and whatever qualifications he made, the proletariat remained for Marx the heir apparent of history.

As for the first of these issues, the question of the source of Marx's concept of the proletariat, further study has revealed that the terms *prolétaire* and *proletair* were beginning to be frequently used in French works of socialism and social theory during the 1830s and 1840s, and less so in similar German works. Lorenz von Stein may have had an important influence on Marx because he drew attention to the novelty of the proletariat, and made the first systematic link between the term and the nascent industrial working class, but Avineri is right to declare that

It would be difficult—and utterly wrong — to choose one writer and make him responsible for moulding Marx's thought. Marx was responding to a *Zeitgeist*, and it was from a common stock far more than from any individual writer, that he drew his ideas and inspiration. [17]

In fact, the debate about the sources of Marx's concept of the proletariat, begun by the Russian liberal, Petr von Struve, and the German sociologist, Werner Sombart,[18] developed at a time when the speculative grounding of Marx's theory was either little known or discounted. To acknowledge that the concept was of a universal class is to transcend the fruitless quest for a definitive source. It is more profitable to ask why the term 'proletariat' was increasingly used, and how Marx's use of it contributed to the *Zeitgeist*.

It should not be forgotten that the choice by Marx of the proletariat as the revolutionary agent of socialism has a parallel in the history of the French Revolution of 1789, for him the paradigm of modern revolutions. The Abbé Siéyès championed the Third Estate in his famous pamphlet as that Estate which was 'nothing' and which desired to be 'everything'. Marx even described the French bourgeoisie of 1789 as a universal class, the true representative of society in its struggle to destroy the last vestiges of feudalism. The Third Estate was the bourgeoisie as universal class. For Marx, the proletariat was the Third Estate of the socialist revolution. Yet its tasks were more thoroughgoing than Siéyès' Third Estate. Could society be regenerated by social outcasts? In effect, Marx's answer was that it could *only* be regenerated by those not implicated in society's guilt, those not besmirched by their acquiescence in 'society'. But like Siéyès, Marx took liberties when

characterizing the proletariat's 'nothingness'. As Marx himself was
wont to argue, man is a social animal. The proletariat was in no
state of nature, however conceived. Indeed, in his politico-economic
ruminations on the proletariat, Marx relied on its integral relationship with modern industry to explain its development as a class and
its revolutionary significance.

The French connection of Marx's concept of the proletariat is
crucial. Marx introduced the concept into his work while discussing
the possibilities of a German 1789. It was the French who revived
the Latin term *proletarii* in the eighteenth century,[19] who employed
it in the French Revolution, and who linked it with the newly
arisen theories of socialism in the 1830s.[20] And it was the French
who dominated social thought throughout the Continent. Among
French users of the term *'prolétaire'*, however, there was little
agreement as to which social group or groups were being specified.
Stein brought some system to this chaos by identifying the
proletariat as the small but growing class of industrial workers.
Such precision was alien to the spirit of the French socialists, who
sought to legitimize their community-oriented projects by appealing
for the broadest possible support and depreciating and deprecating
class divisions. But although French socialists believed their cause
to be that of an amorphous and rightless proletariat, they looked
chiefly to the educated and wealthy for leadership and direction.

Marx, too, may have traded at first on an imprecise social location of the proletariat, yet the point of his early 'rudimentary
sociology', as Lichtheim aptly put it,[21] was confrontation not
conciliation. But Marx was also committed to the proletariat in a
very personal way. He detested bourgeois society and its values,
which he believed degraded and enslaved humans. Marx's was a
personal quest for dignity, inspired perhaps by his early uncertainty
over his religious identity,[22] but given its sharp form in his
university encounters with the philosophies of Kant, Fichte and
Hegel. For Marx, the bourgeoisie came to represent all that was
repugnant and servile in modern society, a true stumbling-block to
progress in the material and moral sense. *Bourgeois* was an epithet
Marx used, sometimes without discrimination, to express a distaste.
Carl Schurz said of Marx in 1849:

I shall never forget the scornful tone in which he uttered the word 'bourgeois', as if he were spewing it out of his mouth; and he stigmatized as 'bourgeois', by which he meant the embodiment of profound moral degradation, everyone who ventured to contradict him. [23]

The proletariat, by contrast, was for him a repository of virtue; we shall see below whether he used the term 'proletariat' with greater discrimination. In its most unguarded and amusing form, we can find this valuation of proletarianism in a letter Marx wrote to Ludwig Kugelmann in 1868.[24] Assuring Kugelmann that he himself could distinguish between furuncles and carbuncles, from the latter of which he suffered egregiously, Marx added that England was 'the land of carbuncles, which is actually a proletarian illness'. England was also the land of gout; but Marx was spared the indignity of suffering from that. The class theory of illness, or at least the correlation of certain illnesses with certain socio-economic backgrounds, is not absurd. Yet one suspects that Marx endured his carbuncles (and the vile treatments prescribed for them) the better for his belief that they conferred on him the status of honorary proletarian, from which his social origins and occupation precluded him.

It may at first seem curious, and it may ultimately be considered untenable, that a class which was originally distinguished by Marx because of its universal suffering and lack of property would be the means and the material for a new, truly human existence. However, the notion that 'the last shall be first' is strongly represented in the Western moral, and particularly Christian, tradition. They may not have been religious, but there were certainly ethical foundations to Marx's choice of the proletariat as humanity's saviour, apart from— and at first superior to—practical considerations. It was not through piety and good deeds that the proletariat would inherit the earth. It suffered, but it was not meek. Marx cherished a rather romantic image of the proletariat during the 1840s. It gained moral stature in his eyes because it endured its suffering without losing its human qualities. Indeed, these human qualities were enhanced because the struggle for life itself introduced a certain simplicity and unaffectedness into the proletariat. The moral issue was simplified into a choice between good and evil, proletariat and bourgeoisie.[25] That such a view was irreconcilable with Marx's social determinism, and that Marx sought to distance himself from ethical formulations of the social problem, did not prevent him from continuing to base his project on the 'primitive ethic' analysed by Kamenka.[26] Marx's conceptual interest in the proletariat's poverty and suffering arose from his belief that they produced in the proletariat an overwhelming human need which would become revolutionary action. He wrote in the *Economic and Philosophic Manuscripts of 1844*,[27] that poverty 'is the passive bond which causes the human being to experience the need of the greatest wealth—the *other* human being' (CW 3,304). Marx's predilection for paradox as a piquant literary device seems sometimes to have obscured his judgement.

The origins of Marx's concept of the proletariat are best understood in terms of the early development of his theoretical system, a subject which has already been well explored. Clearly, the central notion here is of the proletariat as a universal class. So widely accepted is the argument that the 'proletariat' represents the culmination of Marx's philosophical journey (as well as an important turning point in Marx's intellectual journey), that a recent introduction to Marxist views on philosophy begins its chapter on Marx with a discussion of the concept.[28] Marx's concept of the proletariat slotted into his theoretical system like a piece in an almost completed jigsaw puzzle. It was what the proletariat *had to be* that characterized Marx's earliest discussions of it. He cast about for empirical evidence which would confirm and sustain his essentialist view. The evidence he brought to bear, such as episodes from the Silesian weavers' uprising of June 1844, was thin and unconvincing. Where the evidence tended to controvert his conception, he relied on the idealist distinction between appearance and essence to affirm that the proletariat would nevertheless become one with its essence.

It was, in part, the decisiveness of Marx's choice of the proletariat as revolutionary agent and social redeemer which distinguished his from the myriad other socialist and social theories of the 1830s and '40s. He set himself in opposition to the Young Hegelian hope for a philosophy-led social regeneration. His confidence in the proletariat was part of his larger confidence in his theoretical system and, in truth, they share the same strengths and weaknesses. As Alfred Meyer realized, Marxism as the unity of theory and practice is predicated on an image of the proletariat as embodying that unity. Where a radical mass base is lacking, 'the theory disintegrates into independent and mutually exclusive inter-pretations basing themselves on selected parts of the whole'.[29] The question of the revolutionary potential of the working class, there-fore, has been central in the development of the Marxist tradition. Marxists have had to come to terms with the non-revolutionary appearance of the Western industrial proletariat. Those who decided that the real, as well as the apparent character of the proletariat was passive or reformist by and large renounced their claim to being Marxists, although not necessarily to being socialists. Many Marxists, however, devised explanations for the proletariat's recalcitrance. Perhaps the most influential of these is Lenin's theory of imperialism. Lenin built his particular version of Marxism upon, among other things, the idea of a historical detour of the socialist revolution through the colonies of imperialist powers, even though he was a late convert to the idea of imperial-ism, and Tsarist Russia was scarcely a colony. But whether 'imperialism', by postulating a metropolitan labour aristocracy supporting exploitation in the colonies, fully explains working class reformism or not, it makes assumptions about proletarians which are at odds with much of what Marx held about them. Marx's own unsatisfying attempts to explain the limited nature of actual proletarian political activities and goals are not unsatisfying because, as David Fernbach smugly puts it, Marx failed to develop an adequate (i.e. Leninist) theory of imperialism (FIA, 29-30). Rather, Marx's attempts—as we shall see—introduce tensions into his conception of the proletariat itself.

Marx's choice of the proletariat as revolutionary agent also inaugurated the trend in his work away from abstract interests to material interests. The proletariat as a social class in a socio-economic system, with its development and tasks determined by that system, emerged from Marx's speculative concept of the proletariat. The concept was thus a catalyst in his political and intellectual development, even though giving it greater concreteness brought problems as well. Is the proletariat as industrial working class recognizably similar to what Marx saw as a philosophically defined and derived universal class? Was it the proletariat which took up arms against the government in Paris in 1848 and 1871 and, if so, which proletariat? Is the proletariat a social class, and in what sense? A careful analysis of Marx's concept of the proletariat points to issues within and about Marx's theory just as important as the question of whether or not the proletariat is revolutionary. The coherence of Marx's theory is at stake. It is ironic that Herbert Marcuse's *One Dimensional Man*, which discounts the industrial working class and looks to society's outcasts and outsiders for social transformation,[30] is in the spirit of Marx's second Hegel critique while being critical of traditional Marxism.

If Marx was wrong about the industrial working class, then why? Although there are a number of specific objections which can, and will below, be made about his concept of the proletariat, one general explanation suggests itself. Any theory which is based on an interpretation of history, as Marx's ultimately was, must ensure that it has its history right. It must not mistake the peripheral for the central, nor the inessential for the essential. Theories based on an interpretation of history reveal the historical limitations of their authors. Marx, I think, understood this; it was one of the reasons why he refused to set down a blueprint for the future. Marx introduced his concept of the proletariat at a time when the advance of industrialism and protest were closely linked, when workers had begun to organize—occupationally and politically—to protect and advance their interests, and at a time when the lower strata of society began openly to demand that the universal prescriptions of the French Revolution should apply to them as well. Yet Marx mistook artisan protest against industrialism and loss of trade privileges for incipient proletarian self-assertion. He mistook workers' organizational efforts to establish their place in industrial society as efforts to transcend capitalism. And he mistook the last chapter of the French Revolution for the first chapter of the socialist revolution. Adam Ulam has presented this miscalculation as follows:

The *first* reaction of the worker to industrialization, his feelings of grievance and impotence before the machine, his employer, and the state which stands behind the employer, are assumed by Marx to be typical of the general reactions of the worker to industrialization. [31]

That Marx's theory still has the ability to command respect, and even allegiance, testifies to the fine mind of its creator and to the continuing relevance of some of its insights. But that it is an accurate political or sociological account of the industrial working class, or a reliable guide to its future, is a proposition which has now been robbed of its initial plausibility.

The concept of the proletariat in Marx's works has a number of different aspects, some of which were stressed at different times, but not all of which were complementary. From 1844 onward, however, Marx could never question the central role in his theory that he had assigned to the proletariat without bringing his entire project into question. Modifying his conception of the proletariat, from social outcasts to intrinsic products of capitalist industry, Marx nevertheless invites some disagreeable questions. Is the industrial working class of *Capital*, for example, the same as the political class of 1848 or the universal class of 1844? Is it the striving for dignity and freedom which animates the proletariat's struggle, or the calculation of economic benefits and the chance to establish economic rationality? Does Marx develop a positive conception of the proletariat as a carrier of socialism, or does he maintain the negative conception of 1844: the cathartic vision of the proletariat as society's sin and as society's means of redemption? Can this negative, ethically inspired vision allow Marx, consistently, to develop a positive conception of the proletariat?

A careful examination of Marx's concept of the proletariat highlights not just the importance of the role of 'universality' throughout his work, but also certain features of his theory itself: its lack of consistent empirical reference and its internal tensions. For Marx did not simply discover the proletariat, nor invent it: he brought together existing and ideal elements which increasingly threatened to tear apart. That they did not, at least during his lifetime, was due to the systematic character of his theory, and his ability thus to shift from one aspect of the proletariat to another to explain away any shortcomings. Marx never seriously confronted the falsifiable potential of the actual proletariat.

Above all, Marx's concept of the proletariat presents us with a central dilemma for Marx's entire project. It is this: is the proletariat to have a predominantly negative, or a predominantly positive significance? If negative, that is, if the proletariat's historical role according to Marx's theory is determined by its suffering and dehumanization, then how will socialism arise, and what sort of socialism will it be? Will the proletariat not sacrifice freedom for security, enterprise for welfare, the imaginative for the routine? Yet can Marx consistently see the proletariat as bearers of a new civilization, rather than simply as the pariahs of the old? Can he consistently see the proletariat as the bearers of freedom, rather than as simply deprived of freedom? Marx does make an attempt to reconcile these negative and positive characteristics, theoretically, by turning deprivation into a virtue, the lack of particularity into universality, and suffering into stoicism. Ultimately, it is a move which cannot work. Dignity born of despair is a poetic notion, and poets are onlookers, honorary sufferers. Marx's negative conception of the proletariat may have been nearer the mark than even his abstract method had a right to expect. If so, the consequences for his project are disastrous. Kamenka has observed that

In not seeing the proletariat as the bearers of enterprise, as the class of free men, Marx may have been right; but if he was right his vision was doomed.[32]

Marx's concept of the proletariat represented a major step forward in socialist theorizing, and in his intellectual and political development. It was decisive in forging the link between socialism and the working class movement that we now tend to take for granted. But it also gives rise to crucial problems for Marx's theory, particularly the relations between Marx's concept and the industrial working class and whether, in fact, the concept (let alone the industrial working class) is adequate to his project. These issues are examined in the pages that follow.

2

The Dialectic of Universal and Particular

Marx's concept of the proletariat first appeared in his second Hegel critique, published in the *Deutsch-französische Jahrbücher* in 1844. In his earlier newspaper articles, he was concerned not with the proletariat, but with the 'poor', and then not for their own sake, but as indications of social irrationality and the failure to treat people equally. Marx's contributions to the *Jahrbücher*, crowned by the concept of the proletariat, represent a major turning-point in his intellectual and political development.[1] Since about 1840 that development had been sufficiently rapid for us to agree with Avineri that the introduction of the concept into Marx's work came 'at this late stage',[2] despite the fact that Marx was only twenty five years of age. Marx's tardiness in taking up the cause of the proletariat, however, underlines the significance which it had for his theory; the concept meant a new direction for his studies. He left behind the inconclusive intellectual ferment of Young Hegelianism, which had profoundly shaped his ideas. He turned away from ideas about the importance of theory in the making of history, and looked instead to material interests. He rejected liberalism,[3] and proclaimed his adherence to communism. He became a revolutionary. Yet these changes were contained within a theoretical evolution whose major premises and whose inspiration remained virtually constant. Marx's concept of the proletariat itself was, at first, primarily a theoretical construct designed to fulfil the requirements of a theoretical system in the Hegelian tradition.

Marx considered the proletariat to be 'a sphere which has a universal character' (CW 3,186), that is, a universal class. It was the means for making a revolution which would usher in a universal society, defined by Marx as 'the *complete rewinning of man*' (CW 3,186). This formulation, influenced by the work of Ludwig Feuerbach, was meant to denote a state of affairs in which man would be at one with his species-essence (*Gattungswesen*). In such a society, Marx and Feuerbach believed, individuals would be representative of the species, each would see in another an aspect of himself, and harmony would reign between men and between man and nature. Feuerbach's anthropology, derived from the radical atheism expressed in his 1841 *The Essence of Christianity*—the talk of a generation—added a new dimension to Marx's Young Hegelianism. Feuerbach had declared that

Consciousness of God is self-consciousness, knowledge of God is self-knowledge. By his God thou knowest the man, and by the man his God; the two are identical.[4]

Feuerbach's concept of *Gattungswesen* transcended the Young Hegelian preoccupation with the relation between religion and philosophy, and allowed Marx, whose interests were entirely secular, to conceive of a truly human society in terms congenial to his growing awareness of social division. But if Feuerbach allowed Marx a new perspective on the universal society, Marx's intellectual and political development took place within a fairly stable framework of the dialectic of universal and particular.

Universal and *particular* were the two terms of a formula to which Marx kept returning. His intellectual development might be seen as a continuing clarification of the real meaning and logical and social implications of these abstract terms. To understand the universal and the means to achieve it: this was the task Marx in effect set himself early in the 1840s, and which culminated in the concept of the proletariat. Throughout these years, as a student, journalist, editor, and in his study, Marx returned to this issue. There were four major phases in the development which brought him to the concept of the proletariat and to revolutionary communism. The first is represented by his Doctoral Dissertation, completed in 1841; the second by his contribution to the *Rheinische Zeitung* in 1842 and early in 1843; the third by his withdrawal to the study at Kreuznach in mid-1843; and the fourth by his removal to Paris in October 1843, and the publication there in February 1844 of the *Deutsch-französische Jahrbücher*, which he edited with Arnold Ruge.

Marx's Doctoral Dissertation, entitled *Difference Between the Democritean and Epicurean Philosophy of Nature*, is a restrainedly

Young Hegelian work. Its Young Hegelian mottoes are confined to the 'Foreword', sharply distinguishing philosophy and religion and paying homage to Prometheus (CW 1,29-31), and to the 'Notes', which include a discussion of the worldly tasks of philosophy conceived as the theoretical and political tasks of the Young Hegelians (CW 1,85-6). The central topic, however, arose from what Marx believed were inadequacies in Hegel's account, and appreciation of the philosophy of Epicurus. Marx came under the influence of Hegel's work, although not without a struggle, after he transferred to the University of Berlin late in 1836. According to his father, Marx had substituted an ethereal intoxication for the more prosaic one he left behind in Bonn.[5] Berlin, where Hegel had held his chair until his premature death in 1831, remained the centre of his posthumous influence, encouraged by the Prussian Minister for Culture and Education, Altenstein. To fill a gap in Hegel's work on Greek philosophy, Marx reckoned, would open a way for an academic career, such as that followed by his mentor and friend, Bruno Bauer.

Marx believed that philosophers, including even Hegel, had underrated the originality of Epicurus's doctrine of the atom. Marx treated Epicurus as a major and original thinker, superior to Democritus. Hegel, in his *The History of Philosophy*, had presented Epicurus as merely a follower of Democritus who had developed inconsistencies:

Atoms, as atoms [Hegel argued], must remain undetermined; but the Atomists have been forced to take the inconsistent course of ascribing properties to them.[6]

Epicurus had ascribed to atoms qualities such as magnitude, figure and weight.[7] But according to Marx, Epicurus had theorized a dynamic and fruitful and actually existing contradiction. By giving atoms qualities 'Epicurus objectifies the contradiction in the concept of the atom between essence and existence' (CW 1,58). Marx argued that this attribution of qualities was essential to the proper understanding of the atom, and to its development over time:

Through the quality the atom is alienated from its concept, but at the same time is perfected in its construction. (CW 1,61)

Marx attempted to answer, in an entirely speculative manner, a question raised by Hegel on 'the relation of atoms to sensuous appearance'.[8] The world of appearance, Marx argued, 'can only emerge from the atom which is complete [i.e. which has qualities] and alienated from its concept' (CW 1,62).

Epicurus, Marx believed, had made the connection between atoms and appearance. Indeed, Epicurus was 'the first to grasp appearance as appearance, that is, as alienation of essence' (CW 1,64). Universality, for Marx, consisted in appearance being in harmony with essence. Although it is only implicit in the text of the Dissertation, the 'Notes' are clear that the lack of such harmony is the major problem of the modern world. This particularity was to be exposed by philosophy, with its quest for essences. The method of modern philosophy, which for Marx meant a type of Hegelianism, was *critique*: the measuring of an existence against its essence, or concept.[9] Marx already believed that the world of men was not in harmony with its essence. He argued that the party of philosophy, what he called the 'liberal party' and the 'party of the concept', understood the inadequacies of the world which 'has to be made philosophical' (CW 1,86). The 'party' Marx meant was a small group of Young Hegelians, who were in fact attempting to make philosophy more worldly, but who scarcely constituted a political force.[10] Marx believed that simply by exposing particularity, harmony between existence and essence would result. He had faith in the efficacy of reason which invested his subsequent journalism for the *Rheinische Zeitung* with a special purpose; it was a faith weakened with each successive contribution, and it was abandoned when the journal was suppressed by the Prussian censor.

Opinion about Marx's Doctoral Dissertation and its significance within his corpus of writings is far from unanimous. *Qua* thesis, it is difficult to judge. Marx's facility with the Greek and Latin sources, and his attempt to reconstruct Epicurus's doctrine of the atom must be balanced against his dogmatic use of unexamined Hegelian assumptions. It will probably never be satisfactorily resolved why Marx sent his Dissertation to be examined at the University of Jena: whether because it was a recently established university, anxious to grant degrees, or because it was still sympathetic to Hegelianism which was philosophically under attack in Berlin and politically in disfavour. As for the significance of the thesis, it is now widely argued that Marx's stress on the Epicurean notion of the declination of the atom from the straight line, a notion absent from the work of Democritus, lays the basis for the idea of freedom within determinism, and thus sheds light on the larger problem within Marx's theory of the relation between free will and determinism. Maximilien Rubel has argued that the philosophy of Democritus 'renders man the slave of an inexorable, divine fatalism',[11] and Auguste Cornu adds that

Epicurus, by contrast, wishing above all to safeguard human liberty and the mind's autonomy, is brought in to reject determinism.[12]

While the dissertation undoubtedly contains this element, I prefer to see its message in the dialectic between essence and appearance, universal and particular. Marx was committed to universality understood as the unity of appearance and essence, and he believed that the contradiction between appearance and essence was a dynamic one which would lead eventually to harmony. Marx was not precise, however, about just what was alienated from its essence. There are two candidates in the Dissertation: man alienated from himself, through religion and philosophy, a dominant theme among Young Hegelians; and the state alienated from its essence.

For Hegel, according to Karl Löwith, philosophy was 'philosophical theology'.[13] The starting point for Young Hegelianism was the denial of the inseparability of philosophy and theology, as well as a desire to use the works and the method of Hegel to develop philosophy beyond Hegel. Although Feuerbach's early humanism, expressed in his 1830 *Thoughts Concerning Death and Immortality*, was in the spirit of Young Hegelianism, the Young Hegelians emerged only in 1835, after the publication of David Strauss's *Das Leben Jesu*. Feuerbach was influential with the Young Hegelians, but he was never properly one of them. Later Bruno Bauer (an early opponent of Strauss's) published *The Trumpet of the Last Judgement over Hegel the Atheist and Antichrist: An Ultimatum* (1841), which explained Hegel's work as revolutionary and atheist, and presented Young Hegelianism as its proper interpretation. Young Hegelianism emerged as a radical, anti-religious philosophy, centred in the universities. Its involvement in politics arose not simply because of a theoretical development, but because it became the object of political action by the Prussian state. One of the major campaigns of Young Hegelianism was defending Bruno Bauer after his dismissal from the University of Bonn in 1842. The livelihood of Young Hegelians came under threat; Marx was effectively denied the chance of an academic career. The *Hallische Jahrbücher*, the organ of Young Hegelianism edited by Arnold Ruge, began in 1837 by concentrating on issues in art and literature. The accession of Frederick William IV to the Prussian throne in 1840 raised the spirits of liberal-minded Young Hegelians who hoped for the reform of the state, but in 1841 the *Hallische Jahrbücher* was suppressed. Some Young Hegelians, among them Ruge, remained liberals; others, such as Max Stirner, turned to anarchism. Moses Hess, however, had been a communist since 1837, and converted Engels in 1842. The dominant political theme of the Young Hegelians, despite these notable exceptions, was liberal. Hegel's 'mature' political thought, expressed in his *Philosophy of Right*, but especially in his 1831 article 'Über die englische Reformbill' published in the *Prussian State Journal*, was considered to be a defence of the existing Prussian state. Yet just as Hegel's philosophy could be developed against theology, so there were elements of his political philosophy which could be deployed against the Prussian state. The Young Hegelians had a 'cult of the Prussian state', according to Cornu;[14] but they believed that its faults would be uncovered by reason, and that the state would then conform to its liberal essence.

Marx, too, was a radical democrat when he completed his Doctorate and began to search for a profession. He opposed the Prussian state, but believed that it could be made to accord with its liberal essence through critique. He became a journalist. One of the themes of his Dissertation concerned the primacy and efficacy of reason in effecting change in the world. If an appearance was confronted by its essence, he believed, particularity would disappear. Marx as a journalist was a worldly philosopher. Journalism suited his purpose, even if it was the only job he was offered. In 1842, encouraged by Hess, Marx began to contribute to a new journal published in Cologne: the *Rheinische Zeitung*, a journal of industry, commerce and politics. It was sponsored by a group of liberal industrialists and intellectuals, and was initially welcomed by the Prussian authorities as an ally against Rhenish separatism and Catholicism. Its existence was possible as a result of the easing of press censorship late in 1841, but it was tolerated only until May 1843. Von Rochow, the Prussian Minister of the Interior and Police, perceived as early as May 1842 that the tendency of the *Rheinische Zeitung*—'a journal of opposition', as he described it— was for a 'constitutional State'.[15] Hess persuaded the journal's financiers to offer Marx its editorship after Marx had submitted a well received series of articles on the freedom of the press in May 1842.

Marx's articles for the *Rheinische Zeitung* are quite accomplished. They included a series on the freedom of the press, on the Rhenish *Landtag* debates on the law on thefts of wood, an article on the Divorce Bill, and a series defending the analysis made by the journal's Mosel correspondent about the plight of the local winegrowers. Not all were passed by the censor. Soon after his (unfinished) 'Justification of the Correspondent from the Mosel', Marx resigned as editor of the *Rheinische Zeitung*. He had been a good editor. Cornu has argued that Marx displayed 'extraordinary political maturity' during this period,[16] but common sense might be a better term for it. He was prepared to compromise tactically, and to distance himself from the Berlin Young Hegelians, *die Freien*, or 'the Free (and wild) Ones', whose antics he disapproved of, and whose writings he judged irresponsible, and refused to publish. Marx brought a sophisticated and learned tone to his own contributions. His work hinged on the debates in the local Province Assembly, and was directed chiefly against particularism, which he believed was perverting the true nature of the state.

Marx's liberalism was different from that of the industrialists who financed the *Rheinische Zeitung*. They promoted a journal which opposed restrictive trade and customs barriers, but they also wanted a constitutional state which had clearly defined and limited relations with civil society. Marx, however, was not a liberal in the sense of advocating *'guarantisme'*, as Giovanni Sartori has described it;[17] he believed instead that the essence of the state was freedom. Marx wanted what might be described as a 'constituted' state, a state in the proper Hegelian sense, rather than a 'constitutional' state. While the liberals who supported the local assemblies of the estates opposed the predominance of the aristocracy within them, Marx was entirely opposed (as a liberal) to the assemblies themselves, whatever their particular composition. It was perhaps the blurring of this opposition in the tactical alliance between Marx and the financiers against the aristocratic representatives in the assemblies, that allowed him to work so effectively for the *Rheinische Zeitung*.

Marx's journalism was preoccupied with the state. It was a preoccupation not generally shared by the Young Hegelians. Bruno Bauer wrote in 1841 that the state is 'the manifestation of freedom',[18] and Sidney Hook, in an early but perceptive work on the Young Hegelians, avers that 'All of the Young-Hegelians started their careers by singing hymns of praise to the Hegelian conception of the state';[19] yet Marx alone made Hegel's political philosophy the means of his political development. Marx's journalism from this period clearly suggests the need for change in the constitution of the state, but change brought about by reform. Marx no doubt 'pulled his punches': to continue his working relationship with the financiers of the *Rheinische Zeitung*, and thus to retain a forum for his views; to appeal to an ever-broader audience, as growth in its circulation suggests that he did; and not to antagonize the censor. Marx believed that reason would triumph. Characteristic of this view is an incidental remark he made in November 1842: the misguided *Kölnische Zeitung*, he argued, 'will renounce its point of view once it has gained consciousness of it' (CW 1,269).

Marx was a liberal in that he sought for freedom in the state itself, not from the state. He identified the state's essence as 'the realisation of rational freedom' (CW 1,200). The 'pseudo-liberalism' and 'half-hearted liberalism' (CW 1,110)[20] which he criticized was dedicated only to formal, legal freedoms, and regarded the state as the enemy of freedom. The source, or guarantee of freedom, according to liberals of this latter type, were the estates (CW 3,66). Real liberals, wrote Marx, those who believed that the essence of the state was freedom, must support the state asserting itself (and thus the general interest) against the estates and their particular interests (CW 1,306). In the context of the Prussian state, which he had described early in 1842 as an 'unfree state' (CW 1,384), Marx's liberalism was radical and far-reaching, but not revolutionary. His *Rheinische Zeitung* journalism did not, in fact could not, advocate revolution. Marx worked for a new constitution for the

24

state, not for its abolition. He anticipated that the state would renounce particularity, and quash estate attempts to influence state policy. Marx can be described as a liberal until mid-1843 because, following Hegel, he admitted the existence of separate spheres in human life: public and private, political and civic. But unlike 'half-hearted' Lockean liberals, Marx wanted these spheres properly reconciled. He did not accept that the separate spheres were at war with each other, nor that they required a peace treaty for a constitution. His practical campaign in the *Rheinische Zeitung* was to transform a feudal state into a rational state; but a political state nevertheless. In the quest for universality, for the rational state, Marx believed that the press could be an agent of change. He therefore published his criticisms of the Prussian state for allowing private interests, particularity, to become a part of the state and to help determine its laws. The state was not wholly degraded by this external determination, but it would become so, Marx suggested, if it gave the estates any further legislative power. The state could become truly universal, rather than merely claim universality or appear to be universal, if there existed a truly free, i.e. uncensored press.

Marx assumed that the abolition of particularity was fundamentally a question of the dissemination of knowledge. Once committed defenders of self-interest had been exposed to a wider standpoint, the general interest would supplant particularity. Thus he considered particularity as simply a problem of boundedness, or partial knowledge, and saw the free press as a means of education. Campaigning against state censorship, he argued that it fostered particularity. A third force between rulers and ruled was needed: a part of civil society which was not beholden to private interest, and which had the head and heart of a citizen. The free press, Marx declared, 'can make a particular interest into a general one' (CW 1,349).

Marx believed that a free press could also be an effective mediator between spheres in a rational state.[21] Even before his more systematic evaluation of Hegel's conception of bureaucracy as the mediator between state and civil society, he had pointed to the Prussian bureaucracy as a major source of social distress in the Mosel region. The bureaucracy, he argued at the beginning of

1843, was culpable because it identified its own interests too much with those of the state. The free press could contribute to harmony between state and civil society by bringing problems to the attention of the state, thus making them state and, by definition, general problems. The press could turn poverty into a general problem as a prelude to the state solving it. Marx saw a free press in much the same way that Hegel saw bureaucracy. The problem in a state such as Prussia was that the gap between civil society and the state was not being adequately bridged. Marx wanted to bridge the gap. This is what made him a liberal, as well as a champion of a free press and opponent of bureaucracy. His journalism warned against threats to the universal essence of the state from private interests. Although Marx did not say it until his Kreuznach discussion of Hegel, he considered the bureaucracy as one such interest, along with property ownership. Michael Lowy says rightly that for Marx during this period,

private property is always cowardly and egotistical, only those who are dispossessed and who 'have nothing to lose' are capable of courage, revolutionary energy and of identifying with the general interest. 22

Marx certainly began, as Lowy suggests, with the view that private property and the private interest which it generated were inherently limited and particular. He thus opposed the assemblies of the estates as bodies which could not formulate the general interest.

Marx did not begin, however, with the view that the poor were representative of the general interest. Rather, he believed that poverty was a matter of general concern and should therefore be the state's concern, and could be overcome with the state's intervention. His later *Rheinische Zeitung* journalism, particularly that dealing with the debates on the Law on Thefts of Wood, and on the poverty of the Mosel winegrowers, was an attempt to understand what prevented the state from acknowledging poverty as its concern and responsibility, and thus from alleviating distress. The major culprits, he concluded, were the private property owners, with their 'state' or official voice in the provincial assemblies, and the Prussian bureaucracy. The real interest of the state, he urged, lay in assisting those stricken by poverty. Marx did not allocate the 'poor' an active role in social and political change until his second Hegel critique of 1844. The state, he argued in 1842 and early in

1843, was being overwhelmed by private interests: the poor were merely symptomatic of the state's problem. Poverty was proof that the state did not correspond to its essence. A free press, Marx hoped, could not only bring to the attention of the state the plight of those in need, but could also change the limited viewpoints of the private property owners who presently sought to pervert the proper aims of the state. He believed that limited standpoints could not survive the challenge of the general standpoint. His later concept of ideology, which linked limited standpoints with material interests and reinforcements, was his response to the failure of this rather naive approach.

Marx may have been a spendthrift all his life, but he first confronted the problem of mass poverty late in 1842. Like Hegel, he considered this problem within the framework of political philosophy. But for Marx it assumed different theoretical proportions: it became central to his perspective. Avineri relates that 'pauperization and the subsequent alienation from society are not incidental to the [Hegelian] system but endemic to it.'[23] Hegel had admitted that poverty was an unresolved problem in his theory, and he advocated for the management of poverty a limited amount of state intervention. The state could not abolish poverty—which was an unavoidable outcome of the market mechanism—but it could ameliorate the effects. The major difference between Hegel and Marx on this issue was that while Hegel resigned himself to the existence of poverty, Marx could not. For Marx, the problem was a starting-point, not an unfortunate anomaly. But however important was the issue of poverty in convincing him that the rational state was not the solution, but part of the problem, I cannot agree with the claim of Heinz Lubasz that Marx's 'initial problematic' was the 'problem of poverty'.[24] By inverting the usual view that Marx used socio-political evidence to challenge and clarify his philosophical project, Lubasz misreads Marx's early views on the role of the free press and of the poor. Marx's conception of 'the poor' *contributed* to his conception of the proletariat, but they are quite different. Sometimes, it must be admitted, the established view is well-founded. Furthermore, the notion of poverty with which Marx operated should not be conceived too narrowly. A case can be made for the idea that it was the lack of dignity, not the material hardship, which bothered Marx most about the condition of the poor and of the proletariat.

Marx's early conception of particularity is clear. Since his encounters with its powerful influence in 1842, Marx considered private property a form of particularity. Private interest, which he excoriated in the *Rheinische Zeitung*, was the natural corollary of private property. Polluting the true nature of the state, it appeared particularly in the guise of the Assemblies of Estates, and of the Commissions of Estates, which were introduced into Prussia in 1823. (In his 1843 first Hegel critique, Marx extended the charge of particularity to government officials who, as bureaucracy, had the state in their possession, as their private property (CW 3,47).) Estate representation, Marx objected, 'recognises *only* particular elements' (CW 1,300). The outlook of particular estates is narrow-minded (CW 1,179), for particular interest 'by its very nature is blind, immoderate, one-sided' (CW 1,261). Little wonder that he decried the provincial assemblies, 'privileged to assert their *particular limits* against the state', as 'non-state elements in the state' (CW 1,305). Beware, cautions Marx, if an Assembly of Estates 'were ever seriously called upon to make laws' (CW 1,262). Private interest and private property were condemned for their partiality, their inability to formulate a general standpoint. Private interest, he declared, distorted the relations between men because it made 'something inhuman, an alien material essence' into man's supreme essence (CW 1,236). If private interest externally determined man (although this was not yet Marx's central theme), then it was also a danger to the state. The limitations of private interest contrasted with the universality, autonomy and reason which was man's—and until mid-1843 for Marx, the state's—true essence. Marx's abiding hostility towards private property stemmed from his political views. Private property was his *bête noire* as a liberal; his opposition to private property was an important factor in his discarding the goal of a liberal state; and the 'positive transcendence' of private property was the foundation of his communism. For Marx, private property became increasingly not just one of a number of particular interests, but *the* particular interest which divided men from each other and from their true selves.

Marx wanted the political role of the German estates abolished, since they elevated particularity to a general principle of social organization. The *Rheinische Zeitung*, Marx argued in its defence against the censor,

tried to incite every estate against its own egoism and limitations, it has everywhere brought civic reason to bear against estate unreason. (CW 1,363)

His concern for a free press, and for the role it could play in establishing and maintaining a harmonious society, parallels the concerns expressed today about media monopoly. Both views discount the idea of the press as a business, or as something which might have its own interests (or those of its owners) to pursue. It was perhaps not so much a free press which Marx valued, but a means for the dissemination of universal knowledge. Even the free press, he conceded, could make mistakes. But the 'free press remains good even when it produces bad products, for the latter are deviations from the essential nature of the free press' (CW 1,158). Yet 'to abolish the possibility of evil' by state imposed censorship, according to Marx, 'abolishes the possibility of good' (CW 1,158). He idealized the potential of the free press and its contributors:

The writer does not at all look on his work as a *means*. It is an *end in itself*; it is so little a means for him himself and for others that, if need be, he sacrifices *his* existence to *its* existence. (CW 1,175)

Of course, Marx argued, an aspect of the press is trade, but this is the affair only of printers and booksellers. The separation here between writers, whom he considered the essential element of a free press, and printers, who made of the press a grubby trade, is quite artificial. Even Marx's editorial policy for the *Rheinische Zeitung* was subject to review by the paper's shareholders.

Marx remained attached to the idea of a free press even after his conversion to communism, but for rather different reasons. In his speech to the jury in the first trial of the *Neue Rheinische Zeitung* in February 1849, he declared:

The first duty of the press now is *to undermine all the foundations of the existing political state of affairs.* (CW 8,317)

In addition to this revolutionary role, he proposed a long-term role for the press in a society dominated by particularity. The press, he explained to the court,

is by profession the public watchdog, the tireless denouncer of those in power, the omnipresent eye, the omnipresent mouthpiece of the people's spirit that jealously guards its freedom (CW 8,314).

Marx now saw its role in more narrowly liberal terms. As Engels put it on the same day, the primary duty of the press was to protect 'citizens against excesses committed by officials' (CW 8,318).

The third phase in the dialectic of universal and particular which engaged Marx's attention was signalled by his retirement from the *Rheinische Zeitung*, his move to Kreuznach and his marriage to Jenny von Westphalen in June 1843. In Kreuznach Marx undertook a critique of Hegel's *Philosophy of Right*, and as a result abandoned liberalism. Rejecting the division between the state and civil society, he argued that these separate spheres of human activity were really alienated expressions of the human essence which could never be truly reconciled. From at least March 1842 he had planned a critique of the *Philosophy of Right*, to expose Hegel's political ideal of constitutional monarchy 'as a hybrid which from beginning to end contradicts and abolishes itself' (CW 1,382-3). In August 1842, Ruge published a critique of the *Philosophy of Right* in his *Deutsche Jahrbücher*, in which, incidentally, he described the German people as a 'proletariat' becoming indignant that it had no political voice. [25] Ruge wanted to encourage political life in Germany, for he saw a connection between philosophy and politics: the *public* defense of a philosophy under attack would have been a *political deed*. This conflict that Hegel was spared was prepared for later philosophers. The minute philosophy comes forward critically (Strauss broke the ground [with his *Das Leben Jesu*]), the conflict is here. [26]

Ruge did, however, argue that Hegel was not critical enough in his doctrine of the state. It is in this sense that Ruge criticized the *Philosophy of Right*, as David McLellan says, 'for confounding logical and historical categories'.[27] The 'problem that runs through the entire work', according to Ruge, is that *essence*, or *concept*, is never properly distinguished from, and is sometimes actually substituted for *actuality* or *appearance*. As a consequence, Hegel 'wrenches the state out of history'.[28] This was an argument that Marx incorporated into the notes which are described, a little too formally, as his *Contribution to the Critique of Hegel's Philosophy of Law*.

In this first Hegel critique, Marx endorsed Hegel's view that the modern state and civil society were separate and hostile spheres (CW 3,51; 3,72), although Hegel had expounded this separation 'as a *necessary element of the idea*, as absolute rational truth' (CW 3,73). It was a view which Hegel had inherited from Rousseau, and which Marx believed accurately to depict reality. That separation meant the end of the direct influence of property, wealth, religion, etc., on the political sphere. Yet primogeniture, the basis of monarchy, was according to Marx 'the power of *abstract private property* over the *political state*' (CW 3,99). Thus, under a constitutional monarch, 'The political constitution at its highest point is...the *constitution of private property*' (CW 3,98). Constitutional monarchy, he concluded, contradicted the modern separation of state and civil society.

Marx may have won the point against Hegel, but the real importance of the first Hegel critique lay in the application of what Avineri has called Feuerbach's 'transformative method' to Hegel's political philosophy.[29]   Joseph O'Malley observed that 'It is the philosophical form, not the empirical content of *The Philosophy of Right* which is under attack'.[30] Hegel's picture of political reality, Marx believed, was essentially accurate; but Hegel 'uncritically accepts an empirical existent as the actual truth of the idea' (CW 3,8). Hegel, Marx agreed with Ruge, took an 'uncritical' approach to the existing state and law (CW 3,83):

Hegel is not to be blamed for depicting the nature of the modern state as it is, but for presenting that which is as the nature of the state. (CW 3,63)

Feuerbach's method, first outlined in his 'Provisional Theses for the Reformation of Philosophy'—which was published in 1843, and had an enormous influence upon Marx—was used fruitfully by Marx. Feuerbach argued that in Hegel's thought, and particularly in his philosophy of religion,

the thought is made into the subject, but the object, the religion, is made into the mere *predicate* of the thought.... The true relation of thinking and being is simply this. *Being* is *subject* and *thinking* a *predicate* but a predicate such as contains the *essence* of its subject. [31]

Marx therefore insisted that Hegel had inverted the proper relation between the spheres of social life. 'Family and civil society are the premises of the state' (CW 3,8), he declared; they are not products of the state, nor '*spheres of the concept* of the state' (CW 3,7).

Marx now opposed the division he had implicitly accepted: the division between public and private spheres of human existence. He argued that it represented a modern division within man himself which had become institutionalized.

The abstraction of the *state as such* belongs only to modern times, because the abstraction of private life belongs only to modern times. (CW 3,32)

Modern man, Marx complained, must 'effect a *fundamental division* within himself' (CW 3,77) as a citizen of the state and as a member of civil society. These spheres make competing and contradictory demands on man because the state confronts him with one aspect of his existence as something external. Man in modern society is unfree because he is externally determined by an alienated part of his essence.

The political state, Marx declared, is the separation of 'the *objective* essence of the human being from him as merely something *external*' (CW 3,81). The state might present itself as representative of the general interest, but it is an illusory universality. Because the state dominates man, it is a form of particularity. The integration of man into a universal and harmonious society can only be achieved by the abolition of the distinction between state and civil society. True universality consisted in civil society raising itself to '*political* being as its true, general, essential mode of being' (CW 3,121). Man in his everyday life should embody the general interest that he presently reserved for his political self. Marx believed that formal politics was an ethereal realm which should be incorporated into man's real life, his material life in civil society. As he wrote in 1859, he realized in the first Hegel critique that states and legal forms had 'their roots in the material conditions of life', in civil society (SW I,503). It was the prelude to his study of political economy as 'the anatomy of civil society' (SW I,503).

Marx's goal of 'true democracy' required a *constitutional* change which would transform the nature of the political state. 'True democracy' was 'only possible when "man" has become the principle of the constitution' (CW 3,19; 3,57). It was not a question of constitutional change within the 'abstract-political state', but of transcending that state. It had also become a question of revolution: 'for a *new* constitution a real revolution has always been required' (CW 3,56). At about the time he was making these notes on Hegel, Marx wrote to Ruge of the 'impending revolution' in Germany (CW 3,134). His revolutionary model was, and remained, the French Revolution of 1789. As Rubel and others have documented, Marx read histories of the Revolution while preparing for his critique of Hegel. But the Revolution, as Marx was soon to write in his 'On the Jewish Question', perfected the separation of state from civil society. By qualifying the revolution required for 'true democracy' as 'real', he may have been considering the 'inadequacies' of 1789. Furthermore, he did not see a 'real' revolution as a political revolution which established the state—civil society distinction, or modified some aspect of an already established abstract-political state; nor, strictly, was it a social revolution.

While Marx was becoming more interested in social questions and social analysis, he did not yet link revolution with the material force of a social class. A 'real' revolution, it seemed, could grow out of the very process of reform of the state. For civil society begins to merge with the state, and thus to transcend itself, 'only in *elections unlimited* both in respect of the franchise and the right to be elected' (CW 3,121). This, he claimed, 'is the real point of dispute concerning political *reform*, in France as in England' (CW 3,120). Marx accepted that political reform moved within the sphere of the abstract-political state, but he believed that it created a dynamic which might remove the barrier between state and civil society. If everyone were involved in politics their political and civic lives would merge. Universal suffrage, he thought, could become the means for the introduction and maintenance of a universal society, but only if it transcended the abstract-political form in which it would first appear. Universal suffrage had this potential if it was seen not as the periodic link between state and civil society, but as a continuous process of interaction and interpenetration of the spheres. The idea of what an elected representative was, and of how he was representative, would consequently need to change, as Marx explained. Rather than persons or interests, representatives must represent the species: 'He is here representative not because of something else which he represents but because of what he is and *does*' (CW 3,119).

In 1843, universal suffrage existed nowhere and was strongly opposed by those property owners who were entitled to vote. Marx saw this opposition as an attempt by the political state to preserve itself:

Electoral reform within the *abstract political state* is therefore the demand for its *dissolution*, but also for the *dissolution of civil society*. (CW 3,121)

Those who were already entitled to vote, however, saw the introduction of formal political equality not as the beginning of the end of politics, but as a threat to their interests inasmuch as it would lead to demands for other types of equality. In the event, they and Marx were mistaken. Universal suffrage in France in 1848 did not destroy the character of the state (its particularity, as Marx would have said), but produced a conservative government. Under the influence of Feuerbach's method, Marx inverted subject and predicate in (parts of) Hegel's political philosophy, and concluded that civil society was the basis of the state, that the state was the alienated projection and objectification of the universal in man. Civil society, Marx agreed with Hegel, was a sphere of particularity, of competing particular interests, of a *bellum omnium contra omnes*. But unlike Hegel, he considered the state to be a sphere of illusory universality, which only seemed to reconcile the conflicting interests of civil society. The state was a form of particularity masked by the 'general interest'. How these two spheres of particularity merged Marx made (a little) clearer only later, with his notion of a ruling class. For now, he argued simply that the disinterestedness of the state was a facade. In his 'On the Jewish Question' he declared that

the state allows private property, education, occupation, to *act* in *their* way, i.e. as private property, as education, as occupation, and to exert the influence of their special nature. (CW 3,153)

In his second Hegel critique, he added only that

The relation of industry, of the world of wealth generally, to the political world is one of the major problems of modern times. (CW 3,179)

By linking the triumph of the bourgeoisie with political emancipation, as he did in the second Hegel critique, Marx closed the issue but did not much clarify it.

Hegel had used the notions of universality and particularity to denote the spheres of state and civil society respectively. He believed, at least in his 'mature' writings, that these spheres could

34

coexist, but only if there was a mediator between them. The bureaucracy, uniting within itself civic and political roles, was Hegel's 'universal class', the element which served to keep his political philosophy unified. Marx responded to Hegel's conception of the bureaucracy in three ways. First, at a speculative level, he refused to countenance the continued existence of universality and particularity. Particularity was the negation of universality; the two conflicting principles could not simply be confined to separate spheres with a 'universal class' mediating between them. One must engulf the other. This argument was the basis for Marx's belief that particularity reigned in modern society, and that universality did not consist in the state asserting the general interest against the assemblies of estates, but in the abolition of the distinction between state and civil society, the abolition of particularity itself. Secondly, Marx agreed with Hegel that the bureaucracy did indeed unite a civic and a political position; in this respect it was the last of the traditional *estates* (CW 3,80). Thirdly, he argued that trying to bridge the gap between state and civil society simply could not work. It was here that he rejected all forms of liberalism, and liberal means of regulating the interaction of state and civil society: a written constitution, the bureaucracy (Hegel's solution), and a free press (his own earlier solution). Marx did not deny that a free press could be the voice of universality and reason; he now believed that its function could only be oppositional, not mediating. Furthermore, he was coming to the view that undistorted reason alone was not enough to destroy particularity—that particularity of viewpoint was directly related to, or reinforced by, material particularity: private property.[32]

The bureaucracy, wrote Hegel, "*subsumes*" the individual and the particular under the general' (CW 3,48). Hegel, Marx argued,

gives us an empirical description of the bureaucracy, partly as it is in actual fact, and partly as it is on its own estimation. (CW 3,45)

But the bureaucracy, according to Marx, is just another particular interest. Its particularity is based on its relationship to the state: the bureaucracy has 'the state, the spiritual essence of society, in its possession, as its *private property*' (CW 3,47). The bureaucracy, therefore, has its own particular interests to defend, even if it confuses its own interest with the general interest. Particularity,

Marx implied, is based on the possession of private property, because the demands of private property constitute an external determination of man.

Marx's ruminations on the dialectic of universal and particular were the means for his development from liberalism to communism. As long as he had accepted that the state was separate from, and above, the particularity of civil society he could find in it a source of virtue and freedom; he could berate those 'ordinary liberals' who believed that all bad came from government, and all good from the intervention of the estates. He could counter by asserting just the reverse. But once he had discarded the idea that the state and civil society were necessary elements of a truly human community, he had discarded liberalism, however broadly conceived. Once Marx had asserted that the state could not be universal, his abiding commitment to universality led him to search for a way to transcend the division between state and civil society. That way had to be revolutionary. He had, therefore, to clarify his conception of revolution: its methods, agents and objectives. Where Hegel had built his political philosophy on the complementarity of civil society and the state, Marx built his on the transcendence of them, and now conceived of the problem as being broader than politics. Marx's encounter with Hegel's political philosophy convinced him of the derivative nature of political philosophy.

Not only is the first Hegel critique important methodologically because of the application of the 'transformative method', but also because it signifies the adoption by Marx of a new conception of universality. From this point onwards, he differed fundamentally from the mature Hegel in conceiving of universality as the complete absence of particularity. This difference is best seen in their respective attitudes towards the state. Avineri argues that

Hegel's insistence that the state embodies a higher, universal orientation in inter-human relations is premissed upon the preservation of the lower, less comprehensive spheres. [33]

Raymond Plant put it this way: for Hegel, the institutions of the modern state

do not attempt to remove particularity and sectional interest... but [function] rather by recognizing such particularity as being necessary for the development of self-consciousness and building into the state structure this element of particularity but at the same time fusing it with the universal ends of the state. [34]

Hegel concluded that there could be no return to what he saw as the unmediated harmony of the classical Greek polis, the model which had exerted such a fascination over German minds, including Marx's (CW 3,137).[35] Hegel posited a system, a continuing historical and logical relationship, of universality and particularity. Marx, by contrast, saw universality as the annihilation of particularity. Accordingly, the crux of Hegel's problematic is *mediation*; the crux of Marx's is *abolition* or *transcendence*. The question for Marx at the end of 1843 was not what could mediate universality and particularity, but which class could destroy particularity. The role of the universal class in each theory is quite different. There are hints of Marx's thoroughgoing conception of universality in his discussion of the free press as not just a mediator, but an educator, but it was in his notes on Hegel's political philosophy that he began consistently to appreciate its implications. The proletariat may have been 'a kind of logical missing link' for Marx, as Dick Howard has argued,[36] but the puzzle was slightly different from Hegel's.

Marx made a summary of the findings of his first Hegel critique in a review of Bruno Bauer's writings on the Jewish question entitled 'On the Jewish Question' and first published in 1844 in the *Deutsch-französische Jahrbücher*. This work was partly written before he left Kreuznach for Paris in October 1843. In its first part, Marx used the Jewish question as a symbol for all conditions of man dominated by particularity. He argued, against Bauer, that emancipation from particularity was not achieved by a merely political emancipation (the recognition by the state of the right of various types of particularity to exist), but by what he called 'human emancipation', the emancipation of mankind from all types of particularity, including the division between state and civil society. Marx believed that the Jewish question would not be solved if the state granted Jews the right freely to worship and take their place in civil society as citizens, nor by Jews renouncing Judaism. The Jewish question, like all other problems of particularity, would only be solved once universality reigned: when Judaism and all other religions had disappeared. Political emancipation, he declared, is a 'big step forward' to human emancipation (CW 3,155). Yet it created a separate political sphere, formally emancipated from the limitations of man in civil society (such as religion, education and property), without emancipating men themselves from these limitations. Marx listed private property among these external determinants of men, but in the first part of 'On the Jewish Question' private property was merely one of a number of essentially equal forms of particularity which contributed to the division and competition of civil society.

When Marx argued that the 'political annulment of private property not only fails to abolish private property but even presupposes it' (CW 3,153), he was not giving private property special significance, but making a representative point about forms of particularity. But he is also now less sanguine about the possibility of reform within the abstract-political state being able, peacefully, to transcend the state itself. He argued that if political life sought 'to constitute itself as the real species-life of man', to become truly human, universal, life, it would come 'into *violent* contradiction with its own conditions of life' (CW 3,156). Establishing true universality was likely to involve a violent revolution against particularity. Along with this revolutionary conclusion, Marx began to attach importance to material interests in civil society as the basic form and the source of particularity.

In the first part of 'On the Jewish Question', Marx used the condition of the Jews to illustrate his analysis of the modern division between state and civil society, and of the consequent internal division between *man* and *citizen*, *homme* and *citoyen*. Political emancipation, he argued, was not authentic emancipation. In the second part of 'On the Jewish Question', influenced by an article 'On the Essence of Money' unsuccessfully contributed by Moses Hess for the forthcoming *Deutsch-französische Jahrbücher*, Marx identified human emancipation with emancipation from huckstering and money. Here, he used the Jews not simply as representatives of all forms of particularity, but in the vulgar sense of being slaves to money and usury. The 'Jew' is still representative—representative of all men in civil society, pursuing their own interests against one another— and representative of something Marx now considered to be the basic evil of human life.

By using the popular anti-Semitic image for his own ends, Marx

accepts it as an accurate image. He thus, rather ignobly and unfairly, succeeds in satisfying the type of anti-Jewishness then
popular (even among some Jewish intellectuals), while making a
perfectly consistent attack on the inherent egoism of civil society.[37]
The emancipation of the Jews, he now argued, required a human
emancipation conceived as 'the emancipation of mankind from
Judaism' (CW 3,170). It required the emancipation of all humans
from the god, money.

Money is the estranged essence of man's work and man's existence, and this
alien essence dominates him, and he worships it. (CW 3,172)

This was the theoretical prelude to Marx's turn to the study of
political economy. But it also led to him conceiving of social
classes with material interests as the actors of history, and of
revolutions as clashes of material interests, and of society itself as a
congeries of material interests. Society, Marx formerly believed,
consisted of a collection of theoretical interests, in which progress
consisted in the elimination of limitations to knowledge through
education in the universal interest. The role of reason was to
destroy the particularity of viewpoints put forward by different
sections of the population. Once Marx had become convinced that
society consisted of material interests, and that particularity of
viewpoint had a material source in the possession and defence of
private property, he realized that reason was not enough to destroy
particularity. Reason had to be linked with a material force. The
second Hegel critique, by introducing the concept of the proletariat
into Marx's work, turned his attention decisively away from the
problems of political philosophy towards what he now considered
the more central problems of political economy. He turned from
the study of abstract interests to the study of material interests. He
therefore saw no pressing need to prepare the first Hegel critique for
publication. In this sense the second Hegel critique, despite the
'Introduction' of its title, is something of a *conclusion*.

While the notion of material interests had begun to influence
Marx's theory—his use of the concept 'proletariat' being the clearest indication—he still acknowledged the importance of thought, of
philosophy, in the creation of a universal society. Indeed, it was
only when the proletariat had adopted universality in thought, by
becoming the philosophical class, that it would become the

universal class. So Marx argued in the second Hegel critique. At this stage, he saw material interests chiefly as *limits* to the general standpoint. Since the proletariat had no material interests it was subject to no limits to acquiring universality. Marx still claimed that philosophy represented the universal standpoint, and that philosophers (i.e. Young Hegelians) could play a major role in transforming the world of men.[38] His increasing stress on the role of material interests, refracted through Feuerbach's 1843 *Provisional Theses,* began to modify his view of the dialectic between the world and philosophy.

In May 1843, Marx wrote to Ruge that the vehicle for the 'impending revolution' in Germany was 'all people who think and suffer' (CW 3,141). It was still central to this project to 'expose the old world to the full light of day' (CW 3,141) through philosophy. He added:

The longer the time that events allow to thinking humanity for taking stock of its position, and to suffering mankind for mobilising its forces, the more perfect on entering the world will be the product that the present time bears in its womb. (CW 3,141)

This clear division of labour between suffering and thinking humans, repeated in a slightly different form in the second Hegel critique, is a direct result of Marx's reading of Feuerbach. The idea that the development of the world, foreseen by philosophy, is immanent, was common to the Hegelian tradition. In his *Provisional Theses,* Feuerbach had written:

Only what can *suffer* deserves to exist. Only the *entity rich in pain is a divine entity.* An essence without suffering is an essence *without an essence.* An entity *devoid of sensibility, devoid of matter.*[39]

What Marx had earlier thought of as a worldly philosophy must, according to Feuerbach, have a '*passive principle* within itself',[40] that is, a worldly principle; otherwise it would be 'a thoroughly *one-sided* philosophy'. For a complete philosophy, Feuerbach maintained, the philosopher

must consider what in the human being does *not* philosophize, but rather is *at odds with* philosophy and *opposed* to abstract thinking. Thus the philosopher must bring into the *text* of philosophy what Hegel relegated to mere *remarks.* Only in this way will philosophy be *irrefutable* and *uncontested,* a *universal* and irresistable power. Genuine philosophy thus has to begin not *with itself*, but with its *antithesis*, with *what is not philosophy*.[41] Universality of thought, which Marx had earlier considered to be characteristic of philosophy, now required a worldly, non-abstract element: an element Feuerbach treated in an entirely abstract manner as *suffering*, or as the *heart* (as opposed to the *head* of abstract philosophy). This worldly element, soon to be embodied in Marx's concept of the proletariat, took Marx's theory out of the realms of traditional philosophy. Marx had an ungenerous nature; he acknowledged Feuerbach's general contribution to his intellectual development only by writing vigorous and partly unjustifiable attacks on Feuerbach's theories in his *Theses on Feuerbach* (whose very form is Feuerbachian) and in *The German Ideology*.[42]

True philosophy, Marx argued in July 1842, was 'the intellectual quintessence of its time' (CW 1,195). Such a philosophy, he believed, would be taken up by the public, 'which loves truth and knowledge for their own sakes' (CW 1,197). Marx wrote in this spirit, and with this hope, until he concluded that particular viewpoints were nourished and reinforced by particular material interests. He then transferred love of philosophy to suffering humans, who would adopt the universal standpoint because they had no material interests to limit their perception. Up to, and including the time of the second Hegel critique, he conceived the dialectic of universal and particular chiefly as a feature of the realm of thought. Material factors were introduced only in so far as they impinged upon (by limiting or not limiting the perception of) theory. This approach culminated in the second Hegel critique, where the proletariat was introduced as a means of realizing Marx's worldly philosophy not because it was a class of philosophers, but because it was the only class not excluded from philosophy. The proletariat, Marx declared in the spirit of Feuerbach, was the *heart* of human emancipation, philosophy was its *head* (CW 3,187).

Between 1841 and 1844 Marx completely rethought the dialectic of universal and particular, which was the driving element of his thought, the source of his intellectual and political development. Through this development, he altered his conception of the role of philosophy in achieving the universal society by adding to it the non-philosophical element of the sufferers, or the proletariat. He altered his conception of the universal society itself, from the establishment of proper relations between state and civil society to the transcending of the distinction between the two spheres. Certain ideas, of course, remained the same. He was committed to universality—even if he now embraced it as an uncompromising universality; from the beginning he was hostile to private property as a form, and then as the source, of particularity. In general, Marx saw ideas as active, or at least as activators. It was part of his essentially negative conception of the proletariat in 1844 that it had no particular viewpoint, and could therefore be used for implementing philosophy. Lichtheim has thus argued that at the time of the second Hegel critique, Marx 'was then still as it were a German Jacobin for whom the proletariat existed primarily as the instrument of revolution'.[43]

The second Hegel critique was written for, and first published in, the only edition (a double number) of the *Deutsch-französische Jahrbücher* in February 1844. The *Jahrbücher* was designed, as its title suggests, to fulfil the Young Hegelian plan of laying the foundation for the unity of German theory and French practice.[44] But Marx's second Hegel critique, although it might be said to have conceded that the proletariat created a common bond between Germany and France, was otherwise unremittingly German in its style, its assumptions and particularly in its preoccupations. The *Jahrbücher* failed to attract French contributors or a French audience; its programme was stillborn. It nevertheless ignited theoretical and practical issues within Young Hegelianism itself which had hitherto been smouldering. For Marx, the second Hegel critique marks the end of his Young Hegelianism.[45]

The second Hegel critique began with a brief discussion of critical philosophy, particularly its proper object of criticism and its tasks. The criticism of religion, which for many Young Hegelians and even for Feuerbach, was a central and abiding theme, was for Marx simply a point of departure. 'For Germany' he declared, 'the *criticism of religion* is in the main complete' (CW 3,175). Feuerbach's *Provisional Theses* centred on the relationship, 'the *previous mésalliance* ' between philosophy and theology. The very reform of philosophy advocated by Feuerbach was formulated in these terms:

The new philosophy is the *realized idea*, the *truth* of Christianity. But precisely by having the *essence* of Christianity in itself, it abandons the *name* of Christianity. [46]

Marx is a Feuerbachian in so far as he adds, in the second Hegel critique, that 'The basis of irreligious criticism is this: *Man makes religion,* religion does not make man' (CW 3,175). But 'criticism of religion is the premise of all criticism' (CW 3,175), not its end. Where Feuerbach believed that alienation would be solved once religious alienation had been overcome in the realization that God is man, Marx argued that there were more fundamental forms of alienation than the religious. Religion was a product of man in a certain society. 'This state, this society, produce religion, an *inverted world-consciousness* ' (CW 3,175). The distress of men in the real world produced religion; the existing world needed such illusions. But the present task of philosophy, he added, was 'to unmask self-estrangement in its *unholy forms* ' (CW 3,176), and thus to un-cover the real root of self-estrangement in its holy form. Marx wanted to change the world of men so that they needed no illusions to soothe their suffering.

Of what use, then, was a critical exposition of Hegel's *Philosophy of Right* for this very practical task? For isn't Marx dealing only with 'a copy, the German *philosophy* of state and of law', rather than with the actual state and law (CW 3,176)? Marx explained that while German conditions 'are *beneath the level of history, beneath any criticism* ' (CW 3,177), German philosophy apprehends the most modern developments. The critique of Hegel, therefore, represents 'a critical analysis of the modern state and of the reality connected with it' (CW 3,181). But he made an even stronger claim: that German philosophy allowed Germany to tran-scend its *ancien régime* political status:

We Germans have gone through our post-history in thought, in *philosophy*. We are *philosophical* contemporaries of the present without being its *historical* contemporaries. (CW 3,180)

It was clear from the outset of the second Hegel critique that Marx's purpose was not simply, or not even, to introduce a scholarly study of Hegel's political philosophy, but to diagnose the social and political situation in Germany. Having established to his own satisfaction that German philosophical achievements had brought Germany in some respects to the level of modernity, he posed the rhetorical question which reveals his whole programme:

Can Germany attain a practice *à la hauteur des principes*, i.e. a *revolution* which will raise it not only to the *official level* of the modern nations but to the *height of humanity* which will be the near future of those nations? (CW 3,182)

Revolutions, Marx argued, 'require a *passive* element, a *material* basis' (CW 3,183), because the *status quo* was a material force, which could only be overthrown by another material force (CW 3,182). Furthermore, a *radical* revolution required a material basis with *radical* needs. It seems, Marx wrote, as if the 'preconditions and grounds' for a radical German revolution are absent (CW 3,183). Undaunted, he developed two arguments—both essentially negative—to establish that such a revolution was possible, indeed inevitable. The first was that Germany too had radical needs; the second was that a merely political emancipation in Germany was impossible. He concluded that there was no alternative to a radical revolution: it was the 'only *practically* possible liberation of Germany' (CW 3,187).

While Germany has not shared the political and economic benefits of modern development, Marx claimed in the first of these arguments, she has 'shared the *sufferings* ' (CW 3,183). German governments 'combine the *civilised shortcomings of the modern political world*... with the *barbaric deficiencies of the ancien régime*' (CW 3,183). These are the grounds for radical needs. In the second argument, Marx refined his notion of revolution by linking it with social classes. A partial, '*merely* political revolution' occurs when a '*part of civil society* emancipates itself and attains *general* domination' (CW 3,184). The mechanism of this political emancipation plays a vital part in the argument, for

No class of civil society can play this role without arousing a moment of enthusiasm in itself and in the masses, [when it]... is perceived and acknowledged as its *general representative*. (CW 3,184)

The problem in Germany, however, is that there is neither a particular estate which sees itself as an emancipator, nor a particular estate which is considered to be the general stumbling-block to emancipation. The social conditions which preceded and caused the French Revolution, Marx argued, do not obtain in Germany. Analysing the relations between German social classes (with the noticeable and notable absence of the peasantry), he highlighted the limitations of each, their accommodation with one another, and their general timidity. Indeed, he claimed that 'in Germany universal emancipation is the *conditio sine qua non* of any partial emancipation' (CW 3,186). Where then, asked Marx, lies the *'positive* possibility of a German [i.e. a universal] emancipation' (CW 3,186)? It lay, he maintained, in the 'formation of a class with *radical* chains', the proletariat (CW 3,186). The only class which could make the radical revolution, and thus emancipate Germany, did not yet (in some senses) exist; but on it Marx staked the future of Germany.

In outline, this is the argument of the second Hegel critique, an argument for the German radical revolution. Yet it raises serious doubts. One, which became an issue in Russia late in the nineteenth century, is whether a country can 'leap over', or circumvent, a historical stage. The provisional historical schema constructed by Marx in 1843 consisted in the emergence of Europe from the Middle Ages through a political emancipation, to be followed by a human emancipation. His prognosis for Germany, however, challenged this schema, by appealing to Germany's obvious philosophical achievements as a substitute for prosaic historical development. He underlined the exceptional character of Germany's development and revolutionary prospects, ironically as it turned out, by counterposing Germany and Russia (CW 3,180). Hegel's philosophy of the state and law may have owed a great deal to the political realities of France, and may have been revealing about them, but it was no proper substitute for actual German political development. By providing Marx with insights into 'modern' problems, Hegel's philosophy did not make the problems of Germany 'modern'. Nevertheless, Marx believed that philosophy could and did play a major role in the real world.

Another doubt about Marx's argument arises from its style. Marx turns every negative into a positive: he turns disadvantages into advantages for Germany. (Indeed, one sometimes feels that Marx's style encouraged him to present, as a solution to a problem, what was in fact merely a reformulation of it.) This stylistic 'solution' was reserved, for the moment, for the problems of Germany. All that Germany seems to lack of modernity, from his analysis, are its benefits. The dynamic of the radical revolution in other countries is different. The existence of organized politics, at least in France, entails a major difference; Marx described every class in France as '*politically idealistic* ' (CW 3,186), although he did not consider the peasantry. Every French class (with the noted exception)

becomes aware of itself at first not as a particular class but as the representative of social requirements generally. (CW 3,186)

Thus the 'negative' universality which Marx attributed to the proletariat, the universality which arises from lack of particularity and lack of hope, is in fact constructed specifically for the incipient German proletariat.

One of the central propositions of the second Hegel critique is that if Germany cannot have a partial revolution, it must have a universal revolution. It was characteristic of the proletariat that, having no particular interests, it must represent the universal interest. The proletariat, Marx explained in the following well-known passage, is

a class with *radical chains*, a class of civil society which is not a class of civil society, an estate which is the dissolution of all estates, a sphere which has a universal character by its universal suffering and claims no *particular right* because no *particular wrong* but *wrong generally* is perpetrated against it; which can no longer invoke a *historical* but only a *human* title; ... a sphere, finally, which cannot emancipate itself without emancipating itself from all other spheres of society and thereby emancipating all other spheres of society, which, in a word, is the *complete loss* of man and hence can win itself only through the *complete rewinning of man*. (CW 3,186)

Marx may have been a perceptive critic of German social and political reality, and he may have well understood the limitations of the German bourgeoisie, but his conclusion that the only alternative to a French-style political revolution was a revolution for human emancipation is neither logically tenable nor historically prescient. The failure of conventional liberalism in Germany in 1848 prepared the ground for Bismarck, not for the proletariat.

Marx had been deeply impressed by recent French history and by French social and political reality. But despite the insights that class analysis allowed him, his views on France and the French proletariat were abstract and inaccurate. If he could describe swiftly and in a masterly fashion the shortcomings of Germany, he seemed blind to the shortcomings of France. Nevertheless, his move to Paris late in 1843 prompted his adoption of the terminology of 'social class', which distinguished the second Hegel critique from his other contributions to the *Deutsch-französische Jahrbücher*. 'Class' now became a central concept of his social analysis, and the central reference for his notions of political and human emancipation.[47] In 'On the Jewish Question', Marx had treated political emancipation as the perfection of the political principle, whereby the state became formally separated from civil society and its various internal distinctions. In the second Hegel critique, however, a political revolution is defined as a part of civil society gaining general domination, implicitly through its control of the state. Where Marx had seen political emancipation as the introduction of formal political equality and political freedoms, he now considered it to be the domination of the bourgeoisie. How these two frameworks meshed, Marx never precisely explained, but it is clear that he held them both to be valid explanations of modern society.

What characteristics of the proletariat did Marx believe would fit it for the task of establishing the universal, truly human society? Clearly, because it represented universality. How? Marx's arguments on this score are essentially negative. Universality here was the absence of particular interest: the proletariat was the negation of private property.[48] And private property, as Cornu notes, was conceived much more clearly in the second Hegel critique than ever before in Marx's work as the determining element of bourgeois society and as the source of particularity.[49] Universality here also stood for the proletariat's universal, or unrelieved, suffering. Marx argued that the proletariat received none of society's benefits; it therefore had no stake in the existing society (nothing to lose), and had no reason for its viewpoint to be limited or one-sided, except for the absence of education. In this sense, the concept 'proletariat' took on those characteristics which Marx earlier believed resided in society as a whole. Only proletarians loved truth and knowledge for their own sakes. Only the proletariat would respond positively to the presentation of truth. The knowledge of proletarians was 'bounded' only by their inability to acquire it, not by material interests. This essential difference between the proletariat and other classes meant, for Marx, that where his message had been rejected by entrenched particularity, it would be enthusiastically received by the proletariat. Instead of the free press, Marx now required a proletarian press to promulgate the universal standpoint. For it was not the proletariat alone which would emancipate humanity, but the proletariat in alliance with critical philosophy. Marx still believed, as he had in 1842, that intellect was universal (CW 1,303). Critical philosophy represented the universal interest in the abstract; the proletariat represented the universal interest in the material sense. The message of critical philosophy, the need for a universal society, remained the same as in his days with the *Rheinische Zeitung*; only the audience had changed. Those whom Marx had argued would be receptive to the truth were now distinguished by their relation to material interests.

Material interest, Marx argued, not only limited the standpoint of various classes, but constituted an obstacle to universality that could only be overcome by a revolution, which was itself a material act: 'material force must be overthrown by material force' (CW 3,182). And the universal standpoint 'also becomes a material force as soon as it has gripped the masses' (CW 3,182). Philosophy had to take on materiality; it could only do so through the proletariat. It was not enough for philosophy to expose particularity to the 'light of day'; a revolution was required. Material interest in the shape of private property distorted the viewpoint of its bearers, and explained why particularity persisted in the face of reason. Particularity was not so easily given up. Marx might here be seen as accounting for, and trying to overcome, the limitations of abstract philosophy. It should also be noted that the proletariat, as Marx described it in the second Hegel critique, was an element apart from the clash between state and civil society which he had spent many months analysing. The antagonism between state and civil society, Marx implied, took place in a sphere separate from the proletariat. This antagonism may have been the determining element of its own sphere, but Marx believed that there was a more fundamental clash between spheres: between the sphere of the proletariat, and the sphere of (what Marx does not yet call) 'bourgeois society'. For civil society, or perhaps 'bourgeois society', was a sphere of competing particular interests. For Marx,

the proletariat existed outside 'bourgeois society', and therefore outside the individual dialectic he had earlier criticized: the dialectic
between *bourgeois* and *citoyen*. The proletarian was not rent by
this division.

Although it had its origins in Marx's earlier discussions of 'the
poor', the notion that there was a more fundamental division in
modern society than that between state and civil society did not
outlast by many months the second Hegel critique. Nevertheless, it
was essential in forming his view that the political revolution was
only a partial solution to human alienation. The proletarian
revolution, by contrast, was universal in both extensional and
intensional senses: everyone would be liberated from dehumanization.

The universality of Marx's concept of the proletariat was
contrasted, in the second Hegel critique, with another type of universality: that which arises when a particular class sees itself as
standing for, and for a period becomes the actual bearer of, interests
common to the rest of society. Marx introduced this latter notion
of universality to explain the class dynamics of political revolution
and, in particular, the French Revolution. Having declared that
revolutions are made by social classes in their own interests, and
that the French Revolution resulted in the domination of the
bourgeoisie, Marx must needs explain why this bourgeois
revolution was a *popular* event, and why it was successful in a
bourgeois sense. How could only a part of civil society emancipate
itself in what seemed to have been a general emancipation? He
believed that the answer lay with the French bourgeoisie's ability to
become, for a time, a universal class:

No class of civil society can play this role without arousing a moment of
enthusiasm in itself and in the masses, a moment in which it fraternises and
merges with society in general, becomes confused with it and is perceived
and acknowledged as its *general representative* ; a moment in which its
demands and rights are truly the rights and demands of society itself; a
moment in which it is truly the social head and the social heart. (CW
3,184)

The second Hegel critique established the framework for Marx's
sociology of revolution. Modern revolutions, Marx suggested, are
mass events, whatever their outcomes. They involve the

participation of all classes, united around one particular class in the common cause of removing another from power. The notion of what I shall call *revolutionary universality* was introduced to account for what he considered to be the so-far-unexplained paradox of the French Revolution (ostensibly universal but resulting in the reign of particularity), as well as to scotch the idea that the German revolution he anticipated had to follow precisely the French model. For not only did the German bourgeoisie, according to Marx, not have the courage to attempt to become a universal class—society's representative against the old regime—but there was no German estate of general *negative* significance against which it could champion society's interests.

Modern revolution was a dialectic between universal and particular, for Marx, because revolutionary universality arose only in response to what I call 'anti-revolutionary particularity', an enemy characterized by blatant particularity, or selfishness, which had become generally repugnant. Thus modern revolutions are essentially revolutions against particularity, even if they result in the rule of a new type of particularity. Such a result can be explained in terms of revolutionary universality. Revolutionary universality did not inhere in the nature of a particular class; it was a response to the challenge of a particular situation, and only classes which rose to the challenge could embody it. Revolutionary universality lasted only for a historical moment; it was not permanent (although it was a 'real' or 'objective' universality while it lasted) because it soon became confused with particularity. In a sense, revolutionary universality is a way of conceiving leadership in situations where leaders truly represent their followers. Marx had a conception of *representation*, discussed above, as the essential identity of representer and represented. When a particular class *represented* society in this way, it was a universal class.

The universality of the proletariat, however, did not need to be accepted by other classes. Indeed, the universality of the proletariat did not depend on perception at all. The universality of the proletariat, in contrast to revolutionary universality, did not last only for a historical moment; it was part of the concept of the proletariat. The proletariat was a social force progressively realizing its universal essence, its concept. Universality was something which inhered within that concept; once the proletariat realized its essence, through exposure to the truths of critical philosophy, it would put itself forward as the general social representative against the general stumbling-block, the bourgeoisie. For this reason, and in contrast to the *revolutionary* universality which, conceivably, any class might embody (although practically Marx limited it to the bourgeoisie), I shall call the universality of the proletariat *inherent* universality. The essence of the proletariat, according to Marx, is universality. The proletariat has no particular interest to pursue, and thus no particular interest which it might confuse with the universal interest after the revolution it shall lead.

The discussion of the proletariat in the second Hegel critique is conducted primarily in terms of 'essences', or 'concepts'. Even though Marx seems to be discussing real social forces, he was in fact proposing a *concept* of the proletariat not simply in the sense of an entity abstracted from real social forces, but a concept in the Hegelian sense. The dialectic of appearance and essence, with which Marx had been concerned since his Doctoral Dissertation at least, meant that whatever concrete social force he may have had in mind late in 1843 and early in 1844 as the universal class, it was a universal class only 'in itself'. However one-sided its appearance, this social force would realize its essence chiefly (at this stage in Marx's work) by being confronted with a picture of its essence. This potentially universal social force was defined philosophically. The gap between the proletariat's essence and its appearance, conceived in the second Hegel critique as a question of the *formation* of the proletariat, was to become in Marx's later works the problem of the development of class consciousness. That Marx used the term '*Bildung*', which has been translated as the 'formation' of the proletariat (CW 3,186), is itself significant, for '*Bildung*' can also mean 'to educate' and 'to enlighten'. This German term subtly incorporates the role of critical philosophy in turning the existence of the proletariat into an existence at one with its essence. Unlike the other classes of society, Marx saw the contrast between the proletariat's appearance and its essence simply in terms of a lack of knowledge. In this respect, one might say that the *Communist Manifesto*, the *First Address of the International Working Men's Association* and even, perhaps, *Capital*, were the *Rheinische*

Zeitung of the proletariat, although their education by the work-process soon came to outweigh, in Marx's mind, education by the printed word.

Marx's journal of 1848-49, the *Neue Rheinische Zeitung*, re-called its eponymous predecessor not just in its oppositional stance, but also in its educative role. Philosophy, Marx declared in the second Hegel critique, was the *head* of the emancipation of the human being, the proletariat was its *heart*. And, he added,

once this lightning of thought has squarely struck this ingenuous soil of the people the emancipation of the *Germans* into *human beings* will take place. (CW 3,187)

The proletariat was introduced into Marx's work as the class which was receptive to philosophy and which, through philosophy, would realize its essence. Philosophy here was the active principle; the proletariat was passive and material, regarding philosophy as external to it. When, in his 1845 *Theses on Feuerbach*, Marx criticized Feuerbach for dividing society into two parts, 'one of which is superior to society' (CW 5,4), he implicitly condemned his own earlier conception of the relation between philosophy and the proletariat.

Marx selected the proletariat for its role as the agent of the human-emancipating revolution because the proletariat was, for philosophy, a *tabula rasa*, distinguished by what it did not have, rather than by what it had. Because Marx conceived the proletariat as existing in a sphere separate from 'bourgeois society', it is tempting to describe his vision as a contrast between the bourgeoisie in a corrupt and limiting society, and the proletariat in a benevolent 'state of nature', isolated and suffering, yet fundamentally unaffected human beings. There is a constant tension in Marx's conception of the proletariat, as we shall see, between the proletarian conceived as a victim of bourgeois society and the proletarian conceived as an inhabitant of his own sphere. Cornu is right, I believe, to describe the proletariat of the second Hegel critique as 'un peu comme le protagoniste du drame feuerbachien de la destinée humaine'.[50] The Feuerbachian elements of Marx's concept are stronger even than the directly Hegelian elements. Hegel, as Avineri reminds us, relied on a 'universal class'—the bureaucracy—to resolve the tension he perceived in his own system between the state and civil society. But the 'universal class' in Marx's theory does not play an analogous role. Marx's 'universal class' does not exist to reconcile a tension, but to abolish it. I prefer to see Marx's conception of the free press as his response to (and in his radical liberal phase, his substitute for) Hegel's *bureaucracy*. Avineri considers Marx's development of the concept 'proletariat' as a series of theoretical moves, and even as theoretical moves within the framework of political philosophy; but Marx did not formulate his concept of the proletariat by analogy with, and in response to the inadequacies he perceived in Hegel's conception of the 'universal class'.[51] The dialectic of universal and particular, essence and appearance, was Marx's major theoretical tool during this period. With it, he rejected Hegel's concept of bureaucracy; and with it he formulated the role and characteristics of the proletariat. To see the development of Marx's concept of the proletariat within this framework is not to deny the influence of other sources of his concept, such as Hegel's master-slave dialectic, the attitudes of German thinkers to social reform, and particularly the contributions of French socialist thinkers to social and political analysis. These social analyses will be given their due in the next chapter. Hegel's view of the master-slave relationship, with its ironic twist, is best considered briefly here.

Hegel opposed slavery as 'an outrage on the conception of man',[52] even though he saw a certain historical necessity about it. But he argued that although the slave was dependent on the will of his master, the slave's productive activity gave rise to his self-consciousness. Indeed, it is the slave and not the master who is capable of self-realization; the master in this respect is passive and dependent.[53] Hegel declared:

just as lordship showed its essential nature to be the reverse of what it wants to be, so, too, bondage will, when completed pass into the opposite of what it immediately is: being a consciousness repressed within itself, it will enter into itself, and change round into real and true independence. [54]

This discussion operates at two levels. The slave is unfree, but can achieve the consciousness that he exists in his own right. 'Thus precisely in labour... the bondsman becomes aware... of having and being a "mind of his own"'.[55] In a sense, slavery enslaves the master. Neither master nor slave, however, is fully capable of self-realization.[56] Clearly, Marx was aware of this discussion, for he commended Hegel in the Paris Manuscripts for having, in *The Phenomenology of Mind*, grasped 'the essence of *labour* and comprehends objective man... as the outcome of man's *own labour*' (CW 3,333).

The first appearance of the concept of the proletariat in Marx's work marks an important watershed in the development of his thought, the end of his period of Young Hegelianism and the commitment to abstract thought, and the beginning of his turn towards the study of material interests. The dialectic of universal and particular was moved from the realm of abstract interests to the realm of material interests. The concept of the proletariat, emerging from Marx's fertile mind with the birthmarks of philosophy, would become the means of focussing his attention on the struggle of material forces in society. The shift in his theory which the concept 'proletariat' presaged accounts for the curious nature of an 'Introduction' to *A Contribution to the Critique of Hegel's Philosophy of Law* which made publication of the body of the work redundant. The importance of Marx's concept of the proletariat at this point in his work, as well as its central ambiguity, is well expressed by Lowy:

In sum, the conception of the proletariat in the *Introduction* ... is at the same time the point of departure for a politico-ideological evolution closely bound to a reflection upon the European workers' movement, and the point of arrival of a philosophical evolution 'in search of the universal'. Consequently, it has the character of a 'hinge', which explains at first attempt its ambiguity: on the one hand revolutionary and concrete, on the other left-hegelian and abstract....[57]

How 'concrete' one considers Marx's conception of the proletariat in the second Hegel critique depends, of course, on how one weighs the influence on his theory of his contact with workers in Paris. In the next chapter I shall argue for minimizing this influence. Marx still apprehended material interests in an abstract way.

The ambiguity, in fact the tension, between the proletariat conceived as a class without particular interests, and therefore receptive to the universal standpoint, and the proletariat conceived as a social class with a material existence and material interests to pursue, persisted and deepened as Marx's theory developed. As Marx gradually left behind philosophical language, his image of the proletariat as a class open to knowledge and truth did not dim, despite his occasional recognition of the stubborn prejudices of the actual working class. Marx continued to believe that a theoretical universality was possible, but argued that it would grow from the material universality of the proletariat, and through the pursuit by the proletariat of its material interests against the bourgeoisie. From being the handmaiden of philosophy, in the second Hegel critique, the proletariat became the source of the universal standpoint. Yet the proletariat still had an essence to which Marx believed it must conform.

The dialectic of universal and particular, in the years up to 1844, was conceived by Marx chiefly as a confrontation between philosophy and the world. Philosophy took allies against particularity, the chief and final ally being the proletariat. But the introduction of the concept of the proletariat began to alter how he conceived this very dialectic. The concept 'proletariat' served to swallow up philosophy. No longer did Marx see a clash primarily between abstract universality and abstract particularity, reason and limited knowledge; he began to see a clash between two material forces which embodied universality and particularity, and which he soon described as the clash between proletariat and bourgeoisie. Thus Avineri is mistaken when he argues that there is a tension in Marx's concept of the proletariat between universality and particularity, as follows:

This tension between particularism and universality—between a class's appearance as a protagonist of the general will and its search for its own interests—comes to a head, according to Marx, with the emergence of the modern proletariat. It can be overcome only by the simultaneous abolition of the proletariat as a separate class and the disappearance of class differences in general.[58]

While such a tension does arise in revolutionary universal classes such as the French bourgeoisie of 1789, it does not exist in the inherently universal class. What is at issue with Marx's concept of the proletariat is not the tension between universality and particularity, but between universality as an abstract and as a material phenomenon, and consequently, the means by which the inherently universal class recognizes its universality and asserts itself as society's general representative. The realization of its essence by the actual proletariat may involve the intervention of philosophy, as Marx suggested in the second Hegel critique, or it may be a process of self-realization through the class struggle. Whatever the case, the limitations of the actual proletariat—the proletariat's *appearance* as distinct from its *essence*—are considered by Marx not to be essential or irremediable. Thus it is best to talk of the limitations of the proletariat, rather than of its particularity, if we want properly to appreciate Marx's view. For an inherently universal class, no limitation is inherent.

3

Sources

So far I have considered Marx's concept of the proletariat as the culmination of an intellectual development on the theme of the dialectic between universal and particular. This development, of course, was not entirely abstract. As I have noted, Marx's contact with the real world of frustrated academic ambitions, censorship, material interests and, in Paris, workers, was grist to the theoretical mill, and helped to shift the direction of his interests. The choice by Marx of the term 'proletariat' to denote the inherently universal class was probably related to his increasing familiarity with French social, and particularly socialist, thought. Certainly his use of 'class' rather than 'estate' was a product of his shift to Paris in 1843; the language of modern social thought was French. Marx's concept of the proletariat, therefore, drew on two traditions: German philosophy and French social thought. It had no significant economic foundation. Although Marx was schooled in German philosophy, French socialism became an influence—even if, at first, an irritation—in his work as early as mid-1842. Indeed, the introduction of Marx's concept of the proletariat in 1844 put him firmly in the socialist camp, whatever his reservations about particular theorists or theories. It is a forgiveable exaggeration to say that, at this time, there were as many socialisms as there were socialists. Nevertheless, they faced certain common problems, and proposed certain characteristic solutions which stressed *the social interest*. Marx's concept of the proletariat not only arose from this tradition, but can be seen as his attempt to solve one of the fundamental dilemmas it faced: how can the social interest be secured in a society increasingly divided along class lines?

Marx's first serious contact with the radical trends of French social thought probably occurred during his period with the *Rheinische Zeitung*, although his childhood mentor, von Westphalen, was probably a Saint-Simonian, and one of his

57

teachers, Eduard Gans, certainly was.[1] We know that Lorenz von Stein's comprehensive survey of *Socialism and Communism in Contemporary France*—the work which played a major role in bringing socialism to the attention of Germans—was favourably reviewed in the *Rheinische Zeitung* by Moses Hess, himself a Young Hegelian who was already a communist.[2] But Marx was unimpressed by communism. In reply to the Augsburg *Allgemeine Zeitung's* charge that the *Rheinische Zeitung* was flirting with communism, he argued that while it was 'a fact... obvious to everyone in Manchester, Paris and Lyons' that 'the estate that today owns nothing *demands* to share in the wealth of the middle classes' ((CW 1,216), a direct reference to an earlier report in the *Rheinische Zeitung* which Marx did not write), 'communist ideas in their present form' lack 'even *theoretical reality*' (CW 1,220). Such was Marx's world-view that he saw communism as a challenge, or danger, only if it could be theoretically elaborated. Marx indicated, in passing, that he was aware of the works of Pierre Leroux, Victor Considérant, and particularly of Pierre-Joseph Proudhon, but that they were suitable for criticism only 'after long and profound study' (CW 1,220). Marx suggested that he was acquainted with French communism,[3] that he was hostile to attempts at its implementation, but that there might be some critical substance to 'actual communism'. That Marx, in the same statement, limited social distress and social conflict to England and France was doubtless a concession to the censor as well as a defence against the Augsburg *Allgemeine Zeitung*.

In a letter to Ruge in September 1843, Marx described communism as a 'dogmatic abstraction':

I am not thinking of some imaginary and possible communism, but actually existing communism as taught by [Etienne] Cabet, [Théodore] Dézamy, [Wilhelm] Weitling, etc. (CW 3,143)

Marx linked his rejection of this communism with his views on private property and what was required for its real abolition:

the abolition of private property and communism are by no means identical. (CW 3,143)

This phrase is the centre-piece of Marx's opposition to other communisms, even when he himself became a communist. For Marx, 'actually existing communism' was a 'one-sided realisation of the socialist principle' (CW 3,143) since it did not want to abolish private property but to *generalize* it. Marx developed this argument against what he came to call 'crude communism' in his 1844 Paris Manuscripts, but it has a direct parallel in his first Hegel critique. There, Marx presented the case for 'true democracy' (CW 3,30), and advocated for this end '*elections unlimited* both in respect of the franchise and the right to be elected' (CW 3,121). But he differed profoundly from the conventional democrat who supports simply the creation of a republic. To paraphrase Marx, the republican democrat is a 'crude democrat', for

The struggle between monarchy and republic is itself still a struggle within the abstract state. The *political* republic is a democracy within the abstract state form. (CW 3,31)

A true democrat, however, works for the 'true unity of the general and the particular' (CW 3,30): the dissolution of the abstract-political state and of civil society. If 'crude democracy' is the negation of political estrangement 'within its own sphere' (CW 3,31), then 'crude communism', or 'actually existing communism', is the negation of private property within its own sphere. That is, while communism might abolish individual private property, the category 'private property' remains a force external and alien to the community. Such an argument has similarities to Marx's opposition to 'political emancipation' as he outlined it in 'On the Jewish Question': while the state frees itself from restrictions such as religion and private property, man himself remains in bondage to them (CW 3,152). 'Crude communism' frees the individual man from private property only to place the community under its sway. Marx, by contrast, advocated the complete abolition of private property—its '*positive* transcendence' as he put it in the Paris Manuscripts (CW 3,296).

Having stressed in the second Hegel critique the revolutionary transformation of private property and the conflict-ridden nature of class relations, Marx effectively threw in his hand with the small band of French communists. He had indicated in 1843 that he considered communism as a species of the genus *socialism*. But whatever its theoretical limitations, which Marx believed he could overcome in what he might have called a 'true socialism' (had the title not been appropriated by a group of German socialists whose theories he detested), it was the closest of the various French socialist doctrines to his own conception. Actually-existing communist and socialist theories were fairly distinct in France between 1830 and 1848. Communism was revolutionary and often insurrectionist, while socialism was conciliatory and reform-oriented. Communism was dedicated to the abolition of private property or, remembering Marx's injunction, the abolition of individual proprietorship. It took its cue from Rousseau and the more radical groups of the French Revolution. Socialism, through *association*, wanted everyone to become a proprietor. Socialism was inspired by thinkers who were deeply influenced by the French Revolution, but who abhorred violence. Communism was based on a conflict model of social relations, and was more closely allied to the working classes than was socialism. Socialists believed that the bourgeoisie, too, would benefit from social reorganization; they continually attempted to win the bourgeoisie's support as a major part of their strategy. In my view, socialists and communists of this period are not to be distinguished chiefly by their attitudes toward evolution and revolution, but by their links with the proletariat and their advocacy of the proletarian interest. Marx did not adopt an actually-existing communist theory, but the first sketch of his mature theory in the second Hegel critique put him at the communist end of the socialist spectrum. Until then, Marx was closer to socialism than to communism because of his Rousseauan notion of the general interest.

The notion that French practice and German theory were complementary was a common one among German thinkers and, by 1842, had become part of the platform of the Young Hegelians[4] and Feuerbach. It can be traced back to the idea that the work of Immanuel Kant was a revolution in the theoretical sphere to complement and complete the approximately contemporaneous French Revolution. Moses Hess, converted to French communism late in the 1830s, put the 'complementarity thesis' boldly in his 1841 *The European Triarchy*. Ruge, in his 1842 critique of Hegel's *Philosophy of Right*, declared that

The present time seems now to be engaged in the mutual development of 'the abstract theoreticians' and 'the onesided politicians', the *Germans* and the *French....* Germany has just as much sought to appropriate what is necessary from the practical paths of the French as France makes use of the theoretical consequences of the Reformation. But both must go much farther than has happened till now in this exchange of goods.[5]

In his 1843 *Provisional Theses*, Feuerbach asserted that

The true philosopher, the philosopher *identical with life* and *human being* must be of *Franco-German* descent.[6]

And Heinrich Heine supplied the image which Marx used provokingly to end his second Hegel critique: that the 'crowing of the Gallic cock' would usher in a new epoch for Europe, and particularly for Germany.

Marx's liberal background was another point of contact between German philosophy and French socialism. German liberalism during the 1830s and '40s, or 'social liberalism' as D. G. Rohr describes it,[7] tried to strike a balance between individualism and collectivism. One of its leading representatives, Karl Welcker, an editor of the liberal *Staatslexikon*, decried the identification of the liberal principle of individualism with egoism and self-seeking.[8] The second edition of the *Staatslexikon* included an article by Gustav von Struve entitled 'Proletariat', which estimated that three quarters of the German population were propertyless proletarians, earning hardly enough to sustain life. Struve argued that

Our princes, nobles, and lords, our higher dignitaries of church, state, and army, have too much; our proletariat has too little.[9]

Social liberalism, in other words, was sensitive to social distress. It could endorse Marx's remarks in the *Rheinische Zeitung* on the plight of the poor and of the Moselle wine-growers. It could also endorse much of the analysis by French socialisms of the social question, although it rejected socialist remedies.

Marx came to believe that German philosophy and French socialism had essentially the same problem: how to create the universal society. For German philosophy, the task was how properly to conceive of the universal society. Once Marx had lost his faith in the idea of the rational state, the answer lay in 'true democracy' (which was not, in the strict sense, a political concept), and the eventual redefinition of that concept as 'communism'. What German philosophy had believed to be the universal society—the state as the realization of freedom, properly mediated with civil society—Marx claimed was a society determined by particularity.

The distinction between state and civil society itself, he argued, was an expression of the reign of particularity. Universality consisted in the destruction of that distinction. For French socialism, although there were any number of conceptions of the universal society, from *phalanstères* to *Icarie*, the task was how to achieve the goal. It was generally believed that socialism would be a consequence of the union of classes, whose interests were fundamentally the same. Like the Prussian state in which the Young Hegelians had placed so much faith for self-reform, the bourgeoisie to whom most French socialists appealed for support became increasingly antagonistic toward the protagonists of its better nature. The dilemma for French socialists was how to establish a universal society if they could not count on the leadership, or even the support, of the bourgeoisie: the only class they considered to be educated enough to appreciate the wider, social interest. Marx's concept of the proletariat can be seen as a solution to these problems. As a 'universal class', the general representative of society's interest, the proletariat could realize the aims of German philosophy and French socialism at one blow because, in Marx's sense, they were the same aims. The proletariat was the universal class; it could establish socialism against the practical opposition of the bourgeoisie because it embodied the general interest whereas the bourgeoisie represented only its own interests. Marx's concept of the proletariat paved the way, theoretically, for the transformation of socialism from an ambiguously all-class project, with a special concern for the welfare of the working classes, to an unambiguously working class theory and project.

Socialism, for our purposes, is best understood as a modern phenomenon, a product of the French and Industrial Revolutions.[10] From the French Revolution it inherited a goal: Liberty, Equality and Fraternity. From the Industrial Revolution came a new type of social distress and a new social force, the working class, to which, according to socialists, the ideals of the French Revolution had to be extended. Socialism was a response to social disunity and its attendant problems. Its founders elevated the idea of *community* to overcome the egoism and atomism of modern society. But from about 1830, when social disunity was seen increasingly in class terms, socialism helped to define and clarify class cleavages, and tried to overcome them. The link between socialism and the working class, however, was variously interpreted during the period of the July Monarchy in France, from 1830 to 1848. It was only in 1848, and particularly after the June Days, that the view of socialism as an ideology of the working class to be implemented by the working class became pervasive among its critics and advocates alike.

From 1830 to 1848 is not simply a convenient historical segment, enclosed by two revolutions; it represents a crucially formative period in the history of the socialist tradition. Socialism became a distinct current of thought; it had variety and vigour; and it found its most profound exponent in Marx. Socialism even played a role in the transition from 1830 to 1848: the transition from a revolution in the shadow of 1789 to a revolution which signalled a new phase of social relations, class struggle. Marx summed up the change when he described the working class insurrection in Paris on 22 June 1848 as 'the first great battle... fought between the two classes that split modern society' (CW 10,67). But with the defeat of the Paris workers went a defeat for socialism for, in the revolutionary differentiation of bourgeoisie and working class, socialism had become welded to the latter. The alliance between socialism and the working class has been explained in terms of the increasing horror with which the bourgeoisie beheld their rise and growth, and its increasing reluctance to grant or even admit what workers believed were their political and social rights as derived from the slogans of the French Revolution. According to an early work by John Plamenatz, quarrels between moderates and socialists, particularly in 1848,

weakened the sympathies of the bourgeois republicans for the workers, and they made the workers angry and suspicious of the bourgeois: they made the 'class struggle' look more real than any divergence of economic interests could have done.[11]

For socialism did not originate as a doctrine of class war, or of irreconcilable class interests. The language of irreconcilable interests is Marx's. Socialism was not invented in the name of a particular class, although one of its foundations was social (that is, class) analysis; Marx's socialism was.

The early development of socialism largely independently of the working class, their parallel development and interpenetration during the 1830s and '40s, and the identity thrust at them during 1848, call into question some popular notions of the relations between the two. Socialism, in fact, preceded the working class and, in a sense, created it. Socialist theory grew naturally from the universal ideals and unfulfilled promises of the French Revolution; the bourgeoisie of the July Monarchy was ambivalent towards it. That socialism played a major role in forming social reality, in transforming isolated workers and those of disparate trades into a single working class, accounts for the use of the term 'proletariat' during this period, as I explain below.

Before 1848 few argued, and few accepted, that socialism represented solely the interests of labour. It is often assumed that socialism was born into a climate of antagonistic classes, as a reflection of and an instrument in the class struggle. But socialism was dedicated to universality, to the community of all men. One of its prime strands was Romanticism. Socialism originated when the analysis of social classes in the modern sense had not yet appeared. When it began consistently to incorporate the concept of 'class' into its scheme, and to confront the antagonism of classes, by far its most general response was to propose a union of classes. It was Marx who made the audacious claim that the proletariat embodied the social interest and could thus establish the socialist community by itself; it was Marx who eschewed long-term alliance between the proletariat and bourgeoisie. Socialism was not remote from the social struggles of the 1830s and '40s; it participated in them, and developed with them. Furthermore, its analysis of classes changed during this period. From a position of support for the wealthy and enlightened, characteristic of the 'fathers of socialism' (Saint-Simon, Fourier and Owen), it gradually came to rely upon the workers. Except for a few communists, however, most socialists remained faithful to the idea of class reconciliation, to a position that class interests were not irreconcilable. In Marx's analysis, the transition from 1830—when French workers first became a political force—to June 1848—when their insurrection was crushed—represents a transition from conceiving classes as potential collaborators who simply (or wilfully) misunderstood one another, to conceiving of them as rivals and inevitable antagonists.

The real impetus to social analysis in France occurred in 1830, when workers began consciously to claim their political rights and to organize against their employers. A working class of a sort emerged in France in 1830. The event which precipitated its formation was the July Revolution which toppled the Restoration Monarchy, and led to the installation of Louis Philippe as the 'citizen king'. The 1830 Revolution was crucial to the political awakening of the workers because it was widely seen as a second chance for the principles of 1789. In some important ways, 1830 was a second edition of 1789. It raised the same hopes and the same problems. Both revolutions toppled a monarch. Both were made on behalf of the Third Estate by the *menu peuple,* the 'little people', in the belief that all would benefit equally. Both, however, revealed that beneath the slogans of Liberty, Equality and Fraternity lay social tensions, and hope soon turned to disappointment and discord. Both revolutions saw allies in opposition become enemies in victory. And neither revolution crushed the hopes of republicanism, which benefited from the 1830 Revolution at least as much as socialism. The major difference between the two revolutions, apart from their vastly different time scales—ten years, by some accounts, as opposed to three days—was that after 1830 social division began to be seen and analysed in class terms. The hints at class struggle and the inchoate notions of social class in the French Revolution gave way to more developed and ultimately more fruitful notions of class grounded in the emerging science of political economy.

With the overthrow of the Restoration Monarchy, the Third Estate appeared to be in control of its destiny at last, despite a new king. The workers, as part of the Third Estate, began to demand their 'rights'. They became politically active. Like the 'utopian socialists', they thought that their demands would be met by a government they had helped to install. Instead, both government and workers were surprised. The government, because the workers dared to make such demands; the workers, because the government would not countenance their claims. Let there be no mistake. The July Revolution was made by the little people, and in the streets. The people's role was generally acknowledged, and widely applauded.[12] Performance, however, did not match rhetoric; workers grew bewildered as their claims were rejected. After 1830, Jacques Droz argued, the working class which, with some justification 'felt that it had secured the triumph of the revolution, became conscious of its own existence'.[13] The workers, according to Eduard Dolléans, were deceived.[14] A Commission nominated by printing workers called on workers to be moderate. It recalled

the active part that we took in the events of the memorable days of July 27, 28, and 29, when many of our brothers shed their blood for the cause of the *patrie*....[15]

It recommended a calm wait 'until the nation's representatives have appreciated our demands'.

But the new government reacted to the workers' requests with, as William Sewell Jr. put it, 'a mixture of shock, incomprehension, and stern paternal reproaches'.[16] The prefect of police, the liberal Girod de l'Ain, warned the workers that their demonstrations were a 'grave disorder', and added:

Any demand addressed to us requesting that we intervene between master and worker on the subject of fixing wages, or the duration of the working day, or the choice of workers, cannot be admitted, since these are in opposition to the laws that have consecrated the principle of the liberty of industry.[17]

L'Organisateur, a Saint-Simonian journal, declared on 4 September 1830 that in the month since the Revolution, the people had suffered 'all the forced ingratitude that we had predicted'.[18] The Saint-Simonian leader, Enfantin, did not share the hopes generated by the Revolution, and was not surprised at its result. His analysis became widely accepted by socialists after 1830 as the class analysis of the July Revolution:

Who has been conquered? It was the poor class, the most numerous class, the proletarians... the people, in a word.... The people had no leaders; the bourgeoisie can still sleep in peace.... The sacred revolt which occurred spontaneously does not merit the name of revolution; nothing fundamental has been changed in the actual social organization; some names, colours, the national emblem, some titles, some legislative modifications... such are the conquests of our days of sorrow and glory.[19]

The republicans, meanwhile, were puzzled by the new social division, or by the new expression of it, and urged reconciliation. A republican placard of 10 September proclaimed:

National Guards, workshop heads, workers [*ouvriers*], your common interest is the liberty of work. Reunite to reverse a Chamber whose sitting can only perpetuate the discord it has created between you.[20]

Republicans stressed the unity of interests between workers and the rest of society, although they were clear that workers should expect only political rights. But the workers were already disillusioned. They felt isolated, not properly represented. A spontaneous, if short-lived workers' press began to operate from September 1830. A number of journals appeared, among them: *L'Artisan, journal de la classe ouvrière; Le journal des ouvriers; and Le Peuple. Journal général des ouvriers, rédigé par eux-mêmes. L'Artisan* considered that one of its tasks was to instruct 'the workers [*ouvriers*] about their true interests'.[21] But the workers were still to some extent re-living 1789. Just as they had re-enacted the overthrow of Louis XVI, they were enthused by the spirit of a united Third Estate, even if the language of *estate* had neither roused nor accompanied them to action. Perhaps, they asked, this apparent division between workers and rulers, this disregard for workers' interests, is a result of a misunderstanding or a lack of communication? *L'Artisan* itself asked, in an attempt at self-justification:

Without a tribune where they can expose their grievances and their complaints, how can workers make themselves understood by the government?[22]

It was the same logic which prompted workers and their leaders to form themselves into a class, a political force: not to confront and overthrow the bourgeoisie, but to be able effectively to defend and promote their own interests.

Many agree that a new antagonism emerged from the July Revolution. In his early history of socialism, for example, Thomas Kirkup argued that

By far the greatest result for socialism of the revolutionary period of 1830 was the definite establishment of the contrast between the *bourgeoisie* and proletariat in France and England.... Hitherto the men who were afterwards destined consciously to constitute those two classes had fought side by side against feudalism and the reaction.[23]

Eric Hobsbawm agrees that 1830 was a turning-point. It marked a 'radical innovation in politics: the emergence of the working class as an independent and self-conscious force',[24] especially in France. Until 1830, Droz adds, 'social and political life was still dominated... by the aristocracy—bourgeoisie antagonism'.[25] The disillusionment and division which followed the July Revolution were instrumental in forming the modern notion and the modern reality of social class. The history of the 1830s and '40s is one of increasing activity and antagonism of social classes, of events increasingly being interpreted in class terms, and of the ambivalence of socialists towards the working class. Social and socialist analyses fed upon workers' struggles. In this they followed the lead given by the socialist Saint-Simonians.

The *Doctrine de Saint-Simon*, published in 1829, is a seminal document in the history of socialism. Like most socialists, the Saint-Simonians detested disorder and the waste of undirected human energy. They believed that all social activity should be directed 'towards the *same end*'.[26] Their goal, not surprisingly, was '*universal harmony*'.[27] In its pursuit they were encouraged by Saint-Simon's philosophy of history, which they considered scientific in the sense of disclosing social laws by the same methods as those 'employed in... physics'.[28] History had a pattern:

Until now man has exploited man. Masters, slaves; patricians, plebeians; lords, serfs; landlords, farmers; the idle and the productive, here is the progressive history of humanity until now.... [29]

It was a schema endorsed by many socialists during the 1830s and '40s, and it was enshrined by Marx in the *Communist Manifesto*. The exploitation of man by man, the Saint-Simonians continued, must be replaced by 'the exploitation of nature by man *associated* with man'.[30] Unlike Saint-Simon, his socialist followers argued that the worker-master relationship was the historically-crucial antagonism of modern society. The exploited, they argued, now formed the 'immense majority of the population'.[31]

Social conflicts of all types during the 1830s and '40s were interpreted in a 'class' sense, and the notion of social class seemed to be the answer to a longstanding mystery. In November 1831 the silk workers of Lyon, the *canuts*, rebelled. For Saint-Marc Girardin, the struggle had

revealed a grave secret, that of the internal struggle which is taking place within society between the class which possesses and the class which has nothing.[32]

François Guizot perceptively remarked on 22 December 1831 that
The July Revolution only raised political questions, only questions of
government. Society was by no means menaced by those questions. What
has happened since? Social questions have been raised. The troubles of
Lyon have raised them.... [T]oday we have the difficulty of constructing a
government and defending a society.[33]

Republicanism still claimed to have the solution to what was a
growing, or growingly antagonistic, social problem. Its appeal
thrived on a restricted franchise and an obstinate monarchy. Under
the new electoral law of April 1831, it is estimated that of a
population of thirty three and a half million French, there were two
hundred thousand electors.[34] Republicans were generally sympathetic to the plight of the workers as well as to their lack of
political rights. In 1833, the Society of the Rights of Man and
Citizen published a manifesto in which it advocated not only
sovereignty of the people through universal suffrage, but
the emancipation of the working class through a better division of work, a
more equitable distribution of products and association.[35]

Tribune, a republican journal, argued in an issue of November 1833
that 'republicans and *prolétaires* are in the same struggle'.[36]
Workers themselves believed this; they joined republican societies.
In June 1833 Perreux wrote in *l'Echo de la Fabrique*:
All social reform which is not based on a republican political organization,
that is to say just and harmonizing the interests of all, can offer the future
not one guarantee of stability.[37]

That republicanism would harmonize the interests of all classes was
an important part of its appeal. Republicans as much as socialists,
early in the 1830s, sympathetically analysed the condition of the
prolétaires.

One such analysis, by Jean Reynaud in April 1832, incorporated
the idea that the people was composed of two classes, the *prolétaires*
and the bourgeoisie:
Prolétaires are the men who produce all the nation's riches, who possess
only the daily salary of their work and whose work depends on causes left
outside them, who withdraw each day from the fruit of their pain only a
feeble portion incessantly reduced by competition, who rest only their
morrows on the tottering expectation of the uncertain and disorderly
movement of industry, and who only glimpse salvation for their old age in a

place at the hospital or in an anticipated death.[38]

Reynaud's *prolétaires* included not only town workers but peasants; he estimated their number at twenty three million from a total population of about thirty two million. He included France's two hundred thousand electors among her bourgeoisie. But the crux of his argument is that

if we can affirm that the views and interests of the two classes are different, we can also affirm that they are not contradictory, and that the progress which has become necessary for the maintenance of societies can be bought other than by civil war. Bourgeois and *prolétaires* are bound by a powerful necessity....[39]

Reynaud's formulation of the problem, although not socialist, would have been accepted by many republicans and socialists in 1832 and long after. Reynaud urged class reconciliation for the good of France. Since the July Revolution, he explained, the government had issued from, and represented, only the bourgeoisie. But to 'the intervention of the *prolétaires* is attached the future of France'.[40] Truly representative government was the republican solution, and many socialists also accepted the need for universal suffrage.

The 1830 Revolution signalled the end of the Third Estate, and the beginning of the class antagonism of modern society. The July Monarchy was soon branded a 'bourgeois government' by Louis Blanc, among others.[41] Marx scathingly described it as 'a joint-stock company for the exploitation of France's national wealth' (CW 10,50), and as the rule of the finance aristocracy. The July Revolution inaugurated a period of almost undisguised bourgeois political rule. But the decisive break between socialism and the bourgeoisie did not come until 1848. After 1830, socialism can be seen as an attempt to realize the ideals of the French Revolution—to which socialists and the bourgeoisie were putatively committed—in the knowledge that society was divided into classes. Early socialists believed that they could freely cooperate with the bourgeoisie not only because they ostensibly shared the same goals, but because at first and to some extent, the bourgeoisie did in fact cooperate. Plamenatz's study of republicanism in France confirms this,[42] as does Engels' remark that it was not until the beginning of 1843 that English Chartism became sharply separated from the bourgeoisie. Until then, Engels wrote,

The Radicalism of the workers went hand in hand with the Radicalism of the bourgeoisie; the Charter was the shibboleth of both.[43]

Plamenatz maintained that the Society of the Rights of Man, which grew up under the July Monarchy

was the first political association in France, other than a secret society or insurgent organisation, to which bourgeois and workers both belonged.[44]

Even in England, organizations were formed in the 1830s such as the National Political Union and the Birmingham Political Union, which were essentially class alliances. In 1831 the National Union of the Working Classes and Others was formed; among its objectives was the following:

7. To promote peace, union and concord among all classes of people, and to guide and direct the public mind, into uniform, peaceful and legitimate operations....[45]

The prevailing universal ideology of the French Revolution, confronted with classes, chose to minimize their significance and to urge unity. The Society of the Rights of Man issued some declarations which were decidedly in favour of workers' demands and workers' actions, and some of its sections were dominated by workers. Yet its very existence was threatened as workers persistently and sometimes forcefully pursued their goals. It was finally ruined by the Lyon silk-workers' trial of 1835. Throughout the 1830s and '40s many, perhaps most, socialists continued to stress the essential unity of all producers, all classes. But the development of socialism itself was based on an increasing awareness of the importance and the role of social classes.

Within the workers' ranks there seemed to exist a particle of the community socialists wished to establish. Yet the incorporation of the concept of class into their social analyses created a dilemma. To support one class at the expense of another would seem to contradict the notion of community which the socialists valued, and to legitimize the role of self-interest which they detested. Thus many socialists continued to appeal to the wealthy and educated for support, and maintained that there were no irreconcilable differences between classes. They were not united on these points, however. By at least 1832 the idea of a class war had emerged. In a report delivered to the Society of the Friends of the People, Auguste

Blanqui declared that there was no need 'to conceal that there is a war to the death between the classes which compose the nation'.[46] In 1833 the bourgeois journal *Le Semeur* argued that

The war of the inferior classes against the bourgeois class, of workers against masters has lasted for three years, it reappears in one place when it has been stifled in another, it is continued in secret when it does not dare to declare itself openly.[47]

In his *Introduction à la Science de l'histoire*, Buchez denounced the state of 'open warfare' which existed between the two classes of society.[48]

If socialist appeals to the bourgeoisie had little positive effect, socialists were effective in drawing workers together. This was not intended to exacerbate class conflict, but to allow workers to claim their rights more effectively. It is in this context that the use of the term *proletariat* in the 1830s and '40s becomes important. During this period, the term became an integral part of the French political vocabulary. While not unknown before 1830, its significance was enhanced by the social and political realignments which followed the July Revolution. The origins of the term *proletariat* lie in sixth century B.C. Rome, where a census undertaken in the reign of Servius Tullius designated part of the sixth, or lowest, class as the *proletarii*. They were so named because they contributed only their offspring, *proles*, to the maintenance of the state. Montesquieu, incidentally, and Rousseau more substantially, took up the term from Cicero in their analyses of ancient Rome. Professor R.B. Rose has recently pointed out a number of uses of *prolétaire* during the French Revolution.[49] But the most numerous and consistent uses of *prolétaire* occur, as he and Patrick Kessel have discovered, only after 1830.[50] Rose confirms Kessel's view that the term was notable by its absence during the period from 1797 to 1824.[51]

Charles Béranger, in his 1831 'Pétition à la Chambre des Députés', declared:

It isn't as if some of you haven't heard tell of the people. Well here I understand by the people all those who work, all those who have no social existence, all those who possess nothing: you know of whom I want to speak, the *prolétaires*: you have heard tell of them no doubt....[52]

In warning the government to honour the tacit agreement struck among the members of the Third Estate in 1830, Béranger used his *prolétaires* as a barely veiled threat. Historically, he argued, *prolétaires* are rebellious. Among them he numbered Spartacus and Christ, and added: '*Nothing is more dangerous than an eloquent prolétaire!*'[53] Béranger, with many others, felt betrayed by the wealthy. Had the people not overthrown the Restoration Monarchy united? And had not the workers then been told that they were the 'leading people of the world'? He had wondered what this might mean:

Well I said to myself: Without doubt each will be classed according to his capacity and rewarded according to his works. How naive I was! [54]

Act, Béranger advised the Chamber, or beware the 'eloquent' *prolétaires*.

In the context of a predominantly republican appeal for universal suffrage in 1832, Jean Reynaud analyzed the concept *prolétaire*, as we have seen. Pierre Leroux, writing the next year, made a concise distinction between *prolétaires* and bourgeoisie which became almost standard. The former, he declared, are 'those who do not possess the instruments of work', while the latter are 'those who possess them'.[55] Like Reynaud, Leroux argued for representation for the *prolétaires*. Otherwise,

the *prolétaires* are so unhappy and so deprived that a tyrant who promised to free and enrich them might be able, through their ignorance, soon to make them his slaves.[56]

Representation, he believed, would educate the *prolétaires* and make them responsible members of society. For the bourgeoisie and the *prolétaires*, the rich and the poor, at present propound different values: the rich individuality and liberty; the poor security and equality. The resulting 'two exclusive systems of individualism and socialism'[57] split society. The individualistic system 'has as its consequence only the most vile inequality', while the partisans of socialism are evasive about 'how they reconcile the liberty of man with authority'.[58] Liberty and equality, Leroux implied in a discussion which speaks clearly to our day, live at the expense of one another. Political representation of both classes would result, he hoped, in a workable compromise.

The core of the new social analysis, nevertheless, was found in political economy. In this field, the *prolétaires* were championed by Simonde de Sismondi. Sismondi was sympathetic to the plight of the workers under capitalism because he believed that the wages, and thus the conditions of life of the worker were constantly under threat of reduction. Workers under capitalism were *prolétaires* for Sismondi because their suffering was 'so excessive'.[59] The sorts of problems they faced had been recognized by being incorporated into the language, and by being passed from one language to another:

The Romans called *prolétaires* those who had no property, as if, more than the others, they were called on to have children. *Ad prolem generandam.*[60]

But Sismondi did not believe that the interests of the possessors of property and the *prolétaires* were essentially contradictory. That they were considered so, he argued, was a consequence of the 'artificial organization' of society.[61]

The persistence of poverty amid the economic advances of the early nineteenth century was a problem for the relatively new discipline of political economy. In the 1830s, the economist Adolphe Blanqui recognized that a certain anomaly had been left unexplained by Adam Smith: 'Why does private misery grow in our societies at the same time as public wealth?'[62] Around this question grew a debate which became increasingly important for socialists. The study of poverty received an impetus around the turn of the eighteenth century with the publication of the Reverend Malthus's *Essay on Population* and Sir Frederick Morton Eden's *The State of the Poor: A History of the Labouring Classes in England.* Eden concluded that

the miseries of the labouring Poor arose, less from the scantiness of their income (however much the philanthropist might wish it to be increased) than from their own improvidence and unthriftiness.... [63]

The tendency to blame the poor—their wastefulness, morals, or even their supposed limited intelligence—for their own distress, was common. Poverty became the subject of a thriving genre of literature in the first half of the nineteenth century.[64] One of its features was the development of a distinction, sometimes implicit, sometimes explicit, between a traditional and a new poor. The idea of a *new* poor could be used to undermine a belief fundamental to capitalism: that to work is to prosper. For the new poor were generally identified as those who worked for wages, not those who did not work. Socialists defended the interests of these workers, which they felt would be respected only when egoism and the misunderstanding between classes were ended. They rejected Hogarth's 'Gin Lane' approach to the problem of poverty, taken to blame the poor for squandering their resources; instead, they considered the poor to be victims of a poorly organized social and industrial system.

Concern for the poor, an age-old characteristic, was transformed by political economy and by socialism into concern for the working class. Sismondi, in particular, helped to effect this transition. Adolphe Blanqui wrote of Sismondi:

Up to this day no writer has shown a sympathy more notable and more touching for the working classes.... Thanks to him, the worker's condition has become a precious and sacred thing....[65]

As early as 1815 Sismondi sketched his two central, but interrelated themes on the question of the working class. Because workers and employers needed one another, workers should not be reduced to the level of subsistence. The class of day-labourers, he argued, is

more numerous than any other.... They have fewer enjoyments...; they produce wealth, and themselves obtain scarcely any share of it.... Masters and workmen are indeed mutually necessary to each other; but the necessity weighs daily on the workman; it allows respite to his master.[66]

Sismondi succinctly formulated the position of the early socialists on the question of social classes: their interests are different, but not mutually exclusive or necessarily antagonistic.

The rise of the term *prolétaires* in French social and socialist literature in the 1830s and '40s was linked to the analysis of the new industrial working class, but was meant seemingly to convey more: their desperate situation, and sometimes even their propensity to rebel. Lamartine in the Chamber of Deputies in 1835 declared that

The question of the *prolétaires* will create the most terrible explosion in society if governments refuse to investigate and to solve it.[67]

In general, however, it seems to have been used synonymously with 'the oppressed', acquiring a more specific social location and more specific characteristics when the oppression was specified. For many, *prolétaires* were simply those who did not have the right to vote. Since that right was defined, or limited, by economic criteria, it seemed natural that the *prolétaires* formed an economic and not just a political category. But the term also lent itself to vast historical generalizations. In December 1833, Dupont de Bussac declared that 'The nineteenth century has a mission to accomplish: the moral and political emancipation of the *prolétaires*'.[68] According to whom one read, the proletariat might include the artisans or it might not; it might include the peasants or it might not. The concept *proletariat* seems to have been derived, most directly, from that distinction between productive and unproductive members of society: a division used by Siéyès to commend the Third Estate;[69] by Saint-Simon in much the same way; and by some socialists to drive a wedge into the Third Estate by claiming that the bourgeoisie was not productive. Unlike many other advocates of community in the nineteenth century, socialists (with the possible exception of Fourier)[70] welcomed industrialization and based their hopes on it. In 1840 Lamennais defined the *prolétaire* as one who possessed nothing and lived solely from his labour. It 'also... corresponds to the term wage-earner'.[71] Taking as his theme a view that had been outlined a number of times in the previous decade, Lamennais declared:

The capitalist and the *prolétaire* are... almost in the same relation as the master and the slave of ancient societies....[72]

For the capitalist, he continued, the *prolétaire* is merely 'an instrument of work'.[73] Ancient slavery, in a modified form, still existed. And the contrast between the reality of slavery and the rights of man is the real cause of the sickness, of the trouble, of the secret anxiety and of the civil war which today disturbs the world. [74]

History, or historical parallels, seem to have played a major role in specifying the significance of the proletariat. Contemporaries lingered over the lessons of the French Revolution, reliving its victories, defeats and fears. The declaration of affiliation for the *Société des Saisons* contained, *inter alia:*

Who are the aristocrats today? —The aristocracy of birth was destroyed in July 1830; now the aristocrats are the wealthy who constitute an aristocracy as ravenous as the first.[75]

In 1832 Laponneraye argued that there now existed

a continual conflict between the privileged and the *prolétaires* and the revolution will not cease while we have returned to a regime which burdened France before 1789, until the sovereignty of the people is no longer a lie....[76]

With the new struggle interpreted within a framework influenced by the French Revolution, it is no surprise that the proletariat should be interpreted as a new Third Estate. Laurent, a Saint-Simonian, paraphrased the title of Siéyès' famous pamphlet when he asked *Qu'est-ce que le prolétaires?* He wrote:

this class of which the lazy bourgeoisie usually speaks with disdain and which it treats as a humble vassal, also forms the immense majority of the nation; that it peoples the country and the workshops, gives its blood in battles, cultivates the sciences and the arts, furnishes the needs of the State and maintains, charms and embellishes under a thousand diverse forms the existence of the privileged classes which exploit and scorn it.[77]

Nevertheless, for Laurent the victory of the proletariat and the 'exclusive reign of merit and capacity'[78] must be achieved not by violent reform, but by 'a great organic revolution'.[79]

Yet if the proletariat was endowed with immense social and historical significance, its social content remained sketchy and largely unexplored. The proletariat had the potential to destroy modern society, according to Saint-Marc Girardin;[80] it was 'deprived of moral nourishment and of physical well-being', according to Villeneuve-Bargemont in 1834.[81] But of whom was it composed? Fourier's disciple, Considérant, wrote in his 1834 *Destinée Sociale* that

the old professions and the artisans have disappeared to leave only factories and *prolétaires* [82]

and the political economist Constantin Pecqueur linked the proletariat firmly with factory production,[83] but there was no consensus. Dézamy described the proletariat in 1843 in terms identical to those used by Reynaud in 1832.[84] In general, the *bourgeois* was more clearly and consistently located than the *prolétaire* : he was wealthy, an employer, or entitled to vote.[85]

Cabet's *Voyage en Icarie* and Louis Blanc's *Organisation du Travail* appeared in 1839, and Proudhon's *Qu'est-ce que la Propriété?* appeared in 1840. They were, argues Sewell, 'the three most important socialist tracts of the era'.[86] From 1840, socialist ideas became a familiar part of the workers' world. Blanc, in his *Histoire de Dix Ans,* makes a major distinction between the bourgeoisie and 'the people', the latter being those who did not possess the instruments of work.[87] The identification of the proletariat with the wage-earners, and particularly with factory workers, became stronger during the 1840s in France. In 1840 Jules Leroux published *Le Prolétaire et Le Bourgeois*, a fictional dialogue between a worker and an employer on the question of wages. Leroux argued that the lowering of wages benefited no-one, and should be resisted by workers through association. Coalition for an increase in wages, however, must be strongly discouraged. Leroux believed that there was no fundamental conflict of interests between the two classes and, in fact, that 'the master is only a misguided *prolétaire*'.[88]

That the two classes had no fundamental conflict of interests was a position held also by Proudhon, even though he consistently defended the workers' interests. His treatise on property was dedicated to the *'amelioration of the physical, moral and intellectual condition of the most numerous and most poor class'*.[89] In a letter of defence to the Besançon Academy after its publication, he explained that

The education of the *prolétaire* is the mission today entrusted to all men powered by intelligence and fortune, under pain of being overwhelmed sooner or later by an inundation of these barbarians whom we have acknowledged by giving them the name *prolétaires*.[90]

Having noted, in his *Qu'est-ce que la Propriété?*, the contrast of interests between bourgeoisie and proletariat, in his next work, *De la Création de l'ordre dans l'Humanité, ou, Principes d'organisation politique*, Proudhon argued for a new understanding of what he saw as a 'profound antagonism between *worker* and *capitalist*.'[91] But his notion of social class remained non-exclusive and essentially non-antagonistic. Proudhon's concept of the proletariat had two elements. The *prolétaire*, he argued, is 'a minor in society',[92] as is the slave, plebeian and serf. This 'miserable category of humans' appears 'among all the peoples and in all the epochs of history',[93] whatever its particular name. In history, therefore, the proletarian is any youth, minor or apprentice. But the modern *prolétaire* 'is especially... the compartmentalized worker, without industry or initiative'.[94] The proletarian, in other words, is the alienated worker. If history has a logic, it is the

Progressive enlargement of the right of the city and the extension of the political rights accorded to the *prolétaires*.[95]

In so far as I have made a survey of the uses of the concept of the proletariat in France in the 1830s and '40s it is not meant to be exhaustive or definitive, but suggestive. The historian edits history; I have only edited the editors. Nevertheless, I consider it to be a representative survey. I cannot, of course, even hazard a guess about the frequency of use of the concept during this period. Editing enhances its visibility, but uses of the concept seem outnumbered in social and socialist literature by the use of terms such as *workers* (*ouvriers*) and the *working class* (*classe ouvrière*). That very impression raises an important question. Why should socialists employ a term which was vague when they already had terms which were reasonably precise? I believe that there are two major reasons. The first was to try to form the workers into a self-conscious class which could defend its own interests. The second was to appeal to a broad section of the population who were being disadvantaged by the prevailing system and who would clearly benefit from socialism. The very vagueness of the term *proletariat* was of assistance in these two tasks.

Socialism and the working class developed separately but in a parallel direction during the 1830s and '40s, influencing each other. Workers became increasingly conscious of themselves as workers, as having common conditions and interests. As Hobsbawm has put it:

What was new in the labour movement of the early nineteenth century was class consciousness and class ambition. The 'poor' no longer faced the 'rich'. A specific *class*, the labouring class, workers, or proletariat, faced another, the employers or capitalists.[96]

Some argue that from 1830 the working class became a conscious political force. Sewell links the July Revolution with the emergence of class consciousness.[97] The workers' press, Coornaert suggests, is evidence that the workers had begun to identify as a class.[98] The language of 'class', as Asa Briggs has demonstrated, became pervasive.[99] But the development of a unified class, or perceptions of a unified class, requires some explanation.

Workers formed small occupation groups, some of them with long traditions; they had diverse salaries and conditions. Some were active in the defence of their interests; some were not. Furthermore, it is now widely accepted that, in the words of Hobsbawm,

the militants of the French 'working-class movement' in 1830-48 were in the main old-fashioned urban craftsmen and journeymen, mostly in the skilled trades, and centres of traditional domestic and putting-out industry such as the Lyons silk trade.[100]

Christopher Johnson agrees that the *canuts* were, at this time 'man for man, the most mature and politically conscious working class on the continent'.[101] Sewell claims that these artisanal and skilled-worker militants—these 'avant-garde of the working class in formation', as Coornaert calls them[102]—accurately represented a working class which for most of the nineteenth century was dominated 'numerically, politically, and culturally' by artisans.[103] He explains that artisans had the motives, the power and the political skills to make an enormous impact on the workers' movement; in a sense, to establish it:

Artisans... were still proud, numerous, and essential to the functioning of the economy; but they were also financially squeezed, threatened with a loss of skill and status, and provided with virtually no legal form of collective defence against the disordering forces of the free market.[104]

Artisans made higher wages, were more literate, and were more stable—demographically and in their occupations—than unskilled and factory workers: attributes which Sewell believes were requisite for 'serious involvement in working-class politics'.[105]

Simply put, artisans and skilled workers made up the vast bulk of the working class in France (and Germany) in the 1830s and '40s, and probably long beyond; they were the most politically conscious of workers, and the most politically active. Any accurate account of socialism must take this fact into account. Yet artisans were notoriously craft-centred in their aims. Johnson writes about journeymen tailors, for example:

spurred on by dreams of a past independence they never really had, tailors fused together in struggle [particularly in the mid-1840s]. They were artisans whose work and beings were being de-artisanized. With their corporate traditions, long urban experience, a strong sense of self-worth, and—not incidentally—a high level of literacy, they joined one army in the working class war against emergent industrial capitalism.[106]

Bernard Moss argues that the preindustrial values of the artisans gave their movement a particularly critical thrust against industrial capitalism, a thrust which had not developed at this early stage among the ranks of the relatively passive industrial workers, who were essentially rootless.[107] The artisanal character of the early working class movement influenced some of the pre-industrial themes of socialism, such as hostility to the intensified division of labour (and consequent loss of skill) in factories. Socialism, in its turn, tried to remove the craft orientation of the workers, partly through its use of the term *proletariat* as a common identifier. This is a major part of the significance of the term *proletariat* during the 1830s and '40s. Language, Bezucha declares, 'plays a critical role in social cohesion'.[108] And despite its negative connotations (the *Doctrine de Saint-Simon* exclaimed of *prolétaire:* 'What barbarous derision this word implies!'),[109] or perhaps because of them, the term *proletariat* became a point of identity for workers of all types. The similarly derogatory term *canuts*, considered an insult at first by those it designated, also remained and flourished as their rallying cry.[110] The language of the 1830s referring to workers, according to Louis Chevalier, was generally vehement. Terms such as 'savages, barbarians, [and] nomads' were commonly employed.[111] But it was *proletariat* which emerged triumphant from this war of the words, not only because it united workers in opposition, but because it implied that the oppressed and exploited had a common history and mission, and that the sufferers had virtue and dignity because of their suffering.

To this view of the development of a working class in France must be added the fact, noted by Kessel, that the term *prolétariat* first appeared only in 1834.[112] Unlike the term *prolétaires*, which preceded (and accompanied) it, *prolétariat* suggests some degree of cohesion among the individual *prolétaires*. *Pace* Rose, the introduction of the term *prolétariat* points to a shift towards conceiving the working class not as a collection of individuals, but as a unit.[113] Translating this shift in understanding into reality, i.e. turning the workers into a class, became the task of many socialists. Flora Tristan agitated for a union of workers which would aim to 'CONSTITUTE THE WORKING CLASS'.[114] The bourgeoisie, she argued perceptively, had been constituted as a class since 1789. Its rise was an object lesson for the workers:

Observe what force a body united by the same interests can have. —From the moment that class was CONSTITUTED, it became so powerful that it could take exclusive possession of all the powers of the country. —Finally in 1830 its power reached its height.[115]

Tristan's *Union Ouvrière*, published in 1843, is held by Lowy and Rubel to have been seminal in the development of Marx's conception of the proletariat.[116]

The relationship between socialism and the working class is a complex one. It is simply not so, as Tom Bottomore claims, that

The historical connection between socialism and the working class —however complex and diverse its forms—is quite obvious. Working class movements produced socialist ideas.... [117]

The independence of socialism from the actual working class meant that socialism was not simply the reflection of an artisan struggle against industrialization (although it contained such elements), and could thus outlive the disappearance of the artisan. Socialists distinguished themselves not only by their support for working class claims, which were also—at first frequently—supported by republicans, but by their appreciation of the class nature of society and the implications of 'class' for the achievement of the widely-held universal goals of the French Revolution. Socialists brought the notion of 'class' to bear upon society, displacing that of ranks or estates, as well as the more primitive distinction between rich and poor. Lichtenberger argued that the French Revolution was a turning-point in the history of socialism because at its end 'France appeared to be divided, no more as in 1789 into privileged and non-privileged, but into rich and poor'.[118] While socialism may have profited by this clarity, it was the significance which socialists attributed to 'class', confirmed and reinforced by French social experience in the 1830s and '40s, which constitutes the point of departure for socialism as a distinct social and political theory. Throughout this period the development of socialism can be seen as dependent on the development of the concept of class.

While the idea of a union of classes was widely accepted by socialists, there was no unanimity. Marx was the most prominent dissenter. In the 1840s, in particular, the idea that there were no fundamental differences of interest between workers and capitalists became more difficult to maintain, since the bourgeoisie increasingly saw socialism as a threat. The case of Etienne Cabet, as related by Johnson, illustrates the persistence with which some socialists held their belief that a union of classes was the only consistent solution to the social problem. Cabet advocated class unity early in the 1840s, and trusted that the bourgeoisie would apprehend rationally the need for communism. In his 1841 *Ma Ligne Droit*, he argued that

if it is true that the Bourgeoisie can do nothing without the assistance of the People, it is equally true that the People can do nothing without the help of the Bourgeoisie.[119]

According to Johnson, Cabet began to consider the bourgeoisie's hostility towards working class interests as fundamental, rather than as incidental and ephemeral, after a rift between Cabet's journal *Le Populaire* and Ledru-Rollin's *La Réforme*. In September 1845, Ledru-Rollin specifically and vehemently rejected communism. Johnson writes that for Cabet,

bourgeois collaboration no longer seemed visible on the horizon; communism could only be a working class movement.[120]

Cabet turned his energies towards promoting working class solidarity. By November 1845, he still hoped that *Réforme* would appreciate communism, but he was adamant that he would not compromise his principles:

But be firm! if the Bourgeoisie persists in repelling us, we must resign ourselves to being repelled. Then, keep order; march separately by our side. But instead of being the leaders, as before, we must form the rear-guard and the reserve army; leave the Bourgeoisie to make promises, and we will only launch ourselves to decide and direct the victory for our profit as for his.[121]

In *Le Populaire* of 29 May 1846, Cabet argued that 'pleas to the rich' to support communism would not work. Only the spirit of 'fraternity and solidarity' among workers themselves would do.[122] Johnson concludes that Cabet's position on class unity for communism was so undermined by the bourgeoisie that, his abhorrence of revolution considered, he abruptly changed his position around 1847 on the desirability and possibility of establishing a utopian settlement:

the option of revolutionism, because it meant sanctioning overt class conflict, proved to be repugnant to him; the only alternative which appeared viable, therefore, was escape.[123]

Cabet had earlier ridiculed Fourierist attempts to establish utopian colonies. The importance of this analysis is not so much the novel idea that the ill-fated Icarian experiment was an abrupt about-face—

Cabet having had no intention of such an experiment when he wrote *Voyage en Icarie*—but that Cabet had come to view class interests as irreconcilable, and that class compromise could not achieve the social goals to which he was committed. Nevertheless, he clung to the belief that communism would ultimately benefit the bourgeoisie as well as the working class.

The case of Cabet, one of the most popular and influential of the early French socialists, illustrates not just the idea that socialists could feel no contradiction involved in advocating class unity and trying to develop a working class, but that they were reluctant to abandon entirely the idea of class unity. Those who did abandon it were associated with the communist wing of socialism. In February 1841, for example, *l'Atelier* published this: 'It is clear that the interests of the masters is directly opposed to that of the work-ers'.[124] Flora Tristan believed that all bourgeois must be excluded from organizations for workers' emancipation.[125] Such a sentiment was barely thinkable in 1830, and for some early socialists it remained so. Even by 1848, many socialists and workers had not been disabused of what Marx believed was the illusion of a funda-mental identity of interests between the classes. Lamartine, accord-ing to Marx,

baptised the Provisional Government on February 24 [1848] 'un gouvernement qui suspende *ce malentendu terrible qui existe entre les différentes classes.* (CW 10,58)

Was it a 'misunderstanding' which caused the June Days, Marx implied, or an irreconcilable antagonism? Acceptance or rejection of the idea of class unity is one means by which to distinguish communists from other socialists during the 1830s and '40s. Cole, for example, declared:

The 'Socialists' had nearly all appealed, first and foremost, to the brother-hood of men, not to the spirit of class-solidarity.[126]

Communists appealed directly to the working class. Engels conse-quently remarked, in his 1890 Preface to the *Communist Manifesto*, that 'Socialism in 1847 signified a bourgeois movement, commu-nism a working-class movement'.[127] Engels' judgement is un-justly harsh, but his reasoning is clear.

Given that socialism was committed to social unity in a society it had helped to define (and even to constitute) as class divided, use of the term *proletariat* by early socialists might be seen as a means to impress the bourgeoisie about the extent of distress in society. Most discussions of the proletariat during this period stressed its size. Auguste Blanqui, whose use of the term *prolétaire* in January 1832 to describe his occupation did more than any other instance to establish its notoriety, argued that the proletariat represented the condition of thirty million Frenchmen.[128] Ultimately, of course, this extensional universality of the proletariat could be used as a justification for abandoning attempts to make an ally of the hostile bourgeoisie and to establish socialism alone. In an important sense, the way in which the early French socialists used the term *proletariat* made it come to represent a type of universal class. Marx alone, however, drew together the threads of French socialist conceptions of the proletariat, and he alone asserted that the pro- letariat was a universal class. In this he was assisted by his incisive mind as well as his training in German philosophy. To this must be added his pre-socialist sympathy for the poor in Germany, expressed clearly in his work for the *Rheinische Zeitung,* as well as his contact with workers.

It is clear why Marx's adoption of the term *proletariat* to designate his 'universal class' meant that he had more affinity with communists than with other socialists. French socialists were committed to peaceful methods, according to Coornaert, 'sauf une minorité de communistes'.[129] They did not want to exacerbate class struggle. 'All believed firmly in "universal fraternity" in economic as in international life'.[130] The existence of classes had not shaken their faith in fraternity. Moreover, all wanted—'sauf, toujours, certains communistes'—an association of producers. They may have criticized the capitalists as *oisifs*, but they were not yet prepared for the idea of dispensing with them in production. The question of social unity was paramount in the minds of most socialists, and of many others, including Christians. Lamennais, for example, wrote:

What the People wants, God wants; because what the People wants is justice, is essential, eternal order, is the accomplishment within humanity of that sublime saying of Christ: 'Let them be ONE, my Father, as you and I are ONE!' [131]

Private interest, egoism or selfishness were decried on all sides, and the idea of socialism being solely in the interests of one class seemed to violate this widespread commitment to the general interest.

The French Revolution exerted an enormous influence on nineteenth century political and social movements through the proclamation of its goals, as well as its inability firmly to establish them. Of these goals, fraternity seemed to have the greatest ability to continue to generate widespread approval, after liberty and equality had been hedged about with different restrictions by various groups. The historian Augustin Thierry, in his 1840 *Considérations sur l'Histoire de France*, reflected fondly on the social unity of 1789:

In place of the old orders, of classes unequal in rights and in social conditions, there was one society, twenty-five million citizens living under the same law, the same rules, the same order. Such was the new France, one and indivisible....[132]

But even during the Revolution, social unity never approached the idealization represented in this picture; the Hébertistes and Babouvistes, in particular, signified that social tensions still existed. From these roots class analysis emerged, especially after the disillusionment of 1830. Many accounts of socialism rightly highlight the legacy of the French Revolution, but underestimate the importance of the goal of fraternity, concentrating instead on equality. While equality plays an important role in the development of socialism, not all socialists are egalitarians; certainly, Marx was not. In his 1875 *Critique of the Gotha Programme*, Marx endorsed the (Saint-Simonian and inegalitarian) slogan 'From each according to his ability, to each according to his needs' (SW III,19). Nevertheless, it is not surprising that the French Revolution gave rise to two of the major political and social forces of our time—socialism and nationalism—which seek, each in its own way, to substitute for traditional forms of social solidarity a new framework of social meaning and legitimation. For the French Revolution marks the formal victory of the *Gesellschaft*.

Marx's early sympathy for the poor, however, did not mark him as a communist, but simply as a German liberal with a radical social conscience. The circumstances of Marx's upbringing meant that he was unfamiliar with real social distress until confronted by it during the period he wrote for the *Rheinische Zeitung*. The poor then began to assume a special status in his journalism. Marx reported on the debates on the Law on Thefts of Wood in the Rhine Province Assembly in October and November of 1842. He was eager to drive home his central point, that the estates were perverting the nature of the state by turning 'the authority of the state into a servant of the forest owner' (CW 1,253), but he also looked more closely than before at the estate composition of the Assembly itself. Marx realized that while the private interests of the knightly, landowning and burgher estates were represented in the debates, that of the poor was not. When he had reported earlier on the Assembly's debates on freedom of the press, he had not noticed that the voice of the poor was absent. Having now noticed, Marx concluded that the poor did not form an *estate* in the traditional sense because they did not have a political aspect. The Law on Thefts of Wood overthrew a customary right of the poor to gather fallen wood in the forests at no charge. As a customary right, Marx argued, it was no privilege—as enjoyed by the aristocracy—but a right of the 'lowest, propertyless and elemental mass' (CW 1,230). He described the poor as 'the elemental class of human society' (CW 1,234). This class, he explained, has occupation rights and is therefore excluded from all other property (CW 1,233). Marx developed the idea that the poor is not an estate:

up to now the existence of the poor class itself has been a mere custom of civil society, a custom which has not found an appropriate place in the conscious organisation of the state. (CW 1,234)

(Marx used the term *class*, a term popular in France but rarely used in his own work until 1844, probably in order to avoid calling the poor an *estate*.) The poor class had a civil existence without having a political existence. It was a 'social estate' without actually being an 'estate'. It was thus not involved in the state–civil society distinction, or in man's split into *bourgeois* and *citoyen* that this distinction entailed. The poor, in other words, constituted a separate sphere.

The analysis of the position of the poor in society (or outside it), however, was secondary to Marx's intention of measuring the existing state against its essence. The existence of the poor, their distress, was perceived by Marx as *symptomatic* of a society dominated by particularity. In January 1843, for example, Marx implied that poverty is an interest which, when it becomes widespread (i.e. when it begins to affect large numbers of people), becomes a state (i.e. a *general*) interest (CW 1,343):

if it is asserted that there is distress of a *general* character... private misfortune becomes a misfortune for the state and its removal a duty which the state owes itself. (CW 1,348)

Marx exhorted the state to take action: not the poor. Until late in 1843, he did not regard the poor as means for social or political change, nor as the natural allies of philosophy.

There are specific hints in Marx's first Hegel critique of formulations he would use to describe the proletariat in the second.[133] The first Hegel critique is his first serious attempt to discuss the inadequacies of political emancipation. Man in a politically emancipated society must, he argued, make 'a fundamental division within himself' (CW 3,77), a separation between citizen of the state and member of civil society. But Marx was beginning to believe that there were more fundamental divisions, divisions between what he called 'social estates', distinguished mainly in terms of money and education (CW 3,80). One of these 'social estates', 'the estate of direct labour', constituted an entirely separate sphere:

lack of property and the estate of direct labour form not an estate of civil society, but the ground on which civil society moves. (CW 3,80)

Thus the tension between public and private existence does not affect what Marx had earlier described as the 'elemental mass'. Although Marx does not systematically follow this direction, all his comments about civil society, about its egoism, and about the 'atomism into which civil society plunges in its *political act* ' (CW 3,79), all these do not relate directly to the 'estate of direct labour'. Thus the state-civil society distinction is itself one side of a division which has the propertyless labourers as its opposite. The *bourgeois-citoyen* division was used by Marx less as a device to illuminate the condition of man, than as a tool for criticizing constitutions after the French Revolution. In a sense, therefore, Marx's pre-1844 conception of civil society was of a society of wealth: *bürgerliche Gesellschaft* was indeed *bourgeois* society. These considerations, I believe, are the basis for the paradoxical statement in his second Hegel critique, that the proletariat is a class of civil society which is not a class of civil society, an estate which is the dissolution of all estates. (CW 3,186)

It was Marx's developing analysis of the poor as a separate sphere, allied to his conception of the tasks of philosophy—profoundly influenced by Feuerbach's *Provisional Theses*—which fixed the location and character of the class which Marx would call the *proletariat*. He chose the term *proletariat*, I suspect, more because of his contact in 1843 with French socialist literature than because of his contact with workers in Paris. The idea that Marx had significant contact with the advanced French proletariat before he became an advocate of the proletarian cause, seems to have an irresistable attraction for Marxists. Even one of the ablest Marxists writing on this period, Lowy, declares that 'L'exemple du prolétariat français a été décisif pour la dernière étape' in Marx's journey to communism.[134] Rubel argues that it was in France that Marx 'a découvert la classe ouvrière et son mouvement d'auto-émancipation'.[135] Cornu writes that Marx entered 'directement en contact avec le prolétariat' in Paris.[136] He adds, exaggeratedly:

Il y trouvait en effet un prolétariat déjà nombreux, possédant de fortes traditions révolutionnaires et une nette conscience de ses intérêts de classe.[137]

Marx may well have had contact with workers in Paris before he wrote the published version of the second Hegel critique, but they were likely to have been artisans; furthermore, they were probably German artisans on their *Wanderjahre* with whom Paris, at this time, teemed. Evidently, Marx had contact with artisans in Paris at some time during his stay there, for he wrote a panegyric to the results of their association in his Paris Manuscripts (CW 3,313); but how significant such contact was for the development of his concept of the proletariat will always be arguable.

Germans were not entirely unfamiliar with the term *proletariat* during the 1830s and '40s, and Marx may well have encountered it before he read any French socialist literature. In Germany, too, the breakdown of feudal social relations and a (modest) rise in industrial activity had produced a social problem. If anything, the term *proletariat* had a much more specific use and meaning in the German literature than in the French. For most of the German writers on the subject, the proletariat was a threat to society: something which, if it existed, was incipient; and something which must be overcome or avoided. Perhaps because it had such a negative connotation, it behoved Germans to be precise about the social location of the proletariat. Consequently, the proletariat was soon, and fairly consistently, identified in Germany as the industrial working class.

The term *proletariat* entered the German language as part of the language of the social problem. Hegel had realized that a new type of poverty could be distinguished from the existence of poverty immemorial:

When the standard of living of a large mass of people falls below a certain subsistence level... the result is the creation of a rabble of paupers.[138]

This 'rabble', which Hegel designated *Pöbel*, had a special significance. For it consisted not of the ubiquitous beggar, but the discontented and rebellious poor, those who would not accept their poverty as fate:

Poverty in itself does not make men into a rabble; a rabble is created only when there is joined to poverty a disposition of mind, an inner indignation against the rich, against society, against the government, etc.[139]

Hegel's *Pöbel* is a forerunner of Marx's concept of the proletariat. The Germans were eager to describe accurately and to understand properly the significance of this new type of impoverishment which underlay the 'social question'. They chose the term *pauperism* to describe it. The *Brockhaus Real Encyklopädie* introduced *pauperism* as 'a newly invented term for a very significant and fateful phenomenon'. It continued:

Pauperism exists where a numerous class of people can only earn the barest necessities despite working as hard as they possibly can....[140]

Pauperism so defined was the condition of the proletariat. Of course, the poor were often blamed for the misery visited upon them: they were lascivious and alcoholic. But their abstemious critics had to contend with definitions of pauperism such as the one above, as with von Mohl's distinction between individual and mass poverty:

Essentially different from the kinds of poverty which affects individuals and have particular causes is that poverty which grips whole classes of society and which is not the fault of any one individual or the result of extraordinary circumstances, but is rather the consequence of the whole structure of the

relationship between capital and income in that sector of society.[141]
The proletariat was an expression of mass poverty.

Franz Baader in the 1830s, Sagarra claims, was 'probably the first to use the term *"proletair"* in the modern sense of propertyless class'.[142] But the most significant discussions of the proletariat in Germany began in 1842 with the publication of Lorenz von Stein's *Socialism and Communism in Contemporary France*. Stein not only provided an excellent survey of contemporary socialist currents in France, which was a revelation even for informed Germans; he also distilled a distinct conception of the proletariat from the various French 'proletariats', which spoke to German needs and fears. It is not often realized that Stein's own concept of the proletariat was influenced by German social questions of the day. Stein was on a mission for the Prussian government. The proletariat, he argued in the third (1850) edition of his work, was a product of industrial society. Its lack of capital and inability to acquire it 'established an element of bondage';[143] its wage was 'reduced to the level of subsistence'.[144] Stein maintained that the workers' poverty was 'an inevitable consequence of industrial society', which made 'the laborer and the capital owner... inevitable enemies'.[145] This contradiction at the heart of industrial society was exacerbated by the tendency of workers to develop a community of understanding and needs, to become

an independent power, consciously and purposely opposed to the present order of society. As such, that class is called by a new, but appropriate name: the proletariat.[146]

The importance of Stein's work should not be underestimated (although I believe it has often been overestimated).[147] Apart from its influence on German socialists and other social critics, it was perhaps the first systematic discussion of the proletariat in any language. It was, at least, the first methodically to link the proletariat with industrial society, and thus to link its rebellious attributes (which chiefly distinguished it, according to most of its analysts) with the industrial organization of work.

Stein's conception of the proletariat can be seen as a contribution to a larger discussion in Germany about the benefits and dangers of industrialization. It seemed to be widely accepted in Germany that industrialization brought with it distress; the argument was whether that distress could be contained, or offset by benefits. The experience of more industrially developed countries, specifically of France and England, was noted carefully by many Germans. A bailiff drew his master's attention to Engels' 1845 work on *The Condition of the Working Class in England* , saying that Engels

may often paint too lurid a picture, and his bitter resentment of the propertied classes strikes one as being exaggerated. Nevertheless, considering the historical evolution of the proletariat and the conditions in our country, which are in many ways analogous to those in England when it stood at our present stage in manufacture and agriculture, we might... profit by the experience of that great nation and... render the proletariat harmless in its infancy, before it grows (as it has there) into a giant, and threatens the social *status quo*.[148]

Even the official government newspaper, the *Allgemeine Preussische Zeitung,* reviewed Engels' book. It argued similarly: that Germany must learn from England to avoid the evils of proletarianism, the poverty and humiliation of the poor population.[149] Many, of course, saw factory work as inevitable. But humiliation and discontent had to be, and could be, avoided. The economist Friedrich List tried to counter the fear of a proletariat:

It is unfortunate that the evils which in our day accompany industry have been used as an excuse for rejecting industry itself. There are far greater evils than a class of proletarians: empty treasuries, national impotence, national servitude, national death.[150]

The next year, 1843, List insisted that a proletariat was more likely to appear in an agricultural country which failed to industrialize: 'The factories do not give birth to the poor; the poor give birth to the factories'.[151] But List, too, believed that the lessons of England's industrial development should be salutary for Germany.

After Stein's work first appeared in 1842, discussion of the proletariat, its social role, and its connections with socialism and the future of society, became more common in Germany. Unlike France, where there were very few direct, and fewer extended, discussions of the proletariat, in Germany a number appeared before 1848. The same year that Marx published his second Hegel critique, two other important analyses of the proletariat appeared in Germany. Theodor Mundt and an anonymous Magdeburger agreed that the proletarian was either unemployed and willing to work, or employed on the most meagre of wages. The Magdeburger claimed that the proletarian

lives from hand to mouth and what he earns today he spends today. The life of a proletarian is thus a life and death struggle against hunger.[152]

Yet the proletarian is conscious of the injustice of his situation:

This is why he is fundamentally different from the pauper, who accepts his fate as a divine ordinance and demands nothing but alms and an idle life.[153]

The proletariat was a problem, both declared, not simply confined to France.[154] Mundt claimed that the proletariat 'represents the urge for freedom in recent history in addition to the urge for work'.[155] The proletariat, in fact, had universal significance:

This modern proletarian, this self-made giant of modern society, this disowned child of every nation, this great, proud beggar clothed in the purple of freedom, and lying so clothed on the threshold of the future, he is the true picture, the modern personification of our confused life-story always at loggerheads with itself.[156]

Socialism could not become a working class phenomenon, it could not solely advocate the interests of those from whom it derived its major support, and for whom it held an especial sympathy, without undermining its fraternal core. It could not claim to be the rightful heir of the traditions of the French Revolution, nor claim to hold the solution to the troubling problem of social division, if it was seen as merely another factor in that division. Marx, influenced by a different tradition and aware of the parallels between German philosophy and French socialism, seized upon these slender threads and wove a concept of the proletariat as the 'universal class'. By defining the interests of the proletariat as those of humanity, Marx declared that socialism was a working class movement in the fullest sense. If they understood the key, socialists need never be torn between elevating the general interest and elevating the interests of one class.

Marx may have been slightly misled by French socialist uses of the term *proletariat*. Workers' actions in the 1830s and '40s in support of their own interests were undertaken chiefly by artisans, and many workers whom socialism had helped to shape into a class were similarly members of trades which were under threat from industrial progress. It is unfair to call the early socialists poor sociologists, for they did not have the leisure to study and reflect upon the new social struggles; nevertheless, the concept of the proletariat was glaringly imprecise. It was not coined to describe the nascent industrial working class, whose political and social influence was not yet of major importance. The textile industry, from which evidence for a generalized and rapid increase in the proportion of factory and unskilled workers, and for a rapid decline in the proportion of artisans is often taken, now seems atypical. Yet because the concept of the proletariat blurred the distinctions between the various sectors of the 'oppressed' and 'exploited', with which it was almost synonymous, a confusion arose over which sector was responsible for the actions, and particularly the consciousness, attributed to the proletariat, as well as over the motives for its actions. Thus, while Marx could claim the November 1831 rebellion of the Lyon *canuts* as the earliest example of open warfare between the industrial working class and bourgeois society (CW 3,204), Bezucha, a recent commentator, sees it and the rebellion of 1834 as 'a community of artisans who organized in order to resist proletarianization'.[157] The proletariat has been described as 'that child of the Industrial Revolution'.[158] But the Industrial Revolution had many 'children'. If the proletarian is seen as a harassed artisan challenging the rise of industrialism, then the child was prone to tantrums, but died. If the proletarian is seen as an industrial worker, the child became a Peter Pan: it never grew up. Expectations aroused in the socialist by the artisan were dashed by the industrial worker. In general it is true that early analyses which attempted to detail the social content of the proletariat, tended to deprive the 'proletariat' of its aura of rebelliousness and intensified social consciousness.

4

Marx's Proletariat Challenged

To Ruge and the Bauer brothers, Marx's former colleagues and friends, the idea that the proletariat represented the universal interest and could solve the social problem seemed absurd. In July 1844, Ruge published his article 'The King of Prussia and Social Reform' in Paris. He argued that the recent Silesian weavers' uprising (4–6 June 1844) was a futile attempt to solve the social problem in Germany. The uprising, he declared, had revealed a state of 'partial distress of the factory districts',[1] a distress which would become a matter of general concern once Germany had become a political country. Of the poor, he wrote:

nowhere do they see beyond their own hearth and home, their own factory, their own district; the whole question has so far still been ignored by the all-penetrating political soul.[2]

For Ruge, the universality required to solve the social problem would not come from any particular social group, with its limited standpoint, let alone from the poor. The universal standpoint would be achieved only when particular standpoints became conscious of themselves (as particular) and of other particular standpoints, within the political struggles of a democratic republic. Ruge saw politics as an exercise in social education. Through politics the limitations of particular standpoints would be seen and overcome. He defended an idea that Marx had given up: that individuals and groups will adopt the general standpoint once they become aware of it.

Replying to Ruge, Marx re-stated the distinction between 'radical' and 'merely political' revolutions as a distinction between *social* and *political* revolutions. He reaffirmed that the political revolution could not solve the social problem. And he clarified his conception of the proletariat's universality by distinguishing between the *extent* of social (i.e. the proletariat's) distress and its *character*. Marx agreed that distress might be limited to the factory districts, as Ruge had claimed, and thus be partial in extent; yet the nature of the distress in these districts in so far as it represented the dehumanization of man, the estrangement of man from his essence, was universal. No matter how limited in extent dehumanization may be, the suffering of those dehumanized was universal in nature. As Kamenka has noted, Marx made this distinction as early as the first Hegel critique in connection with the issue of representation of the individual in a rational State. Kamenka explained that

The contrast here is between universality as a mere collection, universality treated extensionally, and universality as an intrinsic character, universality treated intensionally.[3]

If the rational State, as conceived by Marx, is intensionally universal because it is an expression of the human essence, then the proletariat is intensionally universal because its demands are universal: to restore man's human and universal essence. Thus the universality of the proletariat lay not in its present dehumanized being, but in what that being compels the proletariat to demand and to do. Universality is conceptually intensional, therefore, when it relates to the essence or intrinsic nature of a thing.

Ruge had written of the 'partial distress' of the factory districts. Allow, Marx wrote, that the distress in Germany is partial in extent, i.e. confined to the factory districts. But in England, he continued,

distress of the workers is not *partial* but *universal*; it is not restricted to the factory districts, but extends to the rural districts. (CW 3,192)

Yet England is a *political* country. Far from supporting Ruge's belief that social distress can be solved only in a political manner, the example of England, Marx maintained, revealed the limitations of political understanding. 'The keener and more lively' the political mind is, the more it thinks within the framework of politics, 'the *more incapable* is it of understanding social ills' (CW 3,199). Marx's theoretical precision marks a rather hollow victory over Ruge: Ruge anticipated, clumsily perhaps, but better than Marx, that the state would intervene to alleviate social distress. The notion of the welfare state did not occur to Marx, and he would no doubt have dismissed it as a contradiction in terms. This is clear when he discussed the nature of the distress suffered in factories in terms of

the fantastic rags worn by the English poor, and the flabby, shrunken flesh of the women, undermined by labour and poverty; children crawling about in the dirt; deformity resulting from excessive labour in the monotonous mechanical operations of the factories! (CW 3,193)

Such labour and conditions, Marx believed, were dehumanizing. Thus the *partial* distress in Germany is a matter of general significance (even though Marx discounted the idea that the state could play a role in alleviating distress), as much as is the *universal* distress in England.

It is well known that Marx argued, on the basis of the discussions in his Paris Manuscripts (to which I shall return), that the worker is isolated not just from the political community—since he has no political representatives—but from '*life* itself', from human nature (CW 3,204). The isolation of man from his essential nature is incomparably more universal, more intolerable, more dreadful, and more contradictory, than the isolation from the political community. (CW 3,205) Because of the nature of the worker's suffering,

however *partial* the uprising of the *industrial workers* may be, it contains within itself a *universal* soul; however universal a *political* uprising may be, it conceals even in its *most grandiose* form a *narrow-minded* spirit. (CW 3,205)

The social revolution made by the workers, Marx argued against Ruge, has 'the point of view of the *whole*' (CW 3,205), however restricted its extent, because 'it represents man's protest against a dehumanised life' (CW 3,205). Making a political revolution, Marx explained, is the tendency of classes which have no political influence 'to abolish their *isolation* from *statehood* and *rule*' (CW 3,205). Making a social revolution, by contrast, is the tendency of men who are separated from their true community, from their human nature, to abolish their isolation from it. The proletariat is the universal class because it is the class of social revolution.

Because the political mind is bounded by politics itself, Marx claimed that the absence of a developed political system in Germany was an aid in solving the social problem there, not a hindrance.

The more developed and universal the *political* understanding of a people, the more does the *proletariat*—at any rate at the beginning of the movement—squander its forces in senseless, useless revolts, which are drowned in blood. Because it thinks in the framework of politics, the proletariat sees the cause of all evils in the *will*, and all means of remedy in *violence* and in the *overthrow* of a *particular* form of state. (CW 3,204)

Not only is Germany capable of a social revolution because of the feebleness of the German bourgeoisie, as Marx's arguments against Ruge suggest, it is in the best position for a social revolution. As Marx put it, Germany was '*classically* destined for a *social* revolution' (CW 3,202). Marx introduced his concept of the proletariat largely in order to explain, or justify, the need for a German 'radical' revolution. The Silesian weavers' uprising confirmed for him the ability of the proletariat to carry it out.

In his second Hegel critique, Marx distinguished between the French and German proletariats chiefly in terms of politics, and thus the way they would each become a (revolutionary) universal class. Because France was a political country, the proletariat soon comes to think of itself as the general representative:

In France every class is *politically idealistic* and becomes aware of itself at first not as a particular class but as the representative of social requirements generally. (CW 3,186)

In Germany, the proletariat is forced by material necessity to liberate itself and thus society; in France the proletariat liberates society and thus itself. The essential difference is the universalizing imperative of politics: in a political system, every competing class is compelled to claim that it represents the general interest, whether or not it does, and whether or not it believes it does. But in a political system, Marx suggested, universality expresses itself as the desire to seize state power, not to abolish it. In a political system, the proletariat enters into the state-civil society distinction. The German proletariat, however, is a sphere separate from the state–civil society sphere, and is thus in a better position to realize socialism. As a separate sphere, the proletariat is not quite a social class—as Marx acknowledged in the second Hegel critique—but as a class, the proletariat is no longer a separate sphere. The unique status of the German proletariat, Marx believed, had to be capitalized upon before there was a political emancipation in Germany (even though he had practically ruled out this event).

Marx praised the '*theoretical*' and '*conscious*' character of the Silesian weavers' actions. He presented Heinrich Heine's *Song of the Weavers* as the battle cry of the uprising in which the proletariat 'proclaims its opposition to the society of private property' (CW

3,201). The fact that he was citing, not the weavers, but Heine's song about them as empirical evidence of what the weavers thought, seems to have escaped his attention.[4] Marx also refused to interpret the destruction of machines and ledgers by the weavers as an instance of Luddism. Instead, he claimed that

The Silesian uprising *begins* precisely with what the French and English workers' uprisings *end*, with consciousness of the nature of the proletariat. The action itself bears the stamp of this *superior* character. Not only machines, these rivals of the workers, are destroyed, but also *ledgers*, the titles to property. And while all other movements were aimed primarily only against the *owner of the industrial enterprise*, the visible enemy, this movement is at the same time directed against the banker, the hidden enemy. Finally, not a single English workers' uprising was carried out with such courage, thought and endurance. (CW 3,201)

Here, the proletariat was not simply the 'heart' of emancipation, but its 'head' as well. For Marx, this disingenuous reasoning proved that 'the German proletariat is the *theoretician* of the European proletariat', and that it has 'excellent capabilities... for socialism' (CW 3,202). He considered the German proletariat, in the guise of some discontented Silesian artisans, to be the standard-bearer of European socialism.

The distaste for violence which Marx expressed in his critique of Ruge was echoed by Engels in the speeches he gave early in 1845 in Elberfeld. Although he remarked upon the absence of the proletariat from his audience,[5] Engels declared that the social revolution was inevitable.

That being so, we will have to concern ourselves above all with measures by which we can avoid a violent and bloody overthrow of the social conditions. (CW 4,263)

Both Marx and Engels cautioned that the proletariat should not exact revenge upon the bourgeoisie. Repugnance for violence was one of the reasons, as I have argued elsewhere,[6] why Marx was taken aback by the ferocity of the suppression of the Paris proletariat in June 1848. Much later, Marx wrote in the Preface to the first edition of the first volume of *Capital* that he dealt with individuals as 'personifications of economic categories':

My standpoint... can less than any other make the individual responsible for relations whose creature he socially remains, however much he may subjectively raise himself above them. (C I,21)

Or, in Engels' badly translated phrase, Communism 'rests upon the irresponsibility of the individual'.[7]

In his second Hegel critique, Marx described the proletariat's universality as a consequence of its suffering and lack of private property. Property, Marx believed, particularizes. The proletariat, therefore, had no particular interest to defend, and its suffering qualified it for a privileged relationship with philosophy. 'This singular philosophical conception of the proletariat', as Tucker describes it, received its meaning and its *raison d'être* primarily in its relations with philosophy. Marx explored the proletariat's 'universal suffering' in his Paris Manuscripts under the rubric of *alienation*, which sought to explain both its material and spiritual poverty as its separation from man's true nature. The proletariat's universality consisted in its need to overcome isolation from the human community, from *'life* itself'. Just as poverty was earlier considered by Marx as a symptom of the rule of particularity, so in the Paris Manuscripts he saw poverty as confirmation of the existence of alienation. Similarly, workers' revolts were now uniformly interpreted by him as evidence of the workers' opposition to dehumanization.

The Paris Manuscripts represent the high point of Feuerbach's influence upon Marx.[8] Feuerbach's notion of man as a species-being (*Gattungswesen*) was used in them as the basis for his argument about the intensional universality of the proletariat. For Marx, as for Hegel, labour—or freely creative activity—was the essence of man (CW 3,333). In the labour process, as man creates products, he creates and recreates himself. Human history, he claimed, is 'nothing but the creation of man through human labour' (CW 3,305). In the Manuscripts, Marx for the first time identified productive activity as the area where the source of alienation was to be found.[9] Unalienated labour is the true expression of man's species essence; it is the true satisfaction of human need:

the productive life is the life of the species. It is life-engendering life. The whole character of a species—its species-character — is contained in the character of its life activity; and free, conscious activity is man's species-character. (CW 3,276)

But for the worker, labour under capitalism is not as it should be, is not 'an *enjoyment of life*' (CW 3,228):

Presupposing private property, my work is an *alienation of life*, for I work *in order to live*, in order to obtain for myself the *means* of life. My work *is not* my life. (CW 3,228)

Marx explained that under conditions of alienated production the product of man's labour appears to him as something alien, an independent power. Private property transforms the expression of man's life into an external determinant of his life. And because human labour also produces man—his relationship to himself and to his species—alienated labour estranges man from the true community of men.

To say that *man* is estranged from himself, therefore, is the same thing as saying that the *society* of this estranged man is a caricature of his *real community*, of his true species-life, that his activity therefore appears to him as a torment, his own creation as an alien power, his wealth as poverty, the *essential bond* linking him with other men as an unessential bond... his life as a sacrifice of his life... his power over an object as the power of the object over him, and he himself, the lord of his creation, as the servant of this creation. (CW 3,217)

It is not unfair to say that Marx's concept of alienation suits his early (German-speculative) prose style; fond of paradox and inversion, of drawing sharp contrasts between essence and appearance, he had now formulated what he believed was the explanatory key.

Marx's concept of alienation tried to explain (but perhaps simply reformulated) the paradox, noted by earlier socialists, that 'The worker becomes all the poorer the more wealth he produces' (CW 3,271). But physical poverty is only one expression of man's alienation from his essence, since man produces not just material goods but also himself as a social being when he labours productively. The general formula of alienation, then, is that the greater the product of man's labour, the less is he himself (CW 3,272). Marx returned to this theme many times in his Paris Manuscripts; one example will suffice:

It is true that labour produces wonderful things for the rich—but for the worker it produces privation.... It produces beauty—but for the worker, deformity.... It produces intelligence—but for the worker, stupidity, cretinism. (CW 3,273)

The worker under capitalism is '*mentally* and physically *dehumanised*' (CW 3,284); he is cut off from a human existence (CW 4,42). Marx believed that this dehumanization was expressed in political economy, of which the Paris Manuscripts were his first serious examination. The categories of political economy such as rent, labour and property, he argued, were not eternal or fixed. But the fundamental category of political economy, generally obscured, was *man*. For Marx, the term *proletarian* was used as a weapon in the struggle against political economists, those 'scientific representatives of wealth' (CW 4,56), to reinstate this category. Political economy, he announced stridently, 'knows the worker only as a working animal—as a beast reduced to the strictest bodily needs' (CW 3,242). Indeed, Marx claimed that the task of political economy had been to maintain the worker '*whilst he is working* and insofar as may be necessary to prevent the *race of labourers* from [dying] out' (CW 3,284). He used the term *proletariat* to highlight the contrast between this approach and his own:

the *proletarian*, i.e. the man who, being without capital and rent, lives purely by labour, and by a one-sided, abstract labour, is considered by political economy only as a *worker*.... It does not consider him when he is not working, as a human being.... (CW 3,241)

Where Friedrich List, for example, had treated the worker as a 'productive force' alongside horses, steam and water, Marx objected:

It is a fine recognition of man that degrades him to a '*force*' capable of creating wealth! The bourgeois sees in the proletarian not a *human being*, but a *force* capable of creating wealth, a force moreover he can then compare with other productive forces—an animal, a machine—and if the comparison proves unfavourable to man, the force of which man is the bearer must give place to the force of which the bearer is an animal or a machine.... (CW 4,286)

In saying that labour under capitalism degrades man, Marx seems almost to object to the removal by machines of some types of degrading labour. In the strict sense, following his argument about labour as an 'unfree, unhuman, unsocial activity, determined by private property and creating private property' (CW 4,279), socialism would be established not by the 'organization of labour' promoted by Louis Blanc and others, but by the *abolition* of labour. Marx may also have been unfair on the political economists by assuming that abstraction for the purposes of study—surely a legitimate approach in most areas—is an accurate reflection of the way that political economists see man, or that their treating of man in this way somehow causes alienation.

Alienation, for Marx, is not simply a question of social psychology, but also and primarily a question of social division. Marx may start from the individual man under capitalism, but he soon moved to social classes:

The estrangement of man, and in fact every relationship in which man [stands] to himself, is realised and expressed only in the relationship in which a man stands to other men. (CW 3,277)

Tucker finds this position 'theoretically untenable',[10] although it explains for him the essential unity of 'original' and 'mature' Marxism. The move from self-estrangement to alienated social relations, however, is essential to Marx's argument, and to his belief that alienation is not a phenomenon of self-consciousness, as in the work of Hegel, but a material fact of social life. For Marx, therefore, the self-alienation of the producers is expressed as a clash between classes, between the workers and the capitalists. 'If the product of labour is alien to me', it must belong to 'a being *other* than myself', to the capitalist (CW 3,278; 3,221).

The relationship of the worker to labour creates the relation of it to the capitalist (or whatever one chooses to call the master of labour). *Private property* is thus the product, the result, the necessary consequence, of *alienated labour*, of the external relation of the worker to nature and to himself. (CW 3,279)

Alienation, however, is said by Marx to affect all men, and not just the proletariat. Under capitalism, all men are dehumanized. The life of the worker is determined by a power outside himself; the worker becomes subject to his products. Yet the owner of these products, the non-worker, is only nominally in control of them; 'his' products also determine his life. The condition of man under capitalism is heteronomy. Neither worker nor capitalist is free, self-determining. Each is under the sway of '*inhuman* power' (CW 3,314). By means of capital, the capitalist 'exercises his governing power over labour'; but Marx also saw 'the governing power of capital over the capitalist himself' (CW 3,247; 3,282; 3,284). That no man is free does not mean, according to Marx, that each suffers;

not all must suffer in a dehumanized society. Alienation, he claimed, produces different effects upon the worker and the capitalist:

The propertied class and the class of the proletariat present the same human self-estrangement. But the former class feels at ease and strengthened in this self-estrangement, it recognises estrangement as *its own power* and has in it the *semblance* of a human existence. The latter feels annihilated in estrangement; it sees in it its own powerlessness and the reality of an inhuman existence. (CW 4,36)

Marx's reasoning here is similar to that in the second Hegel critique: only the proletariat is in a position to see clearly and to feel alienation as the loss of man.[11] The proletariat's authentic perception of self-estrangement was not hindered by deriving any benefit from that estrangement. Marx suggested that only the proletariat can attain to consciousness of self-estrangement, and thus that only the proletariat (as well as philosophers, who are devoted to the abstract universal interest) can attain to the universal standpoint.

The material consequences of self-estrangement also play a major role in the emancipation of mankind by the proletariat:

since man has lost himself in the proletariat, yet at the same time has not only gained theoretical consciousness of that loss, but through urgent... *need...* is driven directly to revolt against this inhumanity, it follows that the proletariat can and must emancipate itself. (CW 4,36-7)

If the material expression of alienation is poverty, and alienated man's physical as well as spiritual needs are denied, human need also has a material dimension. Marx could thus interpret workers' struggles for higher wages as a struggle against alienation. The proletariat is the general representative of mankind because it alone perceives self-estrangement, and fights against it. But the proletariat's emancipation from self-estrangement (which is effectively its emancipation from the rule of the bourgeoisie) contains the emancipation of all men, because

the whole of human servitude is involved in the relation of the worker to production, and all relations of servitude are but modifications and consequences of this relation. (CW 3,280; CW 4,37)

Marx's extended discussion of man's self-estrangement in the Paris Manuscripts clarifies and extends his notion of the proletariat's universality: why it represents mankind, and why its emancipation will liberate all. The proletariat's universality does not rest simply on its being alienated from man's true nature, his species-essence; all men are thus alienated. The proletariat's universality rested on Marx's belief that it is the only section of alienated humanity which can achieve consciousness of man's self-alienation (philosophers excepted, but they were an insignificant material force), and the only section which is driven by 'absolutely imperative *need*—the practical expression of *necessity*' to revolt against inhumanity (CW 4,36-7).[12] Thus the significance of workers' struggles is refracted through the prism of 'alienation' to reveal the struggle for an authentically human life. The intensional universality of the proletariat which Marx defended in his critique of Ruge consisted not just in the estrangement of the proletarian from his species-essence, but in it being the only force capable of abolishing dehumanization. The subtlety of Marx's argument is not apparent in his critique of Ruge; the issue of the capitalist's alienation, for example, was not canvassed.

Marx turned his attention from Ruge to the Critical Critics towards the end of 1844. Bruno Bauer, Marx's erstwhile friend and mentor, was the centre of this circle of intellectuals. Like Ruge, the Critical Critics dissented from Marx's view of the proletariat. Essentially, they believed that only philosophers could represent the universal interest. Edgar Bauer, for example, wrote that 'The modern worker thinks only of himself'.[13] Bruno Bauer was even more emphatic in rejecting the mass: it was 'the true enemy of the spirit',[14] and thus the enemy of historical progress:

All great actions of previous history were failures from the start and had no effective success because the mass became interested in and enthusiastic over them.... [15]

Like Ruge, these Critical Critics emphasized what they saw as the limited viewpoint of the workers. For them, the proletarian standpoint was one of a number of particular standpoints of which society was composed, and above which they, as philosophers, stood as the universal beacon. It was his opposition to this approach which prompted Marx to declare, in an often misunderstood remark, what is simply a reformulation of his view of the proletariat as a universal class: that

It is not a question of what this or that proletarian, or even the whole proletariat, at the moment *regards* as its aim. It is a question of what the *proletariat is*, and what, in accordance with this *being*, it will historically be compelled to do. (CW 4,37)

No single quotation from Marx could more clearly convey the speculative nature of his concept of the proletariat: his belief that whatever the actual proletariat thought about its own interests, it would eventually proclaim itself, and be accepted, as the general social representative. As Kamenka has written, Marx saw in the proletariat 'not just the empirical existence, but the logical category'.[16] There were two things, however, which were integral to this potential. The first was that there was no barrier to the proletariat attaining the universal standpoint: its viewpoint was not bounded by its possession of private property, but limited by its lack of access to education and philosophy. The second was that the proletariat, in becoming one with its concept, was fulfilling a human need.

In a work in which Marx had consciously to contrast the actual proletariat with its concept, he began to link its development with historical and material factors. It was part of his larger campaign against the Critical Critics waged in *The Holy Family* to stress the material nature of man's alienation, and that only material means would end external determination. Marx declared that for the 'Holy Family' (the Bauers and their group), 'The act of transforming society' had been reduced 'to the *cerebral activity* of Critical Criticism' (CW 4,86). He argued that the products of self-estrangement were real, material things which held men in thrall. Self-estrangement could not be conjured away by an act of pure thought. In his Paris Manuscripts, Marx had written:

In order to abolish the *idea* of private property, the *idea* of communism is quite sufficient. It takes *actual* communist action to abolish actual private property. (CW 3,313)

In *The Holy Family*, he counterposed to the Critical Critics the 'mass-minded' communist workers, who

do not believe that by '*pure thinking*' they will be able to argue away their industrial masters and their own practical debasement.... They know that property, capital, money, wage-labour and the like are no ideal figments of the brain, but very practical, very objective products of their self-estrangement and that therefore they must be abolished in a practical, objective way for man to become man not only in *thinking*, in *consciousness*, but in mass *being*, in life. (CW 4,53; 4,82)

Marx's position here is different from that of the second Hegel critique, where he placed greater emphasis on theory and the ability of theory to become a material force 'as soon as it has gripped the masses.' (CW 3,182) Now Marx's emphasis is on theory, philosophy, as a partner of the proletariat. Rather than philosophy realizing itself as the proletariat, the proletariat comes to self-realization with the assistance of philosophy. The partnership of the proletariat with philosophy, it should be noted, was never conceived by Marx as it was by Engels in March 1845:

With the philosophers to think, and the working men to fight for us, will any earthly power be strong enough to resist our progress? (CW 4,236)

Engels seems to take the proletarians as they are; Marx took them as they would be.

To the primacy of the material element in the self-estrangement of man, Marx added a historical dimension which was lacking in the Paris Manuscripts. For real freedom, he argued in *The Holy Family*, socialism 'demands besides the idealistic "*will*" very tangible, very material conditions' (CW 4,95). Marx embraced the idea of 'material conditions' for socialism in response to the Critical Critics' claim that all previous historical actions were failures because the mass had become involved in them. 'Failure', for the Critical Critics, meant that the social problem had not yet been solved. The French Revolution was a 'failure' in their terms because it had not introduced socialism. Yet the very existence of the social problem and the notion of socialism were themselves historical and materially-conditioned products, Marx implied. Furthermore, the Critical Critics had misunderstood Marx's concept of 'revolutionary universality'—essentially his attempt to reconcile the mass nature of the French Revolution with its limited results (a task in which the Critical Critics were themselves involved). It is easy to understand, Marx suggested, that

every mass-type '*interest*'... when it first comes on the scene... is confused with the *human* interest in general. (CW 4,81)

The Revolution resulted in the triumph of the bourgeoisie not because the mass participated in it, but because what at first appeared to be a victory for the general interest was, in fact, only a victory for the bourgeoisie. The 'all-embracing' mass, as distinct from the 'exclusive, limited mass' of the bourgeoisie, 'did not have its *real* interest in the principle of the Revolution' (CW 4,82). But for a social revolution, a revolution in the interests of humanity,

Together with the thoroughness of the historical action, the size of the mass whose action it is will therefore increase. (CW 4,82)

From the time of the Paris Manuscripts Marx had argued that the proletariat included the majority of society (CW 3,239; 3,241), but here he makes a direct link between the general interest and the size of the mass whose direct interest it is. For the first time, he makes it an essential part of his analysis that the social revolution be made by a majority of society.[17]

The Holy Family contains some strong suggestions of what Marx would soon explicitly formulate as the materialist conception of history. By stressing history Marx wanted to devalue the role of critical philosophy, particularly in shaping the proletariat. He substituted a historical development based on needs for a logical and intellectual development based on enlightenment or education. Furthermore, the Critical Critics were vulnerable to attacks on the basis of history, since they argued as if their solutions were applicable at any time. Does Critical Criticism, Marx asked,

think that it actually knows any period without knowing, for example, the industry of that period, the immediate mode of production of life itself?... Just as it separates thinking from the senses, the soul from the body and itself from the world, it separates history from natural science and industry and sees the origin of history not in vulgar *material* production on the earth but in the vaporous clouds in the heavens. (CW 4,150)

Yet the touchstone of the materialist conception of history was the question of Germany's opportunity for social revolution. Only when Marx had rejected, however incompletely, the idea of Germany's privileged opportunity for social revolution could the materialist conception of history fully take shape. Even in March 1845, he had not yet given up the idea that Germany could avoid the historical drill of bourgeois development and move directly to socialism (CW 4,281). The continuing tension in his materialist conception of history between a general (and rigid) scheme of historical development, in which the advanced nations tell the less advanced: *'De te fabula narratur'*, and a scheme which opens up possibilities for less advanced nations—a tension, if you like, within Marx's theory between the claims of France and of Germany —were never entirely resolved by Marx. The tension resurfaced in his work after the defeat of the German revolution in 1848, and in his responses in the last decade of his life to the issue of the character of a Russian revolution. One of the sources of this tension is to be found in Marx's concept of the proletariat, with which Marx originally justified his commitment to a German radical revolution, but which soon became synonymous with a highly developed industrial working class.

If the actual proletariat was not much like its concept, there was no reason Marx could see to prevent it from attaining its concept, and there were a number of human needs which impelled it towards that end. This is not to say that the actual proletariat seemed to him to be devoid of all traces of its concept, or that the actual proletariat or its concept were not used by him in a more positive sense to show what might be achieved in human relations, and as a benchmark to evaluate existing relations. This more positive conception of the proletariat will be examined in the next chapter.

5

A Proletarian Ethic?

As a critique of the abstract and impotent philosophy of self-consciousness of the Critical Critics, *The Holy Family* was soon transcended by Marx's broader critique of ideology in his work of 1845-6, written jointly with Engels: *The German Ideology*. But *The Holy Family* remains perhaps the most important source in Marx's work for a positive, ethically-based conception of the proletariat. Almost a quarter of *The Holy Family* examined the use made by the Critical Critics of Eugène Sue's recent and popular novel, *Mysteries of Paris*. The Critical Critics, Critically transforming it where necessary, used Sue's novel—which for many Germans of the time served as an introduction to the social problem—to clarify their own project of social transformation.[1] The Critical reformation of the Mass, which had found its fictional counterpart in Prince Rudolph's attempts to bring some members of the Parisian underworld to a sense of their own human dignity and worth, was denounced by Marx as a form of dehumanization. As Kamenka has put it:

Each one of Sue's characters who goes through 'moral regeneration' [at the hands of Rudolph], according to Marx, comes out less a *man* (or woman) in a moral sense. Each 'criminal', originally full of vitality, is made dependent or cringing, robbed of his or her talents, brought to anguish and submission.[2]

Marx opposed applying abstract moral standards to the criminals and prostitutes of Sue's Paris, for whom we can substitute the proletariat, by arguing that these people led a more genuinely human life because they did not try to live according to standards which were alien to their species-essence, and externally imposed upon them. The proletariat, we might reasonably infer from Marx's discussion in *The Holy Family*, had a genuinely human ethic which was constantly undermined and negated by the imposition of the abstract standards and imperatives of the reigning morality.

110

The central character of Sue's *Mysteries* is Rudolph, Prince of Geroldstein, a small German principality. To atone for attempting to murder his father, Rudolph goes forth into the world 'to punish the wicked and reward the good' (CW 4,203). Like most moralists, he intends to live his life and achieve his good through others, as a moralizer. *Rudolph* is a literary device, not just in that he is a creature of fiction, or a fictional world, but also in that he functions as the link between descriptions of the lower and higher strata of society. For Rudolph is a man of disguises, who can pass easily from the *haute volée* to which he was born to the level of a wine salesman or a painter of fans. To the members of this lower society (and to them almost exclusively) he applies his ethical standpoint, and from them he exacts his own retribution, attempting to bring them to 'good' and to God.

Rudolph was a prototypical Critical Critic. Herr Szeliga, the Critical reviewer of Sue's novel, declared in the spirit of Rudolph that 'Only *Christianity* and *morality* are able to found universal kingdoms on earth'.[3] 'Criticism' Marx explained, 'leaves the *realisation* of its own *thoughts* to Rudolph' (CW 4,163). Rudolph the moralizer, and through him the Critical Critics as frustrated moralizers, were Marx's targets. Rudolph's moral transformations, Marx argued, were based on an abstract standard and degraded humans. The two criticisms were closely linked: the *abstract* standard was one which did not have the real man as its foundation. Measuring the world, and attempting to change it in the light of such abstraction, he argued, took from man his human dignity, made him dependent on something outside his nature, and meant that he was unfree. The theme pursued in those sections of *The Holy Family* devoted to Sue's *Mysteries* concerns the basic human decency of the proletariat, despite its alleged wrongdoings—wrongdoings only because they were defined in terms of abstract or 'bourgeois' morality. The proletariat does not sin against human nature; it sins against 'bourgeois' morality.[4]

In 'educated society', Rudolph encounters a number of women who are moral hypocrites, and who gossip about their marital infidelities. (The equal and opposite hypocrisy of the husbands is not discussed by Sue.) The Critical Critic—Szeliga—comments that sensuality has taken the place of love for these women. Marx does not deny that love is essential for a true marriage; but he contends that true love is sensual (CW 4,65). Sensuality need not spell the end of virtue. Instead, in at least one case in the *Mysteries* (that of Countess MacGreggor, who schemes to marry Rudolph), virtue is overthrown from calculation (CW 4,67). Marx draws a contrast between such women and those of the lower stratum, the mass. Rigolette, a Paris *grisette*, emerges from the novel, according to Marx, with a 'lovely human character' (CW 4,76). Although she disregards the form of marriage, it is in

her naive attachment to the Etudiant or the Ouvrier... that she constitutes a really human contrast to the hypocritical, narrow-hearted, self-seeking wife of the bourgeois, to the whole circle of the bourgeoisie, that is, to the official circle. (CW 4,76)

The *grisette*, in her relationships, is bound by considerations of love. She is morally superior to the wife of the bourgeois because her actions accord with her human essence (i.e. she acts unwittingly according to a truly human ethic).

Marx's argument is twofold: that bourgeois morality is not a truly human morality, does not accord with the human essence; and that the bourgeoisie does not act according to its own moral abstractions, but hypocritically. These criticisms are intensified as Marx follows the course of Rudolph's moral proselytizing. Instead of uplifting the mass, Rudolph degrades them. Marx found the case of Chourineur instructive in this respect. Chourineur, a butcher by trade, is a murderer. We meet him molesting Fleur de Marie; Rudolph appears and strikes Chourineur, thus winning his respect. Rudolph, according to Sue, instils in Chourineur a sense of self-respect; according to the Critical Critic, Rudolph transforms Chourineur into a '*moral being*'.[5] But Rudolph then persuades Chourineur to become an *agent provocateur*, a police informer, to turn against his friends in the underworld. Marx commented: 'The first lesson Chourineur receives is a lesson in hypocrisy, faithlessness, craft and *dissimulation*' (CW 4,163). Chourineur subsequently lures a friend to his destruction: 'For the *first time* in his life he commits an act of *infamy*' (CW 4,163). The moral transformation of Chourineur, Marx argued, makes him immoral (or perhaps inhuman). This 'moral being' forms an attachment to Rudolph which Chourineur himself likens to the devotion of a bulldog to its master. Rather than making a true man of Chourineur, as Rudolph and the Critical Critic believe, his moral transformation has made him servile. Indeed, Rudolph becomes a god for Chourineur, who dies in Rudolph's defence. Marx ironically concluded: 'What a merit it was for Rudolph to have restored *Schurimann* [Chourineur] to *mankind*!' (CW 4,165)

Much the more interesting discussion with implications for a proletarian ethic, however, centres on Fleur de Marie. Marie is a prostitute,

in bondage to the proprietress of a criminals' tavern. In this debasement she preserves a human nobleness of soul, a human unaffectedness and a human beauty that impresses those around her.... (CW 4,168)

This is her '*original form*', Marx wrote, the better that he might point out her '*Critical transformation*'.

In spite of her frailty, Fleur de Marie at once gives proof of vitality, energy, cheerfulness, resilience of character—qualities which alone explain her human development in her *inhuman* situation. (CW 4,168)

Marie's inhuman situation merely serves to highlight her human qualities; qualities which she struggles unknowingly to protect. Marie has independence and fight in her. In telling the story of her life to Rudolph and his trusty dog Chourineur, she does not repent:

she pronounces on the past the human sentence, at once *Stoic* and *Epicurean*, of a free and strong nature: '*Enfin ce qui est fait, est fait*'. (CW 4,169)

Rudolph, however, is 'itching to moralise' about her situation, eager to impress upon her what a terrible life she has lived. But Marie, Marx's innocent, having admitted that she has contemplated suicide, says that in these moments, 'il me semblait que mon sort n'était pas mérite'.[6] Marie sees her situation as not one of her own making, and besides, she believes she has harmed no-one:

Good and *evil*, as Marie conceives them, are not the *moral abstractions* of good and evil. She is *good* because she has never caused *suffering* to anyone, she has always been *human* towards her inhuman surroundings. (CW 4,169-70)

Marie is good, but her situation is evil, 'because it is not the expression of her human impulses, not the fulfilment of her human desires' (CW 4,170). The proper foundation of morality and its true measure, Marx implied, is man's essential nature, not 'the *ideal of what is good*' (CW 4,170). Marx attacked, under the rubric of 'moral abstractions', *bourgeois* morality. It is 'abstract' not just because it takes the form of universal commandments, but because it abstracts from human nature itself. Marx, however, does not closely link morality with classes, or class interests, preferring in *The Holy Family* to emphasize the distinction between human and inhuman moralities:

In *natural* surroundings, where the chains of bourgeois life fall away and she can freely manifest her own nature, Fleur de Marie bubbles over with love of life, with a wealth of feeling, with human joy at the beauty of nature; these show that her social position has only grazed the surface of her and is a mere misfortune, that she herself is neither good nor bad, but *human*. (CW 4,170)

Marie's inhuman situation has not fundamentally altered her human nature, just repressed the expression of it. Furthermore, her situation appears to be merely circumstantial: the chains of bourgeois life seem not to be mental chains—not, at any rate, until Marie becomes a Christian. For Marx, Marie's conversion to Christianity represents the triumph of abstract morality over her, the crucifixion of her human nature.

Sue's account of Marie, as Marx related it, 'slapped bourgeois prejudice in the face' (CW 4,170) by presenting a prostitute as having an unaffected humanity. But Sue hands Marie over to Rudolph and the priest Laporte, who impose abstract moral notions upon her actions and encourage in her a deep sense of guilt and shame. Marie believes that shame will end when she begins to repent her past; but religion has a different message for her. She believes that she has already been brought back to God; but the priest tells her that her sins are not yet forgiven. 'Soon', he tempts, 'you will deserve absolution'.[7] The priest spoils Marie's vision by transforming the beauties of everything she sees and all her actions into aspects of God. Being devoid of religion, in her natural vision, they were 'impious and godless' (CW 4,172). He tramples underfoot her natural, spiritual resources by Christianizing them. Marie adopts the religious viewpoint which, in Marx's words (echoing Feuerbach), 'in general regards everything human in man as alien to him and everything inhuman in him as *really* belonging to him' (CW 4,173). Religion regards man as inherently sinful and inhuman; it regards God as the only truly moral being—as the only truly human being.

Religion makes Marie less than a fully human being. When she first left Paris to begin her re-education, she had had 'a vague consciousness of... [her] degradation'.[8] But religion showed her that she was 'more guilty than unfortunate'.[9] The priest, she confesses, made her realize '*the infinite depth of...* [her] *damnation*'.[10] She despairs:

From this moment Marie is *enslaved by the consciousness of sin.* In her former most unhappy situation in life she was able to develop a lovable, human individuality; in her outward debasement she was conscious that *her human* essence was *her true essence.* Now the filth of modern society, which has touched her externally, becomes her innermost being, and continual hypochondrial self-torture because of that filth becomes her duty, the task of her life appointed by God himself, the self-purpose of her existence. (CW 4,174)

Marie now conceives of *good*, not as the absence of doing harm, but as nothing but self-torment. She might have said, with the Moor of Venice: 'I swear 'tis better to be much abused Than but to know't a little'.

Marie eventually gives herself wholly to God, convinced that it is the only way to salvation. She enters a convent, where she becomes abbess. But

Convent life does not suit Marie's individuality—she dies. Christianity consoles her only in imagination, or rather her Christian consolation is precisely the annihilation of her real life and essence—her death. (CW 4,176)

For Marx, Christianity is a form of man's inhumanity (to himself). Rudolph epitomized Critical Criticism's inhumanity: he turned Marie into a repentant sinner, then into a nun, and finally into a corpse.

Marx criticized the bourgeois moralist first, for wanting to bring human actions to accord with 'moral abstractions' which do not derive directly from, or seek to promote, the human essence; and second, for wanting the human actor, consciously and continually, to sit in judgement of his own actions using only this inhuman standard. Sin is not sin, Marx implied, until there is consciousness of sin and repentence. It might be said that Marx's discussion of

Marie, far from continuing the fight against the philosophy of self-consciousness, actually incorporates elements of it. For Marx argued that Marie abandons her humanity only when she has adopted an abstract moral standard, Christianity. Her inhuman situation had not made her inhuman; her conversion to Christianity had. Marx at this stage implied that to be fully human is chiefly a matter of having a human consciousness, which need not become inhuman in inhuman surroundings. Being and consciousness are here quite distinct.

But Marx also believed that immorality is a necessary and inevitable part of the system of bourgeois morality or, for that matter, any system of abstract morality. Bourgeois morality fights a losing battle against immorality because it presumes a conscious and free moral agent. In bourgeois society, Marx suggested, there was none; there were simply people whose lives are determined by forces outside, and hostile to, their nature. On this ground, the very idea of morality is inherently flawed. Thus bourgeois morality and immorality, for Marx, actually express differences in the social position of classes in bourgeois society: morality justifies the existing social order. This state of affairs places the proletarian in a condition of moral, and not just material despair. Immorality is also indissolubly tied to morality because morality as a form of external determination is inimical to the human essence. Any attempt to express truly that essence in a system influenced by morality is by definition immoral. Both bourgeois and proletarian are alienated from their human essence, yet social differences translate into differences over how the immorality involved in the inevitable clash between human nature and abstract morality is interpreted. For the bourgeois, transgressions of the moral code are seen as hypocrisy, and are widely tolerated. For the proletarian, transgressions of imposed morality constitute infamy, and are often prosecuted.

As for the absence of free moral agents in bourgeois society, Marx has already implied that the proletariat retains major features of its humanity because it has not internalized bourgeois morality; then he argued, in effect, that proletarians are not free moral agents. Marx opposed bourgeois morality, in other words, on its own grounds. The basis of his argument is a rather crude determinism.

116

Marie is a prostitute; Marx implied that she had no choice in the matter. Of the priest who thought that it would have been easy for Marie to preserve her virtue in Paris, Marx wrote:

The hypocritical priest knows quite well that at any hour of the day, in the busiest streets, those virtuous people of Paris pass indifferently by little girls of seven or eight years who sell *allumettes* and the like until about midnight as Marie herself used to do and who, almost without exception, will have the same fate as Marie. (CW 4,172)[11]

Marx suggests that proletarians are not responsible for their actions. Chourineur becomes a murderer, he explained glibly, 'Owing to a concourse of circumstances' (CW 4,163). And the *Maître d'école*, the leader of a group of criminals, also had no choice:

This passionate athlete comes into conflict with the laws and customs of bourgeois society, whose universal yardstick is mediocrity, delicate morals and quiet trade. He becomes a murderer and abandons himself to all the excesses of a violent temperament that can nowhere find a fitting human occupation. (CW 4,176)

Marx does not explain why not all proletarians, or even unemployed proletarians, are prostitutes or murderers. It is also interesting that he expands on the idea of a basic human ethic only in the case of Fleur de Marie. On his own account, none of the characters he treats is a free moral agent, and none can be judged by the abstract moralist. This approach should apply irrespective of the actions these characters have performed. Yet Marx adopted a different standpoint when he reports Marie as saying that she had harmed no-one. His acceptance of her statement is part of the ground on which he builds his notion of her humanity. Such a standpoint encounters certain difficulties with the case of a murderer. Expressing the human essence, as Marx conceived it, consisted partly in recognizing other humans as aspects of oneself. Murder is a complete negation of this essence. Indeed, except in cases of self-defence or accident, murder is widely condemned by most systems of morality. Marx cannot oppose this prevailing view, even if he might disagree with its condemnation on moral gounds. So in discussing the case of the *maître d'école*, Marx focussed on the morality of punishment, rather than on the morality of the foul deed.

Prince Rudolph, who captured the *maître d'école* to punish him, tries to link *vengeance* against the criminal with *penance* and consciousness of sin. Rudolph promotes punishment as a means of moral education. Thus he has the *maitre d'école* blinded, shutting him up with consciousness of his sin. When the criminal in despair shouts 'Mon Dieu!', Rudolph believes he has succeeded in turning all the criminal's thoughts into prayers. Marx commented:

Compared with this Christian cruelty, how humane is the ordinary penal theory that just chops a man's head off when it wants to destroy him. (CW 4,179)

The Critical Critics ascribed to Rudolph the theory, which had its origins in Hegel's work, that punishment must make the criminal the judge of his own crime. But Hegel's was only a speculative interpretation of current punishment practices, according to Marx. Hegel thus 'leaves punishment as it is' (CW 4,179). In a sense, Hegel tried to convince the criminal that the violence done to him by others as punishment is violence which he does to himself. In a truly human society, Marx argued by contrast, 'punishment will *really* be nothing but the sentence passed by the culprit on himself' (CW 4,179). He will see in other men natural saviours from the punishment he has imposed on himself, not as the instruments of a punishment externally imposed. The theory of punishment proposed by Rudolph and endorsed by the Critical Critics: to reward the good and punish the wicked, unCritically considered, Marx declared, is 'nothing but the theory of society as it is today' (CW 4,188). Punishment and reward consecrate social differences. A man who is truly self-determining, and who is therefore in a free, truly human society, needs no external regulation, no law.[12] Yet it is not clear why the need for (self-) punishment will ever arise.

Having disposed of, or neutralized, the 'badness' of these characters of the Parisian underworld, Marx turned his attention to Rudolph, the self- and Critical-appointed paragon of (bourgeois) virtue. Rudolph confronts and measures the world with 'his *fixed, Christian* ideas' (CW 4,201); but what sort of a man is he? He is a hypocrite, Marx argued, because

he manages to see and make others see the *outbursts of his evil passions as outbursts against the passions of the wicked*.... (CW 4,206)

In three major instances, Marx charged, Rudolph was motivated by petty personal concerns such as revenge. Marx questioned

Rudolph's morality by contrasting his motives with the *human* motive of concern for the general interest:

The 'good' Rudolph! Burning with desire for revenge, thirsting for blood, with calm, deliberate rage, with a hypocrisy which excuses every evil impulse with its casuistry, he has all the evil passions for which he gouges out the eyes of others. Only accidental strokes of luck, money and rank in society save this '*good*' man from the *penitentiary*. (CW 4,209)

Rudolph is challenged on his own moral ground. The aristocrat's prejudices of good and evil coincide with real differences between rich and poor (CW 4,203). But where one might wish to see morality made universal, Marx wanted a universal morality. That is, far from arguing that the prevailing morality should subject all *equally* to its strictures, he wanted an entirely different morality: a morality which corresponded to the human essence; a morality in which, therefore, there will be no external *strictures* properly so-called; a morality which, in a sense, is no morality at all. But while Marx linked morality with social differences, he did not say whence morality came, or why many of its features were constant over long periods of time.

The Holy Family contains the clearest expression in Marx's work of a conception of the proletariat as a repository of human values in an inhuman world. In this respect, it builds upon characteristics of the proletariat which may first have attracted Marx to them, and which dovetailed with his belief that the cause of the proletariat was the cause of humanity. This positive conception of the proletariat is found in the Paris Manuscripts:

When communist *artisans* associate with one another, theory, propaganda, etc., is their first end. But at the same time, as a result of this association, they acquire a new need—the need for society—and what appears as a means becomes an end. In this practical process the most splendid results are to be observed whenever French socialist workers are seen together. Such things as smoking, drinking, eating, etc., are no longer means of contact or means that bring them together. Association, society and conversation, which again has association as its end, are enough for them; the brotherhood of man is no mere phrase with them, but a fact of life, and the nobility of man shines upon us from their work-hardened bodies. (CW 3,313)

Marx enthused about 'the nobility which bursts forth from these toil-worn men' in a letter to Feuerbach in August 1844 (CW

119

3,355). Shortly thereafter, in *The Holy Family*, he added that

English and French workers have formed associations in which they exchange opinions not only on their immediate needs as *workers*, but on their needs as *human beings*. In their associations, moreover, they show a very thorough and comprehensive consciousness of the 'enormous' and 'immeasurable' power which arises from their co-operation. (CW 4,52-3)

These visions of the proletariat are in stark contrast to the picture more common in Marx's work of a suffering and mentally and physically dehumanized proletariat. Production under capitalism, Marx argued, produces man 'as a *mentally* and physically *dehumanised* being' (CW 3,284). Condemning the rule of private property, he had claimed that

Light, air, etc. — the simplest *animal* cleanliness—ceases to be a need for man. *Filth*, this stagnation and putrefaction of man—the *sewage* of civilisation (speaking quite literally)—comes to be the *element of life* for him. Utter, *unnatural* depravation, putrefied nature, comes to be his *life-element*. None of his senses exist [sic] any longer, and [each has ceased to function] not only in its human fashion, but in an *inhuman* fashion, so that it does not exist even in an animal fashion. (CW 3,308)

The proletarian is dehumanized under capitalism because his activities are dictated by an external necessity, or are limited and abstracted expressions of internal necessity, so that the truly human needs of his whole personality are not met.[13] Marx further suggested that even these limited needs of the proletarian were sometimes not met. How, then, does a physically dehumanized proletarian come to have a 'work-hardened' body? And how does a mentally dehumanized proletarian come to have a 'thorough and comprehensive consciousness'? This contrast between the worker as a degraded human being and as a noble human (perhaps even a noble savage), in touch with his true needs, points not only to a larger tension in Marx's concept of the proletariat between the proletariat as a separate and as an integrated sphere of society, but to a question about the motive for Marx's commitment to the proletariat. Was Marx concerned chiefly about the proletariat's poverty, or with its degradation? Did he see the proletariat as the inheritors of a society of immense wealth, or as the truly human, noble men of the future? Was the basis of his commitment to the proletariat an ethical or a material one? Although he often stressed their poverty, and the material basis for their emancipation, Marx was concerned primarily with proletarians as agents of a truly human society, however he described or named that society.

The link between those quotations in which Marx extols the nobility of the proletariat is their common reference to the association of workers. Like Fleur de Marie in the countryside, the workers in association find themselves in *natural* surroundings (CW 4,170), in which their true nature can emerge. In association workers can become indignant at the contrast between their human nature and their conditions of life, which are 'the outright, resolute and comprehensive negation of that nature' (CW 4,36). Instead of seeing in the organization of the workers simply an expression of limited, money-oriented preoccupations, Marx saw the potential for, and the expression of human dignity. The association of workers for whatever ends had a profound influence on them: it was a means by which they constituted themselves as a separate sphere. The motives for association, Marx argued, were relatively unimportant, although all the examples he cited involved workers already committed to socialism (and thus arguably atypical). This is the basis for his later claim that trade unions, formed to fight for limited goals, would be a prelude to the organization of the workers as a class to destroy bourgeois society. Marx could thus reconcile the *particular* aims of the workers (although *material* aims might be a better expression) with the universal outcome of a workers' revolution.

For Marx, part of man's dehumanization consisted in his isolation from other men. He detested the individualism of civil society, which he had discussed in 'On the Jewish Question', following the example of Hobbes and Hegel, in terms of a *bellum omnium contra omnes* (CW 3,155). He returned to this theme in *The Holy Family*. In civil society, he argued, men treated others as means to their own narrow ends. Marx believed that a natural necessity held men together, even in civil society where they were unaware of it, and where it had assumed a perverted form:

The *modern state* has as its *natural basis* civil society and the *man* of civil society, i.e. the independent man linked with other men only by ties of private interest and *unconscious* natural necessity, the *slave* of labour for gain and of his own as well as other men's *selfish* need. (CW 4,113)

This mediation between men in civil society, and man's subsequent isolation, affected the worker as much as the capitalist.

Marx noted and deplored the competition among workers (e.g., CW 3,235). But the association of workers as a class and the association of individual bourgeois as a class, he suggested, were entirely different. The class expression of the bourgeois is a form of external necessity:

However much the individual bourgeois fights against others, as a *class* the bourgeois have a common interest, and this community of interest, which is directed against the proletariat inside the country, is directed against the bourgeois of other nations outside the country. This the bourgeois calls his *nationality*. (CW 4,281)

The bourgeois class is an alliance for the protection of the individual interests of every bourgeois. The proletariat, however, formed a different type of association, a different type of class, because its class-bond was an expression of human nature, human necessity. The proletariat as a class fought for the interests of humanity. And while proletarians nowhere yet formed a class, Marx glimpsed in their limited associations such a class, and the truly human society itself.

It should be noted in relation to the discussion of *class* in *The Holy Family* and his earlier works, that Marx sometimes operated with a distinction which he only made explicit in his 1847 *The Poverty of Philosophy*: a distinction between the proletariat as a class in itself (*an sich*), and as a class for itself (*für sich*) (CW 6,211). Therefore, in the discussion above, Marx does not strictly counterpose the bourgeois class (as a form of external necessity) to the proletarian class (as a form of human necessity). He did have a conception of the class position of the proletariat as a form of external necessity, as a set of material circumstances into which the proletarian was born and which determined his life; but he saw in the conscious association of the workers the potential for the recognition of human necessity. For Marx, *class* as external necessity was the class in itself; *class* as human necessity was the class for itself. Only the proletariat as a class could develop from the former into the latter. Of course, the bourgeoisie during the French Revolution became for a time a class for itself; but being universal and being conscious of the character of one's class and its role coincide only in the proletariat. This was another reason why Marx introduced the proletariat as a class of civil society which was not a class of civil society: the proletariat as a class for itself consciously embodied and expressed the human bonds which were mediated in civil society. The proletariat as a class for itself formed a sphere separate from civil society, a sphere which could include all men only by the abolition of civil society.

Marx's enthusiasm for the cause of the proletariat was fired by his (probably limited) contact with groups of socialist artisans in Paris. He seemed to be impressed chiefly by their human dignity. Rather than claiming that adversity often brings out the best in man, he defended the idea that the proletariat formed a separate sphere. The importance of *The Holy Family* is not just the incipient critique of ideology which it contains, nor its development of Marx's primitive ethic, but also the light it sheds on his notion of a separate sphere. Marx's condemnation of the ethical standpoint of the Critical Critics was based, after all, on the idea that the Parisian underworld was a separate sphere, progressively contaminated by the imposition of bourgeois morality. In ethical terms, the separateness of the Parisian underworld was threatened by its acceptance of bourgeois moral norms. But how separate is this underworld? Marx did not consider whether the actions of its figures are based on a rejection of prevailing morals, or have no reference at all to external moral strictures. The difference is important. Just as Feuerbach rejected the designation *atheist* for his own position, because it involved the negative recognition of God, so a rejection of prevailing morals, an amoralism on the part of these underworld figures, would have involved a negative recognition of morality. Such a view would not have helped Marx's case. By acting without reference to moral commands, Marx suggested instead, these figures lived out a truly human ethic.

Marx's discussion seems to assume, on the part of the Parisian underworld (and by implication, the proletariat), a sort of simplicity or unaffectedness. Its members are not burdened by moral abstractions as external 'rules' or 'principles' or 'commands'. To burden them so is the task of the bourgeois moralist. Thus the underworld figures act according to their own (human) lights, until they collide with the morality of bourgeois society (in the shape of the law, for example). These criminals then become conscious of their actions in the light of bourgeois morality, and attain consciousness of their guilt. 'Consciousness of sin' and 'penance', according to Marx, are important parts of the inhuman ethic. But this model assumes a separation of society into separate *worlds*, which come into contact only formally through systems of laws and ethics: not that these systems permeate the whole of society, and are expressed and reinforced in innumerable ways. Marx's model contradicts the idea that no action in society is prior to 'moral abstractions'.

The suggestion by Marx that the proletariat lives in a different moral world from bourgeois society, even if its ethic is not—and perhaps cannot be—formulated, leads to the idea that certain aspects of the proletariat's existence are authentically human. It is as if the proletariat, or certain aspects of it, exist in a beneficent 'state of nature', of the type constructed by seventeenth century political philosophers to describe the pre-political state of man. But which aspects of the proletariat's existence were separate? And how separate is separate? Marx wants to have it both ways: to blame bourgeois society for the physical and mental degradation of the worker (i.e. to stress that the worker's condition is an integral product of bourgeois society); and to rely for the foundation of the truly human society on the separation of the proletariat from the contamination of bourgeois society. On Marx's reasoning, the proletariat can only liberate itself from its inhuman condition because it does not lead an entirely inhuman existence.

The manifest nature of Marx's ethical standpoint in *The Holy Family* forms a natural progression from the ethical element of the Paris Manuscripts. Alienated man, Marx had argued there, was not truly or fully human. The criteria of what it was to be human, genuinely to express the species-essence, were inextricably ethical. To be human was to be autonomous, to be self-sufficient and self-determined; it was to consider and to treat all one's fellows as aspects of oneself.[14] Marx's ethical standpoint was one in which man was the sole standard, by which all activities and social arrangements would be judged. This standpoint, or disposition, was constant throughout Marx's work. His rejection of *morality*, about which paradox there has grown a vast literature,[15] was quite consistent with this position. (Indeed, consistency in following the logic

124

of an argument was one of Marx's major strengths, as well as a weakness. It allowed him to detect flaws in arguments, as well as to push beyond them to sometimes startling conclusions. In being consistent with the idea of man's species-essence, Marx was led to reject the state, law and morality. Politics, law and morality are devices with which we attempt to cope with conflict—and Marx was right to see that they presume and institutionalize conflict. They are ways of reconciling the individual and society. Marx, however, did not conceive of the individual as a fundamentally different type of unit from society. For him, the truly human society was the universal individual writ large. Where the individual and society were in a dynamic and conflicting relationship, man was not in harmony with his species-essence. The notion of species-being seems to dispose much too quickly of important problems. It even allowed Marx to link hypocrisy, his main charge against moral society, with the nature of existing morality itself: 'moral abstractions', because they do not express the human essence, will naturally be contravened. Hypocrisy, the inherent tendency to contravene morality as external determination, is taken by Marx as evidence that the human essence endures.) Morality as a form of external determination cannot be a human ethic. The very existence of abstract morality represents for Marx a contradiction between man's appearance and his essence, a contradiction which will disappear in a truly human society.

Once the problem is put into the terms of what Marx considered to be a logical relation between appearance and essence, an alienation which had logically to be overcome, he could consistently disavow that he was preaching a new morality. Marx did not see the idea of the truly human society as normative in the traditional sense: because it corresponded to the human essence, the truly human society was logically necessary. Marx took his stand, as Kamenka has put it, on 'logico-ethical criticism'.[16] The traditional distinction between *is* and *ought*, according to Marx, was an expression of a disjunction between existence and essence; a disjunction whose solution was logical, not exhortative. Indeed, to try to impose the *ought*, as abstract morality tries, is implicitly to accept the disjunction between appearance and essence, and even to reinforce it by a new form of external determination. Although

Marx soon substituted history for logic as the motor of the necessary unity of appearance and essence, he did not alter his rejection of the abstract moral standpoint.

In *The German Ideology*, Marx declared that the emergence of communist views had 'shattered the basis of all morality' (CW 5,429). Thus to change society it was not 'merely a matter of a different morality' (CW 5,419), to which the world must conform. 'The communists' he wrote, 'do not preach *morality* at all' (CW 5,247). In slightly altered language, Marx here repeats a point he had made as early as 1843: that he did not confront the world with a new principle before which it must kneel, but showed the world what it had to become (CW 3,144). He conceived of the distinction between *is* and *ought* as a seeming contradiction determined by the material life of individuals in alienated society, a contradiction which disappears when alienation is overcome. Marx thus believed that his ethical standpoint, which he based on his conception of the nature of man, was not a morality. Thus his 'human ethic' was expressive of the nature of man, not a new external determinant. That he had correctly apprehended the true nature of man, he did not question. When he declared that the communists preach no morality, he meant that they set up no arbitrary standpoints by which capitalism will or should be judged. His insistence that communism was an actually existing movement was essential to this rejection of morality:

Communism is for us not a *state of affairs* which is to be established, an *ideal* to which reality [will] have to adjust itself. We call communism the *real* movement which abolishes the present state of things. The conditions of this movement result from the now existing premise. (CW 5,49)

Practical criticism was proof enough for Marx that the disjunction between appearance and essence had been grasped by communist workers. The communist movement was Marx's ethico-logical criticism in action: its standpoint was 'real' or human, not abstract. By the time of *The German Ideology*, however, Marx had linked the question of morality more closely with the issue of the dangers of abstraction (for professional abstracters, or *ideologists*), rather than with the issue of external determination. This change of focus, which subsumed the question of 'morality' under the rubric of 'ideology', has given rise to some confusion over the subject of

Marx's ethical disposition. When he began to use the existence of the communist movement as evidence for the disjunction between man's appearance and his essence, and as the materialization of the logical movement to establish harmony between them, he also began to do away with the philosophical arguments which under-pinned his position. This is not to say that he rejected them, merely that he thought it impolitic to associate himself too closely with the German philosophical tradition. The reasons for this tactic will be examined in the next chapter.

Marx did not mean to suggest that a truly human society would be amoral or immoral. In a human society ethics would be an expression of the life of man, not an abstract standard to which he would always aspire but never fulfil. But how does this ethical standpoint relate to the proletariat? Rubel has argued that 'Marx came to the proletarian movement by ethical vocation',[17] and that the original Marxian definition of the proletariat

is essentially situated in an ethical standard, and the contents of which Marx later enriches with sociological and historical properties.[18]

This view of the inherently ethical nature of Marx's conception of the proletariat, to which I also subscribe, seems to conflict with the material content which Marx soon gave his concept. As Anthony Skillen has written,

there is a strong current in Marxism which scorns moralism, not in favour of a free, living, materially rooted socialist 'ethic' ('spirit'), but in favour of the 'material interests of the working class'.[19]

This is a current not just prevalent in the Marxist tradition after Marx, some of whose members argued for a socialist morality by drawing on traditions outside Marxism (such as Kantianism)[20] and seeing them as supplements to an ethically deprived Marxism, but occurs in Marx's work as well. The contrast is between conceiving of the workers fighting for socialism because they were motivated by the spirit of a truly human society, or workers fighting for socialism merely because they pursue their own material interests, whose realization happens to coincide with a truly human society. This contrast Skillen presents as one between 'sheer necessity' of the workers (or the 'quasi-utilitarian vision' of Marxism)[21] and the pursuit of a socialist ethic. He concludes that 'As long as the "particular" interests of particular workers do coincide with the

127

"general" interest of "man"... there is little problem'.22 But as I have argued above, to see the workers as having *particular* interests is to misunderstand Marx's concept of the proletariat. The proletariat, according to Marx, has *material* interests (and it was with these that he was ultimately concerned in his work), but these interests are an expression of *need*, or *human necessity*. Marx did not conceive of the proletariat as an 'interest group' in the sense that political scientists use that expression. Such real dilemmas as 'interest groups' can face did not exist for his proletariat. Even were proletarians to conceive of their material interests narrowly, and to begin to pursue them single-mindedly, the logic of their position in society and the logic of their association would bring them to see that they were fighting for a human end, according to Marx. Their very movement would be an expression of the human ethic. Yet once that ethic is formulated, it inevitably becomes what Skillen would call a 'command form of morality'.23 It is not difficult to see why Marx dropped talk of the human ethic: just talking about the human ethic tended to undermine it by helping to convert it into its opposite, an abstract moral standard.

While Skillen's interesting discussion of the 'proletarian ethic' in Marx can be seen as another element in that debate which explores the implications of seeing the proletariat as the representative of humanity and as the working class (between the proletariat as a concept and as an interest), it also adds to the discussion about Marx's enthusiasm for the workers as the creators of a truly human society. Was it merely the association of workers which encouraged the expression of the human ethic, and what was the content of this ethic? As Georges Sorel asked:

how is it possible to conceive the transformation of the men of to-day into the free producers of tomorrow?24

Is it the activity of production, which Lenin believed produced the disciplined workers needed for socialism? Or was it the heroism and creativity Luxemburg believed would be fostered by the workers' opposition, particularly the mass strike? Yet, as Skillen points out, the productive discipline of capitalism is a form of servility, an external determinant. The collective self-discipline of the workers, in strike activity for example, is anti-productive:

The strike rather than the take-over presents itself as the typical mode of struggle, and, if it is easy to see why working class organisation is the first enemy of authoritarian capitalists and managers, it is not easy to see the struggle for hegemony as the proletariat's destiny.[25]

Rather, Skillen believes that Sorel's 'ethic of the producer' is a better preparation for the triumph of socialism. The capacities for self-emancipation which Marx believed the proletariat would gain in the struggle against capitalism, Sorel implied and Skillen argues, may require more than simply the mechanics of opposition. The virtues required for the expression of a human ethic, therefore, may be unaccounted for in Marx's conception of the proletarian ethic in *The Holy Family*. Did Marx conceive the proletarian ethic as developing in a fundamentally *reactive*, or in a fundamentally *creative*, manner? Indeed, is Marx's account of the proletarian ethic sufficient for an account of the human ethic?

The outline of a human ethic which Marx developed in *The Holy Family* had two relatively limited purposes. The first was to undermine the abstract moral standpoint of the Critical Critics, and to present this standpoint as an instance of Criticism's proposed reformation of the mass turning out as a degradation of man. The second was to defend the idea of the proletariat's universality in terms of the proletariat's more authentic human existence in its *natural* setting, i.e. in association. The proletariat as a separate sphere, and as the representative of the human interest were central ideas here, even if they create more problems than they solve. Marx's case for the proletariat rested on the idea that universality was not simply an attribute of philosophers. Universality did not consist, as Bruno Bauer believed, in the '*generality of self-consciousness* ',[26] which generality is to be attained by rising above the limitations of particular standpoints. These limitations were based, Marx believed, on material factors—on the possession of private property—and they could not be transcended entirely by an effort of will. The standpoint of 'the standpoint', Marx argued, believed that it had overcome the objective world and its real limiting factors in thought. He concluded:

Just as in Rudolph's opinion all human beings maintain the standpoint of good and bad and are judged by these two immutable conceptions, so for Herr Bauer and Co. all human beings adopt the standpoint of *Criticism* or that of the *Mass*. But both turn *real human beings* into *abstract standpoints*. (CW 4,193)

Marx's defence of treating the proletariat as a universal class, as the material complement of philosophy, had begun to turn into an attack on German abstract philosophy itself, an attack which culminated in Marx's next major work: *The German Ideology*.

6

A Proletarian Ideology?

In the years between the first appearance of his concept of the proletariat in 1844, and 1847, Marx defended it against attacks by those who had shared his own philosophical background: Young Hegelianism. First against Ruge, then against the Bauers and their Critical School, and finally against Max Stirner, Marx insisted that the proletariat was the universal class, the revolutionary agent for the truly human society. In *The German Ideology*, he tried to settle accounts with the entire German philosophical tradition. He dismissed as a form of ideology German speculative philosophy and its approach towards social reality and social change. While developing his critique of ideology, Marx clarified the relations between his concept of the proletariat and German philosophy, its native soil. For Marx, formulating a concept of ideology involved examining closely philosophical assumptions about the relations between ideas and material reality, and about the role of ideas in social change.[1] As philosophers, his early critics believed that only those with a special intellectual aptitude and training and with the leisure for reflection—namely, philosophers—held the key to social harmony. For them, universality was chiefly a question of intellect: the ability to grasp the general standpoint. They disdained the proletariat; proletarians were dullards.

Until *The German Ideology*, Marx disputed with his critics very much on their own ground, although he neglected his earlier view of the complementarity of philosophy and the proletariat at the expense of the idea of the proletariat's comprehensive competence. He consistently praised the intellectual ability of the proletariat, for example, even though he singled out some rather unrepresentative proletarians for special merit. Marx had described Wilhelm Weitling's *Garantien der Harmonie und Freiheit* as 'this *vehement* and brilliant literary debut of the German workers' (CW 3,201); and he had mentioned 'the great scientific advance' made by Proudhon in

Qu'est-ce que la propriété? (CW 4,32). By 1847, he considered them both as exemplars of petty bourgeois stupidity.[2] In *The German Ideology*, however, Marx distanced himself from the philosophical assumptions in terms of which he had earlier defended his position. He constructed an argument for seeking the universality of the proletariat in the material conditions of its life. He argued that the universality of the standpoint was dependent upon, and subordinate to, a material universality which only the proletariat could fully construct.

In *The German Ideology*, Marx attempted to 'step outside' the debate among German philosophers: to see it in a broader context. Why? Marx's earlier responses to his critics were largely ineffectual. Although he seemed prepared to entertain the idea that his critics wilfully misinterpreted him, or were plainly stupid, he settled for the notion that philosophers' viewpoints were limited by philosophy itself. Marx turned the tables on German philosophers: their extended learning and preoccupation with abstract thought, rather than developing the universal standpoint was a barrier to it. Besides trying to account for the irrationality—as he saw it—of professional reasoners, Marx developed his critique of German philosophy in response to the challenge of Max Stirner.

After *The Holy Family* had been written, but before it was printed in February 1845, Stirner published *Der Einzige und sein Eigentum*.[3] Although the largest part of *The German Ideology* is a direct rejoinder to Stirner, Marx's critique of ideology owes much more to the method adopted by Stirner and derived from Feuerbach, than to Destutt de Tracy. Stirner argued that the Critical Critics were ruled by abstract ideas. He believed, in general, that man was possessed by ideas and ideals which were man's own products: *fixed ideas*, including freedom and communism. Communism, according to Stirner, was a religion with the '*faith* that labour is a man's "destiny and calling"'.[4] It enslaved man:

Man, your head is haunted; you have wheels in your head! You imagine great things, and depict to yourself a whole world of gods that has an existence for you, a spirit-realm to which you suppose yourself to be called, an ideal that beckons to you. You have a fixed idea![5]

Stirner believed he had freed his thought from the arbitrary and dogmatic premises which undermined German philosophy. This attempt at extrication from inconclusive discussions in the realm of ideas, by reflecting on that abstract realm itself, was emulated by Marx. Marx too rejected the 'dogmatic' premises of the philosophers, substituting for them what he called 'real premises': 'the real individuals, their activity and the material conditions of their life' (CW 5,31). These premises, Marx believed, could be 'verified in a purely empirical way' (CW 5,31), a statement which echoes Destutt de Tracy's hopes.[6] At the same time, Marx attacked Stirner as the consummate representative of 'German ideology', not its destroyer.

The decisive factor in Marx's decision to describe the German philosophic tradition as 'ideology', however, was his rejection of what he alleged was Feuerbach's still philosophical and passive materialism. Marx based his critique of the Critical Critics on Feuerbach's materialism, but by the (Northern) spring of 1845 he had come to see it as simply another philosophical standpoint, theoretically and practically as inconclusive as any other. As long as disputes were conducted within the separate sphere of human activity devoted to abstract thought, i.e. within philosophy, no progress could be made. In his eleventh Thesis on Feuerbach, Marx claimed that 'The philosophers have only *interpreted* the world in various ways; the point is to *change* it' (CW 5,5). The alternative demand to change consciousness, which Marx attributed to the 'German ideologists', is simply

a demand to interpret the existing world in a different way, i.e. by means of a different interpretation. (CW 5,30)

Feuerbach as a philosopher, Marx charged, 'merely wants to produce a correct consciousness about an existing fact' (CW 5,58), not to change that fact. This criticism of Feuerbach's philosophy as passive, however, is unjust; Feuerbach believed that to change ideas *was* to change the world, since some social arrangements depended for their continued existence on reigning ideas. Despite the fact that the concept of ideology is the focus of the lengthy *The German Ideology*, the logic of Marx's position is that ideology is peripheral to society, since it is the obsession and illusion of only a small section of society, and peripheral to the class struggle, which develops inexorably on the basis of the clash of opposed material interests. To explain the failure of the Western working classes to make a socialist revolution by citing the enhanced role of ideas in reconciling them with capitalism, as a number of influential Marxists in this century have done,[7] may be an obvious and largely correct move; but it cannot be sustained by appeal to Marx's work. Ironically, this move is a Feuerbachian one. Indeed, to follow it consistently would ultimately undermine Marx's conception of history, which was formulated in opposition to it. Marx's work would suggest that such Marxists were themselves ideologists.[8]

The two philosophers who most influenced Marx were Hegel and Feuerbach. Of the two, Marx continued to respect only Hegel; his infatuation with Feuerbach turned sour. He unfairly criticized Feuerbach's materialism as contemplative (CW 5,3–4). And his consequent treatment of Feuerbach as, in effect, a Young Hegelian did not properly reflect on the empiricism inherent in Feuerbach's philosophical position, or on his distance from the Young Hegelians. What Feuerbach considered to be his proper role, Marx saw as a limitation. Feuerbach, he wrote, 'is going as far as a theorist possibly can, without ceasing to be a theorist and philosopher' (CW 5,58). The justice of Marx's treatment of Feuerbach aside, the thrust of *The German Ideology* consisted in equating Feuerbach's materialism (and strictly philosophical materialism in general) with philosophical idealism as aspects of ideology, and going on to understand social life through its material foundations, not through philosophical concepts.

Marx here argued that philosophy could only be realized materially, and that philosophers misunderstood, and were powerless alone to implement, the realization of philosophy. To reject philosophy as a specialized discipline, to say that its viewpoint was inherently limited, spelled the end to his earlier conviction that philosophy could represent the universal standpoint. He had not argued that it did, but that it could; now he rejected even the possibility, on account of the nature of the philosophical enterprise. Marx based his argument on the notion of the division of labour, which took on the role that was earlier played in his work by the concept of alienation.[9] For 'within the division of labour social relations inevitably take on an independent existence' (CW 5,78); 'man's own deed becomes an alien power opposed to him, which enslaves him instead of being controlled by him' (CW 5,47). Under the division of labour, each man has an 'exclusive sphere of activity, which is forced upon him and from which he cannot escape' (CW 5,47). Thus the product of co-operating men appears to them as an alien force. The division of labour was a form of external determination. The communist regulation of production, Marx believed, would lead to the abolition of this estrangement between man and man, and between man and his products (CW 5,48); it would reveal to men that their co-operation could be voluntary, not imposed by the capitalist. In communist society, the division of labour would be abolished: there,

nobody has one exclusive sphere of activity but each can become accomplished in any branch he wishes, society regulates the general production and thus makes it possible for me to do one thing today and another tomorrow, to hunt in the morning, fish in the afternoon, rear cattle in the evening, criticise after dinner, just as I have a mind, without ever becoming hunter, fisherman, shepherd or critic. (CW 5,47)

The division of labour, by contrast, creates the individual 'who has been crippled... at the expense of his abilities and relegated to a one-sided vocation' (CW 5,292). It affects the philosopher as much as anyone else: 'philosophers have given thought an independent existence' (CW 5,447). Indeed, the existence of philosophers and their ideological creations is for Marx the distinguishing feature of the division of labour:

Division of labour only becomes truly such from the moment when a division of material and mental labour appears. From this moment onwards consciousness *can* really flatter itself that it is something other than consciousness of existing practice, that it *really* represents something without representing something real; from now on consciousness is in a position to emancipate itself from the world and to proceed to the formation of 'pure' theory, theology, philosophy, morality, etc. (CW 5,44–5) [10]

The 'division of labour' is one of the chief explanatory tools of *The German Ideology*, accounting for the limitations of philosophy and the illusions of the ideologists. Almost all men, in his view, were capable of advanced and abstract thought, but only the philosophers (and others who worked with abstract ideas, such as priests and lawyers) were prone to illusions about the products of their thinking process, and to propagating these illusions as truth.

In principle, a porter differs less from a philosopher than a mastiff from a greyhound. It is the division of labour which has set a gulf between them. (CW 6,180)

Marx wanted to overcome the separation of philosophers and philosophy from real life, and in general to abolish separate and exclusive spheres of human activity. Stirner, like the Critical Critics, believed that 'innately limited intellects unquestionably form the most numerous class of mankind'.[11] Marx might have responded that Stirner meant simply that few men were philosophers, and that this did not mean that the proletarian's thoughts were 'innately limited', just undeveloped. Indeed, Marx argued that the limitation was precisely on the philosopher's side, *because* the philosopher was a philosopher. The proletarians had no chance to develop their capacity for thought because of the division of labour.

If the circumstances in which the individual lives allow him only the [one]-sided development of one quality at the expense of all the rest, [if] they give him the material and time to develop only that one quality, then this individual achieves only a one-sided, crippled development. (CW 5,262)

Where Marx had earlier decried the 'alienation' and 'dehumanization' of man under the rule of private property, he now stressed the 'one-sided, crippled development' of man under the division of labour. The 'species-essence' of man consisted in his all-round development on the basis of certain material preconditions.

Marx argued that the thought of his opponents was ideological and thus mistaken. In the case of philosophers, the division of labour led them to illusions about the power and place of ideas in social life; in effect, the philosophers' ideas had come to dominate them. Ideology, then, was the product of a one-sided activity, and was itself one-sided. It was not the content of particular ideologies that concerned Marx in *The German Ideology*, but the general form of ideology: the inversion of what he saw as the real relation between thought and being; one-sidedness; and the subordination of man to an external imperative. Marx had rejected bourgeois morality as a form of external determination in *The Holy Family*—he now saw morality as a particular form of ideology. His own theory, he believed, expressed the real movement of the working class, rather than positing an abstract ideal to which the working class *should* aspire; he thus denied that it was an ideology. Marx, as Martin Seliger rightly points out, held a 'restrictive' (and pejorative) conception of ideology, rather than an 'inclusive' conception.[12] I shall examine the basis for Marx's restrictive conception of ideology in terms of its relationship with universal thought, not in terms of the truth or falsity of its contents. Whatever the particular functions of ideologies in a social system, and whatever their actual contents, Marx argued that they were all forms of one-sidedness or particularity. Ideology was particularity in the realm of thought.

The starting-point for Marx's analysis of ideology is his claim that ideas and systems of ideas reflect, or are determined by, the material conditions in which they are produced, and the material conditions of their producers. But Marx did not explain precisely what he meant by terms such as 'reflect' or 'determine', even if they were central to his argument. His conception of ideology lies somewhere between epistemology and social theory. Nevertheless, in *The German Ideology*, he declared that 'It is not consciousness that determines life, but life that determines consciousness' (CW 5,37). He added that

The ideas of the ruling class are in every epoch the ruling ideas: i.e. the class which is the ruling *material* force of society is at the same time its ruling *intellectual* force. (CW 5,59)

Unfortunately, Marx never turned his attention systematically towards what has become a vital question for Marxists: how important are these ruling ideas in maintaining the ruling material force in power? Yet this 'sociology of knowledge', as Karl Mannheim would later call it,[13] was not entirely novel to Marx's work. It expressed in a positive and direct way what he had believed at least since his journalism for the *Rheinische Zeitung* : that the particular interests of the estates limited their viewpoints. That the proletariat had no private property, no particular material interest to limit its viewpoint, was a major reason why Marx saw it as the universal class.

Furthermore, this sociology of knowledge does not exhaust the content of Marx's conception of ideology; rather, it was a preparatory step in the development of that concept. Ideology is a form of consciousness; it is therefore related to class (or material) position, as are all forms of consciousness according to Marx. But are all forms of consciousness ideological? If all thought is ideological, what makes one ideology 'better' or 'truer' than another? If ideologies are reduced to being the theoretical expressions of competing classes, will one ideology be deemed superior to another when the class which champions it is victorious? Marx avoided this relativist dilemma, and this version of 'might makes right', by maintaining not only that 'being determines consciousness' but that not all consciousness is ideological.[14] Ideological consciousness is by its nature one-sided and partial, reflecting the condition of the class which shaped it. Non-ideological consciousness is all-sided and universal. Marx still believed that it was possible to attain universal consciousness (all-sided, rather than all-knowing) in specific conditions. Until *The German Ideology*, he had exempted philosophers from his argument that certain ideas were shaped or limited by the social location of the individuals or groups who advocated them. Now he claimed that philosophers, being subject to the division of labour, were ideologists. Marx did not abandon the idea that there could be universal consciousness; it simply required for its development a situation in which the division of labour was overcome or negated. This situation obtained, according to him, in communist society, and in the life of the proletariat (for reasons I shall examine later). Proletarian consciousness was, or could be, universal—non-ideological. The consciousness of communists, reflecting on the situation of the proletariat, could also be non-ideological. Marx, as I have explained, thought that his own theory was not ideological: not because it was not determined by the conditions of life of his own time, but because those conditions had created a sphere of material universality which had found its expression in his (universal) theory. Yet although the idea would not have been congenial to Marx, it still required an effort of will for him (in his own terms) to overcome the limitations of his particular social and intellectual background, and his development to communism was almost entirely abstract or theoretical.

For Marx, ideology represented the 'cult' of abstract concepts (CW 5,363), the alienation of thought. The products of men's brains 'have got out of their hands [sic]. They, the creators, have bowed down before their creations' (CW 5,23). Ideologists, he believed, made two central errors. First, they did not perceive the social and material basis of all ideas. Second, they held the illusion that ideas and systems of ideas were independent of social life, had a life and development of their own, and were pre-existing, 'natural' imperatives (which they had simply discovered) to which man must conform. By stressing that ideology consists of all those disciplines in which ideas appear to be sovereign—especially morality, law, theology and philosophy—Marx could argue that the proletariat had no ideology and was largely immune to its influence. In Marx's communist vision there are no philosophers, no moralists, and no lawyers to set up abstract and inhuman standards for men. The preoccupation with abstract and dominating ideas will cease when the division of labour disappears:

with a communist organisation of society, there disappears the subordination of the artist to local and national narrowness, which arises entirely from division of labour, and also the subordination of the individual to some definite art, making him exclusively a painter, sculptor, etc.; the very name amply expresses the narrowness of his professional development and his dependence on division of labour. In a communist society there are no painters but only people who engage in painting among other activities. (CW 5,394)

Similarly, in a communist society there are no philosophers but only people who engage in serious and systematic thought among other activities. Thus the subordination of the individual to abstract ideas will cease. The end of ideology does not mean that communist man will be unthinking, lawless and immoral; people will simply live in a human manner, as Marx conceived it, and whatever arrangements they make will be an expression of their humanity, not a negation of it. Ideology subordinates man to abstract (and, by implication, not fully human) ideas. It is not an expression of a fully human life. In this connection, Marx introduced the metaphor of turning reality *upside-down*. Ideology, by demanding that man's behaviour conform to some abstract ideals, turns reality 'upside-down' (CW 5,359; 5,361; 5,460).

The ideas of the ruling class, expressed in law, morality, etc., may be ideological, but the ideologists of that class give them 'a sort of theoretical independence' (CW 5,420). Instead of seeing ideals as expressions of the ruling class interest, ideologists see the dominant political and social arrangements as expressions of these ideals:

as in general with ideologists... they inevitably put the thing upside-down and regard their ideology both as the creative force and as the aim of all social relations, whereas it is only an expression and symptom of these relations. (CW 5,420)

The illusion of the ideologist is that various ideas have created various conditions of life: this is the 'illusion of politicians, lawyers and other ideologists which puts all empirical relations upside-down' (CW 5,355). For Marx, it was important not only to stress the social basis of all ideas, but to deny that ideas are independent and determining. Thus ideological attempts to solve the social problem (as with the 'German ideologists') by an alteration of consciousness were futile:

The alteration of consciousness divorced from actual relations— a pursuit followed by philosophers as a profession, i.e. as a *business*[15] —is itself a product of existing relations and inseparable from them. This imaginary rising above the world is the ideological expression of the impotence of philosophers in face of the world. Practical life every day gives the lie to their ideological bragging. (CW 5,379)

Marx devoted an entire volume to denouncing the impotent illusions of the 'German ideologists', and campaigned from 1845 to 1848 against their political representatives, the True Socialists, because, as he candidly admitted in the *Communist Manifesto*, True Socialism had 'spread like an epidemic' (CW 6,512).

Why did Marx believe that he and the proletariat could escape the enervating and distorting influence of ideology? The distance between reality and the ideological ideal, he argued, would disabuse the proletariat of the prevailing ideology. For the proletarian, 'Law, morality, religion are... so many bourgeois prejudices, behind which lurk in ambush just as many bourgeois interests' (CW 6,495). Marx considered the proletarian to be immune from ideology, and to be able to discern the material interests which ideology served. The absence of national sentiment among the proletarians, in particular, was axiomatic for Marx at this stage. Engels had earlier, in *The Condition of the Working Class in England*, made the same point (CW 4,298). Both were later more cautious. But was immunity from ideology the same thing as having universality in the realm of knowledge (intensional, not extensional, universality)? Such universality, according to Marx, could only be the product of universality in all aspects of man's existence: the product of an integrated man.

In the case of an individual, for example, whose life embraces a wide circle of varied activities and practical relations to the world, and who, therefore, lives a many-sided life, thought has the same character of universality as every other manifestation of his life. Consequently, it neither becomes fixed in the form of abstract thought nor does it need complicated tricks of reflection when the individual passes from thought to some other manifestation of life. (CW 5,263)

Where did such a situation obtain? Could the proletariat escape from the particularizing effects of the division of labour, and could individual theorists? Marx held that there were exceptional individuals, although he discounted their historic influence in the following—rather unfortunate—parallel:

It is perfectly 'possible' that what individual persons do is not 'always' determined by the class to which they belong, although this is no more crucial to the class struggle than an aristocrat going over to the *tiers-état* was crucial to the French Revolution. (CW 6,330)

For Marx, individuals such as himself were exceptional in so far as they could anticipate the development of history on the basis of incomplete or faint evidence. Such individuals could transcend ideology since the material conditions for universality existed (or existed in embryo):

That under favourable circumstances some individuals are able to rid themselves of their local narrow-mindedness is by no means due to individuals imagining that they have got rid of, or intend to get rid of their local narrow-mindedness, but is only due to the fact that in their real empirical life individuals, actuated by empirical needs, have been able to bring about world intercourse. (CW 5,264)

Marx's own thought, he believed, had the character of universality for this reason. It was a point of view predicated, as many of his thoughts were, on an imminent proletarian revolution.[16]

Marx's explanation of why some thinkers can transcend, in thought, particularity does not fully account for what he saw as the imperviousness of the proletariat to ideology. Of course, proletarians were not professional thinkers, and were therefore not liable to develop illusions about the power of ideas; but the same might be said of the mass of the bourgeoisie. There seem to be two possible connections between the proletariat and ideology. First, proletarians may be influenced by bourgeois ideology. Second, those of their own thoughts which manage to gain currency among them might be ideological by reflecting the influence of the division of labour to which workers were subject. Marx denied both.

It might seem reasonable to expect that proletarians will be influenced by the prevailing ideology. Yet Marx insisted that it could not have a positive effect on them, primarily on the grounds that relations between people under capitalism—and particularly the worker-capitalist relation—had become simple matters of economic calculation. Marx wrote in the draft of his lectures on wages, in December 1847, that 'the money relationship [is] the sole relationship between employer and workers' (CW 6,436).[17] No longer, he declared, were there any patriarchal relations between the two, no feelings of deference, no illusions:

the halo of sanctity is entirely gone from all relationships of the old society, since they have dissolved into pure money relationships. (CW 6,436)

Marx had argued similarly in *The German Ideology* that for the proletariat social relations had become transparent, and thus that ideology had no control over them:

For the mass of men, i.e. the proletariat, these theoretical notions do not exist and hence do not require to be dissolved, and if this mass ever had any theoretical notions, e.g., religion, these have now long been dissolved by circumstances. (CW 5,56)

The simplicity and non-ideological nature of relations between people was a characteristic of capitalism alone. The advent of manufacture, Marx argued, established simple monetary relations. Universalized competition, with the resultant centralization of capital,

destroyed as far as possible ideology, religion, morality, etc., and, where it could not do this, made them into a palpable lie.... [It] took from the division of labour the last semblance of its natural character... and resolved all natural relations into money relations. (CW 5,73)

Marx believed—at this stage—that the work relation was the greatest educator of the proletariat, the best antidote to ideology. It was the major reason why Marx claimed that for the proletariat 'nationality is already dead' (CW 5,73), and why he always seemed surprised when the working class adopted with alacrity certain forms of bourgeois ideology.

The ideas that the character of relations between people under capitalism is becoming increasingly more obvious, and thus more repulsive, and that the proletariat cannot be deceived because of the conditions of its existence, are quite prominent in the *Communist Manifesto*. The bourgeois epoch, Marx claimed, had so simplified class antagonisms that society splits 'into two great hostile camps, into two great classes directly facing each other: Bourgeoisie and Proletariat' (CW 6,485). For the bourgeoisie itself has ended the illusion about social relations by its own activity. Ideology had become patently false in the face of material reality:

The bourgeoisie, wherever it has got the upper hand, has put an end to all feudal, patriarchal, idyllic relations. It has pitilessly torn asunder the motley feudal ties that bound man to his 'natural superiors', and has left remaining no other nexus between man and man than naked self-interest, than callous 'cash payment'. It has drowned the most heavenly ecstasies of religious fervour, of chivalrous enthusiasm, of philistine sentimentalism, in the icy water of egotistical calculation. It has resolved personal worth into exchange value, and in place of the numberless indefeasible chartered freedoms, has set up that single, unconscionable freedom—Free Trade. In one word, for exploitation, veiled by religious and political illusions, it has substituted naked, shameless, direct, brutal exploitation. (CW 6,486–7)

The bourgeois epoch, according to Marx, was the end of all illusions about social relations, and thus the end of all illusions. Partly in support of this thesis, and partly by way of demonstration, he claimed that the makers of illusions had plainly become creatures of the bourgeoisie:

The bourgeoisie has stripped of its halo every occupation hitherto honoured and looked up to with reverent awe. It has converted the physician, the lawyer, the priest, the poet, the man of science, into its paid wage-labourers. (CW 6,487)

Marx also believed that even the family relation had become a 'mere money relation' (CW 6,487).

Marx's attack on ideology downgraded the role of abstract ideas in social life and social change. In the second Hegel critique, by contrast, German philosophy was seen as bringing Germany up to the level of modern nations, and religion was considered as *consolation* —a sort of distorted need in an inhuman society. Furthermore, the notion that the wage relation destroys the illusions of the proletariat faces an objection that Marx himself developed. In 1851, in an interesting notebook discussion, he wrote that

in a society with a completely developed monetary system, there is... actually real civil equality of individuals insofar as they have money, irrespective of their source of income. (CW 10,590)

By possessing the universal medium of exchange, not only is the class position of the worker blurred, but workers are 'in a better position to acquire the universal powers of society, such as the intellectual ones' (CW 10,591). The worker is in quite a different position from the slave or the serf on this score. Money has a 'universal levelling power' (CW 10,591). Thus, although money 'is the supreme expression of class contradiction', it also 'obscures religious, social, intellectual and individual differences' (CW 10,592). Such a qualification became important later in Marx's work, as I shall demonstrate in Chapter Eight.

Marx gave another reason for believing that the proletariat was immune from ideology. Instead of stressing that ideology was illusion, he concentrated on its innately one-sided character. Particularity was a product of the division of labour, but he now argued that the division of labour was being overcome within the bounds of capitalism itself. The universalization of the productive forces established the '*universal* intercourse between men', and the proletariat as a 'world-historical class' (CW 5,49). Individual proletarians 'with the broadening of their activity into world-historical activity, become more and more enslaved' to the world market (CW 5,51). But world intercourse is the basis for the abolition of local narrow-mindedness (CW 5,264). In *The German Ideology*, this analysis was applied chiefly to individual thinkers. In *The Poverty of Philosophy*, however, Marx extended it to the proletariat. Inside the modern workshop, he explained, the division of labour 'is meticulously regulated by the authority of the employer' (CW 6,184) and, ultimately, by the instruments of production to which the workers must conform. In bourgeois society, unlike the feudal and guild systems, the division of labour inside the factory was not expressed by fixed social rules, and generally did not extend beyond the factory. In civil society, individualism reigned; changes within the workshop were not hindered by social restraints. The introduction of machinery, which in its first stages engendered 'specialities, specialists, and with them craft-idiocy' (CW 6,190), eventually caused labour to lose its specialized character.

But the moment every special development stops, the need for universality, the tendency towards an integral development of the individual begins to be felt. The automatic workshop wipes out specialists and craft-idiocy. (CW 6,190)

Capitalism, Marx implied, developed not only the objective material preconditions for communism, but the preconditions for the development of a universal consciousness among the proletariat. Machines begin to end the one-sidedness of workers' lives. Engels put it bluntly in his *Principles of Communism* when he wrote that the division of labour 'has already been undermined by machines' (CW 6,353).[18] Thus does capitalism undermine itself.

Marx believed that the proletariat did not need to be disabused of illusions and one-sided thought, but he made no such claim for the theoreticians of the proletariat. He considered communists to be liable to ideological errors, because they operated with abstract ideas and could thus lose touch with the real movement of the working class. *The German Ideology* included an attack on True Socialism— 'German philosophy in its socialist disguise' (CW 5,460)—which maintained that socialism was the 'most reasonable' social order, and was not a question of 'the needs of a particular class at a particular time' (CW 5,455). The Brussels Communist Correspondence Committee was established partly in order to counter the True Socialists, and other so-called friends of socialism. In a letter from the Committee to G.A. Köttgen, Marx and Engels explained that 'Communists must first of all clear things up among themselves' (CW 6,54). Engels later declared that 'The Communists... must ever be on their guard against sharing the self-deceptions of the bourgeois' (CW 6,356). One of the guiding threads of Marx's work was the belief that the struggle against ideology within communist ranks was vital to the socialist revolution, because of the importance he attached to the role of the communists.[19]

Marx believed that communism was not a question of abstract ideals. He relied on the idea that consciousness was determined by the material conditions of life of classes. But that did not mean (for him) that all consciousness was limited and one-sided, i.e. ideological. Philosophers, Marx argued, believed that their ideas were universal because they stood aside from the social struggle. But it was not in independence from society that a universal consciousness would develop. All-sided knowledge required a society whose material conditions were universal. Marx argued that capitalism was rapidly creating such a society. Its development threw up theorists who could overcome one-sidedness, and created a class whose conditions of existence precluded it from having illusions about its situation.[20] Marx denied that abstract philosophy could represent the universal interest, even in the theoretical realm, by claiming that a universal theory was an integral part of the universal man shaped by universal material conditions.

* * *

In the last three chapters, I have followed Marx's response to abstract objections to his concept of the proletariat. Two central points emerge. The first is that Marx rejected such criticisms by denying the validity of the abstract philosophical approach itself. If professional philosophy was intrinsically one-sided, how could it recognize the proletariat's universality? Second, he reaffirmed the idea that the proletariat constituted a separate social sphere. Both are fraught with difficulties. Marx praised the proletariat's intelligence, as well as extending Feuerbach's notion that those who suffer were a necessary complement to philosophy. He argued that the proletariat had a human need for the universal society, again drawing from Feuerbach's notion of the species-essence of man. Marx at first saw the material and intellectual spheres as relatively independent. The proletariat represented a material universality; philosophers represented abstract universality. Only the proletariat had a pressing human need for communism, and only the proletariat unburdened by the limiting influence of the possession of private property could appreciate abstract universality. One of the most important, if most arguable, propositions of *The German Ideology*, however, is that 'being determines consciousness'. Thus did Marx subordinate the intellectual to the material sphere. The major feature of the latter is the division of labour, which gives rise to intellectual one-sidedness. Only the proletariat, and certain of its theoretical representatives, who have escaped from the limiting effects of the division of labour can represent universality. In *The German Ideology* Marx made a significant shift in his argument by establishing a historical and objective basis for universality. *The German Ideology* marks the transition in his work to a more concrete and empirical approach to the proletariat. Yet Marx never rejected the speculative or developmental conception of the proletariat.

Marx developed his concept of the proletariat chiefly in the German context in which the proletariat had no political representation and could therefore be seen as a separate sphere. In France, where the proletarians were potential citizens until 1848 (and actual citizens afterwards), they formed a class of civil society which was not a class of civil society because they had no particular interest to assert against other classes. In *The Holy Family*, Marx implied that the proletariat constituted a separate sphere because in natural surroundings it began to live a truly human life. In *The German Ideology* he added that the proletariat was immune from ideology because within its sphere the division of labour was, or was being, overcome. Yet while he sometimes stressed the proletariat's separation, it was precisely their integration into bourgeois society which made a human society necessary. In his conceptual treatment of the proletariat, Marx vacillated between seeing them as thoroughly dehumanized and therefore as the agents of a human society, and seeing them as preserving humanity within their own sphere. There seems, in other words, to be some tension within Marx's conception of the proletariat between these positive and negative aspects.

7

The Proletariat as a Political Class

As Marx distanced himself from the speculative construction of the proletariat, he increasingly concentrated on the proletariat as a political and as an economic class. He saw the political as important both in constituting the proletariat as a class and in distinguishing modern from earlier social arrangements. Politics compelled social classes who would rule to present their interests in a universal form. In developing into a class *for itself*, therefore, the proletariat had to aim at the capture of state power partly by presenting its interest as the general interest. Politics, Marx now believed, was the medium in which communists, as representatives of the proletariat, could proclaim the proletariat as a universal class, thus uniting the proletariat and attracting allies to its cause. Between 1846 and 1850, communists had a central role in Marx's conception of the proletarian revolution;[1] most of his work at this time, therefore, was directed at them and against their 'deviations'. Until just after the 1848 Revolutions, he conceived of the socialist revolution in rather traditional (i.e. French) terms: as a political revolution inaugurated by communist seizure of state power, the introduction of universal suffrage and a programme of gradual nationalization of industry, universal education for the young, etc. The capture of state power by the communists would precipitate the formation of the proletariat into a class for itself. Yet Marx was no Leninist *avant la lettre*. For him, communists possessed no knowledge that the proletariat could not attain to. Nevertheless, he treated communists quite differently from workers: he demanded more from them, and he was generally intolerant of them. He believed that communists were prone to ideological illusions. As proletarians came, peacefully, to have a political voice in the 1850s and '60s with the extension of suffrage, the insurrectionary role Marx had envisaged for communists became less relevant. Proletarians needed access to politics to develop into a class.

Marx had not always been this clear about social division, or about the role of politics in preparing a class to take power. He first began to use the French term 'class' instead of the German term *Stand* (estate) late in 1843. In the second Hegel critique, they were still synonymous. But soon Marx recognized that the contrast between the terms expressed the difference between a society which gave no political (i.e. state) recognition to social differences (France), and one that made them legally constituted parts of the (German) nation. The political abolition of the estates with the collapse of the Estates-General in 1789, and the adoption of the 'Declaration of the Rights of Man and Citizen' did not signify the abolition of classes. The 'freedom of the individual', the ethos on which capitalism was being built, disguised the fact that human lives were more than ever determined by material factors over which they could, but did not, have control. Unlike slaves, whose bondage was palpable, and enforced by the might and right of the state, and unlike the lower orders of feudal society, whose social and political position was fixed by the state, and who deferred to their superiors, the proletariat faced a new situation. What separated the proletarian from the capitalist was wealth, not legal restriction. Individuals were bound together as a social class, then, if they had a common life situation, and common interests against other classes. In *The German Ideology*, Marx argued that workers were brought together as a powerful material force by their aggregation in ever-larger factories, and their struggles for higher wages. He had previously seen workers as uniting on the basis of a commitment to socialism; now, their commitment to socialism would grow from a more prosaic quest.

In *The German Ideology* social class was presented as a modern phenomenon, a product of capitalism. Marx used the term 'class' in two different senses, however: as a paradigm or ideal type, present in all societies, and as a social grouping peculiar to capitalism. In the first sense, social class denotes any (significant) social group throughout history—slaves, serfs and nobles, for instance, as well as the proletariat and bourgeoisie. In the second sense, social class was peculiar to capitalism; it was just as real a limitation on the lives of its members as earlier social groupings, even if its boundaries were not formally defined. All of the central terms

149

employed in *The German Ideology—class, state, civil society* and even *division of labour*—are used in these two senses. Thus, Marx used the term 'civil society' to denote any type of economic or material relations, as distinct from political relations, when he spoke of 'civil society in its various stages' as 'the basis of all history' (CW 5,53). Yet the separation of economic and political spheres was also a product of political emancipation: 'Civil society as such only develops with the bourgeoisie' (CW 5,89). So, in the second sense of the word, was class. It

assumes an independent existence as against the individuals, so that the latter find their conditions of life predetermined, and have their position in life and hence their personal development assigned to them by their class, thus becoming subsumed under it.... (CW 5,77)

As an alienated social relation, class 'is itself a product of the bourgeoisie' (CW 5,78). Individuals may seem freer under capitalism than ever before because their conditions of life seem accidental. In reality, Marx argued, they are less free: class is a form of external determination.

Together with affirming the intensional universality of the proletariat, discussed above, Marx claimed that capitalism created the proletariat as an extensionally universal class. Communism can only arise, he argued, when capitalism has 'rendered the great mass of humanity "propertyless"' (CW 5,48), and when the productive forces have developed on a 'world-historical' or 'universal' scale (CW 5,49). Under capitalism, it is inevitable that such development 'finally puts *world-historical*, empirically universal individuals in the place of local ones' (CW 5,49). This material universality of the proletariat explained, for Marx, their developing universal consciousness.

In *The Poverty of Philosophy* , Marx anticipated the transition by the proletariat from a class in itself to a class for itself (CW 6,211). He thus drew attention to the unfolding of the proletariat's intrinsic universality into a conscious, revolutionary force. This process, which he had earlier described as *Bildung*, was now a product of workers' conditions under capitalism and of their association to protect their interests. Marx had begun to treat the proletariat more as a class in the political science sense, as a material interest with its own dynamic, than as a philosophical class, as an essence realizing itself. But though the proletariat now had material interests, it still did not have *particular* interests. One of the major differences between Marx's approach, and that of political science, is that Marx saw the proletariat not as a fixed, but as a changing entity. The proletariat need not conceive of itself from the outset as a universal class. The class struggle had its own dynamic of classes defending their prosaic interests against one another and having as their aim the capture of state power. To become the ruling class was the natural goal of the proletariat in the class struggle. But to turn its localized struggles against bourgeois into a political struggle against the bourgeoisie, the proletariat had to present its class interest as the general interest (which, in fact, it was):

it follows that every class which is aiming at domination, even when its domination, as is the case with the proletariat, leads to the abolition of the old form of society in its entirety and of domination in general, must first conquer political power in order to represent its interest in turn as the general interest, which in the first moment it is forced to do. (CW 5,47) 2

Marx presented publicly this dynamic of the class struggle in *The Poverty of Philosophy* and especially in the *Communist Manifesto*. The development of the proletariat as a class for itself was the product, he argued in the former work, of a long process. Capitalism, and particularly large-scale industry,

concentrates in one place a crowd of people unknown to one another. Competition divides their interests. But the maintenance of wages, this common interest which they have against their boss, unites them in a common thought of resistance—*combination*. (CW 6,210)

From the standpoint of economic calculation, combinations and strikes may cost the worker more than he gains. But such associations are not simply means for fixing wages: 'they are the means for uniting the working class' (CW 6,435). Once the proletariat is united, 'association takes on a political character' (CW 6,211). The idea that the proletariat must become *politically* constituted was central to Marx's work during the 1846-48 period, as he re-examined his views on a German revolution. According to him, the German bourgeoisie had not yet taken 'political shape as a class. The power of the state is not yet its power' (CW 6,318). He believed that the next German revolution would be a bourgeois revolution.

Developing the material aspects of his concept of the proletariat led Marx to this changed expectation for Germany. There, he argued, 'one can speak... neither of estates nor of classes, but at most of former estates and classes not yet born' (CW 5,195). The German bourgeoisie, he continued, 'has now got almost as far as the French bourgeoisie in 1789' (CW 5,196). Marx had lost his enthusiasm for immediate proletarian uprising, seeing instead the historical necessity of a bourgeois victory in Germany; this change was matched by a new appreciation of the role of politics. In the second Hegel critique, and the 'Critical Marginal Notes on the Article by a Prussian', Marx argued that politics was a diversion:

Because it thinks in the framework of politics, the proletariat sees the cause of all evils in the *will*, and all means of remedy in *violence* and in the *overthrow* of a *particular* form of state. (CW 3,204)

Instead of obscuring its vision, he now believed that politics forced the proletariat to present itself in a universal form. It was the form of politics which he thought important for the proletariat's cause, and in the dynamic of the class struggle he added the stage of conquering state power: not just so that the proletariat could wield a useful implement in the construction of socialism, but so that it could recognise itself as the founder of the new society.

In June 1846, Marx and Engels wrote to Köttgen that if the German communists could not get bourgeois support for their petition, they should join the bourgeoisie: 'for the time being in public demonstrations, proceed jesuitically' (CW 6,56), i.e. deceptively. Engels claimed that the German workers were too dispersed over the country to 'constitute themselves into *one* class'; he thought them 'thoroughly petty bourgeois' (CW 6,84). Marx argued that the German aristocracy 'cannot be overthrown in any other manner than by the bourgeoisie and the people together' (CW 6,233). A Diet which demanded liberal constitutionalism, he added, 'could count on the strongest support from the proletariat' (CW 6,228). He also declared that the True Socialists 'must accept the *bourgeois revolution* as a precondition for the *workers' revolution*' (CW 6,333). The *Communist Manifesto* declared that Germany was 'on the eve of a bourgeois revolution' (CW 6,519), but the weakness of the bourgeoisie was cited as a reason why it would be the immediate prelude to a proletarian revolution.

What was the role for the proletariat in the coming German revolution? Marx considered that revolutionary universality of the type acquired by the French bourgeoisie is 1789 was central to all modern revolutions. In *The German Ideology*, for example, he wrote:

The class making a revolution comes forward from the very start, if only because it is opposed to a *class*, not as a class but as the representative of the whole of society, as the whole mass of society confronting the one ruling class. (CW 5,60-1)

This universality, because it involves a common (and for a time, genuine) perception on the part of the opposition classes that they are one, could be undermined by the claim that the common interest it presupposed was an illusion. By insisting on the proletariat's independent support for the bourgeois revolution, Marx lessened the chance for the bourgeoisie to emerge as a universal class (however ephemeral), and thus for the bourgeois revolution itself. The existence of Marxists in countries which have not had a '1789' seems to ensure that a bourgeois revolution will never occur or be successful; the timidity of the bourgeoisie is increased by the knowledge that a section of the proletariat will not unite unconditionally with it, and will challenge its claim to be the general representative. The bourgeoisie will not trust the proletariat; and vice versa. Of the latter point, Marx wrote:

The people, and in particular the communist section of the people, knows very well that the liberal bourgeoisie is only pursuing its own interests and that little reliance should be placed on its sympathy for the people. (CW 6,222)

Marx's discussion of the political constitution of a class suggests that he conceived of the class *for itself* as a product of state control by the proletarians or their representatives, not its necessary precursor. Hence, in the three or four years before the 1848 Revolutions, Marx endeavoured to set forth the correct communist position and to convince other socialists of it. After 1850 he changed direction: he began to write works of political economy, not chiefly as polemics against other socialists; and he attempted, without much success, to get a working class audience. There were a number of reasons for this change. First, hopes for revolution dimmed after 1850. The working class movement went through a period of decline, when the influence of Marx and of his socialist rivals was diminished. Furthermore, the 1848 Revolutions put an end to the idea — which Marx and Engels shared with the bourgeoisie, among others—that the rule of the bourgeoisie could not co-exist with democratic political forms. The hopes and fears inspired by universal (manhood) suffrage were laid to rest when its implementation in France produced a conservative government. Universal suffrage, however, gave the workers a means of political expression, and thus a means to constitute itself politically as a class without first taking state power. Finally, after 1850 Marx gave greater significance to the trade union struggle under capitalism, which culminated in his involvement with the International Working Men's Association in the 1860s and early '70s.

In its first edition, the *Manifesto* declared:

The proletarian movement is the independent movement of the immense majority, in the interests of the immense majority. (CW 6,495)

But Engels added in the 1888 edition that the proletariat was the 'self-conscious' independent movement of the immense majority (CW 6,495). In the 1840s, Marx believed that the socialist revolution would precede, and be a factor in, a proletarian change of consciousness. Only in revolution, he wrote, could the proletariat 'succeed in ridding itself of all the muck of ages and become fitted to found society anew' (CW 5,52-3). In 1895, Engels wrote that he and Marx in 1848 had been 'under the spell' of the previous French Revolutions (1789 and 1830): insurrection-oriented, the work of minorities. In 1895, he continued, this mode of struggle was 'obsolete'. Engels concluded that

The time of surprise attacks, of revolutions carried through by small conscious minorities at the head of unconscious masses, is past. (SW I,190)

Before 1848, however, Marx and Engels stressed the role of communists in the development of the proletariat as a class *for itself*. An important aspect of this development was the implementation of democracy. By 'democracy', Engels meant chiefly universal suffrage, although Marx's earlier discussion of 'true democracy' and passive representation disinclined him to embrace democracy as openly as did Engels. In 1846, for example, Engels declared that '*Democracy nowadays is communism....* Democracy has become the proletarian principle' (CW 6,5).[3] For

Engels, the bourgeoisie had become paramount in the political sphere through restricted suffrage: bourgeois electors elect bourgeois deputies, who constitute a bourgeois government (CW 6,346). Could the bourgeoisie also rule through universal suffrage? Engels thought not. Universal suffrage, according to him and Marx, would give the communists their opportunity to transform the proletariat into a class. In the *Manifesto*, Marx wrote that the communists' aim was 'formation of the proletariat into a class, overthrow of the bourgeois supremacy, conquest of political power by the proletariat' (CW 6,498). For Engels, their aim was 'the unification of the proletariat into a closely knit, militant and organised class' (CW 6,357).

Marx saw the 1848 Revolutions as an opportunity to influence history, and to confirm his class analysis; they represent the first real confrontation of his theory with reality. He had a rare insight into these Revolutions as well as a certain detachment from them: unlike most other socialists, his hopes were not dashed by the failures of 1848. His class analysis and perspective sustained him. But Marx mistook the nature of the Revolutions. His political and revolutionary outlook had been shaped (but also limited) by the vivid image of 1789. From it he derived his understanding of the alliances, mechanics and stages of modern revolution. His conception of the proletariat grew in part by analogy with the Third Estate. Marx saw in 1848 the revitalization of the traditions of 1789, when they were coming to an end; he saw social concerns where there were chiefly liberal concerns; and he saw—although only until 1850—the beginning of an epoch of revolution instead of decades of prosperity and relative stability.

Marx was living in Brussels when the February 1848 revolution broke out in Paris. The French Provisional Government invited Marx to the revolutionary capital just before the Belgian government expelled him from Brussels. In Paris, Marx opposed a move by other German *émigrés* to form armed units to export the revolution on their bayonets to Germany. These attempts ended in military fiasco,[4] but Marx may have been less concerned about that possibility than about Herwegh's leadership and nationalist united front declaration. On March 18, a revolution broke out in Prussia, as Marx had hoped. Frederick William IV, embattled King of

Prussia, promised a constitution and elections to a Constituent Assembly. Marx moved to Cologne early in April, and began to publish the *Neue Rheinische Zeitung* on June 1.[5] It was a consistent critic of the half-hearted decisions and indecisiveness of the constituent assemblies which were formed throughout Germany after March. In particular, it carried attacks on the timidity of the liberal majorities in the Prussian National Assembly (meeting in Berlin) and the all-German National Assembly (meeting in Frankfurt), both of which had begun to sit in May. Marx used the *Neue Rheinische Zeitung* to try to prod the bourgeoisie into action against the monarchy, so as to complete the bourgeois, or political, revolution. The liberal bourgeoisie who dominated the Berlin and Frankfurt Assemblies, Marx claimed, had turned them into mere debating clubs. Many liberals believed that they must come to an agreement with the monarchy over a constitution, instead of implementing a constitution with the backing of the revolutionary people; Marx contemptuously called the Berlin Assembly the 'Agreement Assembly'. Instead of openly acknowledging the revolutionary origins of the constituent assemblies most German liberals—prominent among which were the Prussian leaders Camphausen and Hansemann—urged that there be an unbroken line of legal continuity between the old monarchical and new 'constitutional' order. They tried to establish a constitutional monarchy on the condition that it was accepted by the King, and repudiated the revolutionary origins of their power. Frederick William IV regained his power as the liberals lost theirs; eventually he vetoed the constitution that was offered to him, and sent the Berlin Assembly packing to Brandenburg.

The German bourgeoisie failed to use the power presented to it by the people, and blundered by retaining the old executive arm of the state. They believed that civil servants would work loyally for those who paid them, that allegiance could be bought. Marx warned that the executive was thus merely given time to regain its power and to prepare the counter-revolution. The German liberals were effectively hoist with their own petard. Their aim was the rule of law, but they did not believe that a revolution could provide sufficient authority for such a rule. That authority, they thought, had to be grounded on the long and continuous progress of the law.

Revolution was a break in legality. For the new constitution, as they found to their cost, could not be based on the old legality which had served the crown. When the Prussian King refused to accept the constitution drafted by the Berlin Assembly, the Assembly at last realized its situation and appealed to its revolutionary base—the urban population. It refused to vote taxes for the government, and advised the people not to pay taxes. This line was taken up enthusiastically by the *Neue Rheinische Zeitung* (so much so, that the newspaper declared 'No More Taxes' across its front page a few days before the Berlin Assembly dared to become defiant). The *Neue Rheinische Zeitung* plainly asked members of the police and army in Rhenish Prussia to declare whether they stood for the legality of the National Assembly, or for that of the crown (CW 8,38). But the doomed Assembly had already alienated most of its popular support, and had strengthened the instruments for its own destruction: the bureaucracy and the army of the old regime.

Marx suggested that the failure of the German bourgeoisie to become a revolutionary universal class was not simply a local problem of timidity or cowardice, but was bound up with the development of class society itself:

In both revolutions [of 1648 and 1789] the bourgeoisie was the class that *really* headed the movement. The *proletariat* and the *non-bourgeois strata of the middle class* had either not yet any interests separate from those of the bourgeoisie or they did not yet constitute independent classes or class subdivisions.... (CW 8,161)

The existence of social classes with recognisably different interests, Marx implied, undermined the attempt to form a revolutionary universal class. The revolutions that offered classic examples of revolutionary universality heralded class divided society. They were revolutions of a European type:

They did not represent the victory of a *particular* class of society over the *old political order;* they *proclaimed the political order of a new European society.* (CW 8,161)

The bourgeoisie could thus not play its 'traditional' role in those societies which did not possess the new European political order. In Germany, for example, Marx claimed that the 'bourgeois revolution' was impossible, and the only possibility was a 'feudal

157

absolutist counter-revolution or a *social republican revolution* ' (CW 8,178). The social and political character of this latter revolution was not specified, and seems akin to Lenin's 1905 compromise formula of the 'revolutionary-democratic dictatorship of the proletariat and peasantry'.[6] Marx used a number of means in order to fudge the distinction between bourgeois and proletarian, political and socialist, revolutions in countries such as Germany. Like Lenin, Marx put politics first, not theory. Marx's dissimulating approach was cast aside as he turned from a minimalist into a maximalist,[7] finally advocating the proletarian, in default of the bourgeois revolution.

This shift in Marx's attitude to the German revolution was accompanied by a series of tactical shifts in his theory. From the outset, he saw 1848 as the chance for a rapid and proletarian transformation. But he proceeded cautiously, advocating alliance with the bourgeoisie as a first step, realizing that only the bourgeoisie could get enough support to launch a successful revolution. In the ensuing enthusiasm, he hoped, a proletarian revolution could be launched. The phlegmatic German bourgeoisie infuriated Marx. He declared that Germany would have a proletarian revolution as part of a European-wide revolution. At first, he claimed that a Russian invasion of Germany would compel the bourgeoisie to take decisive action (CW 7,51). Soon after, he declared that *'The Tsar will save the German revolution by centralising it* ' (CW 7,90). He also hoped that an upsurge in the French Revolution would stiffen the resolve of Germans. For Marx, by 1849, socialism had become a European possibility. A new revolt by the Paris proletariat had to be supplemented by an English revolution:

England dominates the world market. A revolution of the economic relations in any country of the European continent, in the whole of the European continent without England, is a storm in a teacup. (CW 8,214)

Marx also began to link closely revolution and war. The 1848 Revolution in France failed, he explained, partly because there had been 'no *national* enemy to face', nothing which could 'hasten the revolutionary process' (CW 10,58). The Revolution had been disarmed. Every fresh proletarian upheaval in France, he concluded, must involve a world war: the European terrain was the soil 'on which alone the social revolution of the nineteenth century can be accomplished' (CW 10,70). Consequently, he declared in the first edition of the *Neue Rheinische Zeitung* for 1849 that

The table of contents for 1849 reads: *Revolutionary rising of the French working class, world war.* (CW 8,215)

Marx could thus anticipate a proletarian revolution in Germany without having any precise discussion of the German proletariat, which he described in *The German Ideology* as a 'latent proletariat' (CW 5,75). He did, however, claim that revolution itself was a major factor in the development of classes. Revolution was a hothouse in which the proletariat matured. Of France, he wrote:

in this vortex of movement, in this torment of historical unrest, in this dramatic ebb and flow of revolutionary passion, hopes and disappointments, the different classes of French society had to count their epochs of development in weeks where they had previously counted them in half centuries. (CW 10,97)

For this reason, Marx described revolutions as '*the locomotives of history*' (CW 10,122).[8] Above all, his impatience with the German bourgeoisie turned him from a minimalist into a maximalist, against the clear advice of *The German Ideology*. As a minimalist, he had broken with the leader of the German Workers' Association in Cologne, Gottschalk, who was firmly in control of the workers' movement, and had joined the Democratic Association, an alliance of workers and bourgeois. When Gottschalk was imprisoned, Marx took control of the Workers' Association and turned it in the maximalist direction he had previously opposed. The importance of tactics should not be underestimated in Marx's theoretical developments of 1848–9.[9]

By the time Marx realized that the 1848 Revolutions had been defeated, he restored the schema of the materialist conception of history, became a minimalist, and turned on his colleagues who continued his maximalist line. On 15 September 1850, he broke with Willich and Schapper, and effectively split the Communist League, by arguing that

We are devoted to a party which, most fortunately for it, cannot yet come to power. If the proletariat were to come to power the measures it would introduce would be petty-bourgeois and not directly proletarian. Our party can come to power only when the conditions allow it to put *its own* views into practice. Louis Blanc is the best instance of what happens when you come to power prematurely. (CW 10,628)

At about this time, Engels made a similar point in *The Peasant War in Germany* (CW 10,469). Like Marx, Engels alluded to the proletariat's representatives in the French Provisional Government of 1848. Marx and Engels trimmed their arguments. Affairs of the moment had encouraged their maximalism; they couched their minimalism on appeals to history. Marx had glimpsed that the instability of the revolutionary moment created opportunities for political manoeuvring, for novel and unexpected alignments of forces, for the most skilful party. Perhaps to acknowledge that there is nothing mechanical or certain about revolution, and to be prepared to take every advantage, is simply to be a revolutionary. In this sense, Marx was very much the revolutionary in 1848–9.

The strengths and weaknesses of Marx's analyses are nowhere more apparent than in his treatment of France: his model for European political development. Revolutionary events there had not gone as he expected. The monarchy was still widely considered to be the general stumbling-block to progress; the bourgeoisie still had the ability to attract allies, partly by appealing to the spirit of unity of 1789. The unsuccessful and short-lived June uprising of Paris proletarians was for Marx perhaps the single most important event of 1848. He cited those three days to confirm his class analysis. They represented, in his words, 'the first great battle... fought between the two classes that split modern society' (CW 10,67). As long as his hopes for European revolution survived the June defeat, Marx looked to the French proletariat to take the lead.

In February 1848 the monarchy of Louis Philippe fell under the weight of a popular revolt, and a Provisional Government was established under the leadership of Lamartine. In this coalition of social forces, the workers were represented by Louis Blanc and Albert. The coalition, however, soon threatened to tear apart. The Paris proletariat forced the Provisional Government to proclaim a republic, and by its frequent mobilizations forestalled attempts to re-establish a monarchy. Elections were organized for a Constituent Assembly, effectively taking power away from the Paris proletariat. Marx described this as an attempt by the Provisional Government to 'appeal from intoxicated Paris to sober France' (CW 10,53). In his writings on revolutionary events in both Germany and France, Marx had a sure feel of the relationship between assemblies and popular masses (or, more precisely, urban masses). He understood that the sitting of an assembly in a city such as Paris or Berlin could embolden it; he understood how the masses could directly intervene in the proceedings of an assembly, and how they could protect or destroy an assembly. A revolution, in Marx's terms, was an interplay between 'representatives' and extra-assembly masses, perhaps closer than any other example to his 'true democracy'. Thus Marx objected to the Provisional Government's attempt to isolate the Constituent Assembly from the revolutionary populace of Paris by giving it a 'more democratic' authority, by turning it into a passive representative of France. Similarly, he opposed Frederick William IV's proposal to transfer the Prussian National Assembly from Berlin, whose people were the real source of its power, to Brandenburg, where it could decline in obscurity. The choice before the Berlin Assembly, Marx stated succinctly, was 'Intimidation by the unarmed people or intimidation by an armed soldiery' (CW 7,438).

The deputies to the French Constituent Assembly were chiefly liberals. When the Paris proletariat perceived that its interests were threatened by the new Assembly, they rose against it. From the outset, Marx and Engels saw in the June Days a proletarian essence. On June 25 Engels peremptorily proclaimed that 'The decidedly proletarian nature of the insurrection emerges from all the details' (CW 7,124). The revolution had not begun as a proletarian revolution, Marx explained, because the proletariat had been dominated by the bourgeoisie with its appeal to *fraternité*. According to Marx, many workers believed that after the February Revolution there would be an end to class rule. Louis Philippe had been known as the 'bourgeois monarch', and under his rule suffrage to national assemblies was restricted to a propertied few. Marx claimed that the entire bourgeoisie did *not* rule in France during the 1830s and '40s—a claim which distinguished him from other socialists[10]—but only the 'finance aristocracy'. Thus the February Revolution was not an anti-bourgeois revolution, but an attempt at power by the industrial bourgeoisie. Engels emphasized this aspect of Marx's analysis, although Marx introduced it only upon the defeat of 1848. After the June uprising itself, Marx claimed that the proletariat and

161

(entire) bourgeoisie had fallen out from their alliance against the monarchy (CW 7,147). Engels, however, wrote later:

With all historians of the last twenty years' events in France, it has been a thing generally agreed upon, that under Louis Philippe, the bourgeoisie, as a whole, was the ruling power, in France.... Under Citizen Marx's pen, these assertions, although not directly and absolutely denied, yet undergo important modifications. (CW 10,357)

Why Marx made such modifications is apparent. He was required to give a class content to the French monarchy, but also to explain why there was a popular notion that after February *fraternité* between classes had been established or restored. He also had to explain why the proletariat was defeated—a problem, in his own terms, of why the proletariat was not yet ready to take power. This he did by stressing the essentially industrial nature of the proletariat. He argued that because the industrial bourgeoisie had not actually ruled in France, and the preconditions for socialism (a mature proletariat and industrial capitalism) were not established, socialism could not have been achieved.

The February Revolution, according to Marx, had been made in the name of *fraternité*, a *fraternité* which found its appropriate dénouement in the civil war of June 1848 (CW 7,147). There was a common interest among proletarians and bourgeois when they had had a common enemy: 'capital on the throne' (CW 7,147). The result was perhaps a nominal abolition of bourgeois rule, yet the bourgeoisie—or a different section of it—continued to rule. The people soon lost their illusions:

Nothing is more understandable, then, than that the Paris proletariat sought to assert its own interests *side by side* with the interests of the [industrial] bourgeoisie, instead of enforcing them as the revolutionary interests of society itself, that it let the *red* flag be dipped before the *tricolour*. (CW 10,57)

Workers believed that the republic had put an end to class rule. According to Marx, this illusion was shattered by the June Days. Soon after them, he wrote:

The momentary triumph of brute force has been purchased with the destruction of all the delusions and illusions of the February revolution.... (CW 7,144)

In November 1848, Marx argued that the counter-revolution,

ascendant since June, had educated the proletariat: 'All the illusions of February and March have been ruthlessly crushed' (CW 8,104). The 'loss of illusions' was Marx's constant theme as he waited for a new upsurge in the revolution.[11] Even universal suffrage, he suggested, tore from the exploiting class its 'deceptive mask' (CW 10,65).

Marx's theory, as it emerges from his writings of 1848-50, is complex and more realistic than before. Instead of two classes, there were more, and even fractions of classes now had independent roles to play. Instead of a proletariat made clear-sighted through the work process, Marx believed that the proletariat was freed from illusions by the revolutionary process itself. It is tempting to consider his theoretical moves during this period (and perhaps even after)[12] as primarily instrumental or manipulative exercises designed for tactical advantage. But Marx also made an interesting addition to his notion of revolutionary universality. Until 1848, he had argued as if the proletariat had no need of revolutionary alliances. In 1848, however, he conceded that the proletariat was a minority in all the countries of Europe, and thus any hope of proletarian revolution rested on its ability to attract to its universal cause other social forces. Politics, with its universalizing form, ensured that the proletariat could frame its interests and demands so that it would be recognised as the general representative of society. Marx looked, in particular, to an alliance between the proletariat and peasantry.

Marx believed that the peasantry was vital to the bourgeois revolution. It was the inability of the Prussian bourgeoisie to support the demands of the peasantry against feudal obligations which sealed its fate as a class with no major historical role to play. The peasantry, therefore, could now become a supporter of the proletariat, since

Only the fall of capital can raise the peasant; only an anti-capitalist, a proletarian government can break his economic misery, his social degradation. (CW 10,122)

The peasants, according to Marx, would find their 'natural ally and leader in the *urban proletariat*' (CW 11,191). If the proletariat must encourage alliances, the tasks of the proletarian party were increased. It had to formulate a programme which would not only unite the proletariat, but court potential allies. Marx wrote to Engels of the alliance between proletariat and peasantry, and argued that the success of the German proletariat depended on a sort of second edition of the Peasant War. In his March 1850 address to the Communist League, he referred to its role in making revolutionary alliances:

In the case of a struggle against a common adversary no special union is required. As soon as such an adversary has to be fought directly, the interests of both parties, for the moment, coincide, and, as previously so also in the future, this alliance, calculated to last only for the moment, will come about of itself. (CW 10,282)

Marx was concerned that the League maintain its independence, so that the proletariat would not submit to the leadership of transient allies. Engels even argued that all modern revolutions involved momentary coalitions of classes (CW 11,32). In December 1852, he wrote of the League's preparation for the revolutionary universality of the proletariat: it had

applied itself to the study of the conditions under which one class of society can and must be called on to represent the whole of the interests of a nation, and thus politically to rule over it. (CW 11,389)

Marx was careful not to identify the interests of the proletariat with those of the peasantry. It is reasonable to assume that after such a temporary alliance, the proletariat would give precedence to its own claims. The March 1848 'Demands of the Communist Party in Germany' proposed not the abolition of peasant property, but the abolition of feudal dues, nationalization of princely estates and of peasant mortgages (CW 7,3). Yet the victory of the proletariat would ultimately entail the abolition of peasant property. In his 1847 *Principles of Communism,* Engels anticipated that after an alliance of the proletariat and peasantry to inaugurate the 'democratic constitution', there may be the need for a 'second fight' to ensure that the interests of the proletariat predominated (CW 6,350).

During the 1848 Revolutions, Marx stressed the industrial character of the proletariat. He could thus separate the proletariat from the lumpenproletariat, the material force of counter-revolution. He could relate the proletariat's revolutionary potential and development as a class to its conditions of existence. He could also oppose the notion of an independent revolutionary role for the peasantry. And, he could explain why the revolutions had failed to introduce socialism.

In *The Holy Family*, Marx used the criminals and prostitutes who inhabited Sue's *Mysteries of Paris* and the streets and taverns of Paris and elsewhere, as symbols for his proletariat. Max Stirner had even described the proletariat as consisting of 'rogues, prostitutes, thieves, robbers and murderers, gamblers, propertyless people',[13] a conception Marx now rejected as the view of burghers and officials. For Stirner, Marx declared,

the entire proletariat consists of ruined bourgeois and ruined proletarians, of a collection of *ragamuffins*, who have existed in every epoch and whose existence *on a mass scale* after the decline of the Middle Ages preceded the mass formation of the ordinary proletariat. (CW 5,202)

In the *Communist Manifesto* the proletariat is presented as the 'special and essential product' of modern industry (CW 6,494). Those who must sell their labour as a commodity are concentrated into a powerful social force by modern industry. Lumpenproletarians are not so shaped. In November 1848, Marx accused the lumpenproletariat of defeating the proletariat in Paris in June and in Vienna:

In Paris the mobile guard, in Vienna 'Croats'—in both cases *lazzaroni*, lumpenproletariat hired and armed—were used against the working and thinking proletarians. (CW 7,505)

Already in June 1848, Engels had criticized the *lazzaroni* as counter-revolutionaries (CW 7,25). Marx maintained this view in *The Class Struggles in France*, and emphasized the educative role of large-scale industry for proletarians. He argued there that the Paris bourgeoisie decided after February '*to play off one part of the proletariat against the other* ' (CW 10,62). The Provisional Government thus formed the Mobile Guard, distinguished by Marx from the bourgeois National Guard. The Mobile Guard was composed of lumpenproletarians,

which in all big towns forms a mass sharply differentiated from the industrial proletariat, a recruiting ground for thieves and criminals of all kinds, living on the crumbs of society, people without a definitive trade, vagabonds, *gens sans feu et sans aveu*, varying according to the degree of civilisation of the nation to which they belong, but never renouncing their *lazzaroni* character. (CW 10,62)

The Paris proletariat, according to Marx, was deceived: it thought that the Mobile Guard was a proletarian guard. Recent research tends to support the Paris proletariat's view against Marx's.[14]

Marx used the industrial character of the proletariat to explain its cohesion and combativeness.[15] He used it also to explain the failure of the French Revolution of 1848 to produce socialism. In *The Class Struggles*, he argued that the proletariat of 1848 could not have become a revolutionary universal class because it was not yet a class 'in which the revolutionary interests of society are concentrated'; thus 'it was still incapable of accomplishing its own revolution' (CW 10,56). The development of the industrial proletariat was 'conditioned' by that of the industrial bourgeoisie. Only under the rule of that bourgeoisie

does the proletariat gain that extensive national existence which can raise its revolution to a national one, and does it itself create the modern means of production, which become just so many means of its revolutionary emancipation. (CW 10,56)

The French proletariat, according to Marx with hindsight, was not prepared enough to rule. To explain the abortive proletarian uprising of June, he resorted to the idea that the bourgeoisie provoked the proletariat into premature confrontation (CW 10,69).

Marx's post-1850 return to historical determinism blurs the distinction between two issues. The first is the political ability of the proletariat to take power in a revolutionary upheaval. The second is its economic readiness for power. In revolution, all is in flux; opportunities are created; and revolutionaries—the tacticians of revolution—seize them. The proletariat may take power, but can it retain power and implement its programme: when is a country historically 'ripe' for socialism? There is a tension in Marx's work between his emphasis on tactical opportunities and his larger historical vision: between his more considered remarks, and those forged in the heat of revolutionary struggles.

Marx also used the notion of an *industrial* proletariat to distinguish the revolutionary potential of proletarians and peasants. The rural population, he believed, would gradually disappear, while the proletariat would grow along with vast productive forces (CW 11,531). Industry immunized the proletariat from 'rural idiocy', fitted it for its revolutionary role, and for its role as the future ruling class. The peasants could play no independent revolutionary or historical role. They could not organize themselves as a national class to propose or defend their interests, and thus they could not become the general representative of society. Just as, for Marx, there were historic nations, so there were historic classes; the peasantry was not among them.

The great mass of the French nation is formed by simple addition of homologous magnitudes, much as potatoes in a sack form a sack of potatoes. Insofar as millions of families live under economic conditions of existence that separate their mode of life, their interests and their culture from those of the other classes, and put them in hostile opposition to the latter, they form a class. Insofar as there is merely a local interconnection among these small-holding peasants, and the identity of their interests begets no community, no national bond and no political organisation among them, they do not form a class.... They cannot represent themselves, they must be represented. (CW 11,187)

Or, as he put it in *The Class Struggles*, the peasantry is 'absolutely incapable of any revolutionary initiative' (CW 10,134).

The industrial character of the proletariat suited Marx's earlier views about the productive nature of man (Tucker notes that it was man as frustrated producer, not as dissatisfied consumer, who would make the revolution),[16] but it was also suitable to explain the defeat of the 1848 Revolutions. Yet it did not seem to account for the absence of proletarian revolution in England. Late in 1848, Marx suggested that a new revolution by the Continental proletariat would lead to a revolutionary war between England and Europe. Such a war would give the Chartists courage to take power (CW 8,215). By 1850, however, when he was beginning to take seriously the influence of economic factors in precipitating revolution, Marx attributed the quiescence of the English workers during 1848 and 1849 to the upsurge of English industrial activity (CW 10,497). By 1850, he argued, the prospect for revolution in Europe itself had receded:[17]

With this general prosperity, in which the productive forces of bourgeois society develop as luxuriantly as is at all possible within bourgeois relationships, there can be no talk of a real revolution.... *A new revolution is possible only in consequence of a new crisis. It is, however, just as certain as this crisis.* (CW 10,510)

In August 1849, Marx arrived in London as an exile. In

December, still with high spirits, he wrote to Joseph Weydemeyer about his plans for the *Neue Rheinische Zeitung. Politische-ökonomische Revue*:

I hardly doubt that after the publication of three, or perhaps two, monthly issues, the world conflagration will intervene and the opportunity of provisionally coming to terms with the economy will cease.[18]

But he was wrong on both counts. The prospect of revolution did not revive, and for the next five years Marx—never able properly to manage his financial affairs —suffered great poverty with his family in the slums of London. At first he tried to reorganize the Communist League. His study of political economy, however, convinced him that the revolutionary situation had passed, and in September 1850 he and Engels withdrew from it. The League's Central Committee split between the supporters of Marx and Engels, and those of Willich and Schapper. Marx was instrumental in having its headquarters transferred to Cologne, thus ending its effectiveness. Marx remained in London, close to the British Museum, while Engels went to Manchester to work in the family business so that he might materially assist Marx.

In the 1850s and '60s, there were not many opportunities for Marx to pursue political activities, even had he sought them. Chartism rapidly declined after 1848; English workers began to organize in legal trade unions; and they began to be protected by special legislation, notably the Ten Hours Act. English workers still had political demands and waged political campaigns: they wanted an extension of the franchise to include them (which they got in the 1867 Reform Act, about which Marx said almost nothing), and they helped to dissuade the government from intervening in the American Civil War on the side of the Confederacy early in the 1860s. From these activities Marx was isolated as a foreigner and as an intellectual. In 1864, however, he turned his skills to account, and ended his isolation by influencing the International Working Men's Association (hereafter, the First International) from its inception.

The First International was established on the initiative of trade union leaders and workers' representatives from England and France. Its period of effective existence was from 1864 to 1872, although it expired officially in the United States in 1876. The designation

'First International' does not mean to suggest that like the Second, Third, and various Fourth Internationals, it was committed to some form of Marxism. Although Marx was the First International's chief theoretical guide until 1872, it was formally bound to no particular socialist theory.[19] Its major addresses, resolutions and reports, however—most of which were written by Marx—from the first put forward conceptions of working class activities, tasks and emancipation which were distinctively his. Conceptions such as the necessity for working class political action lay fallow until Marx was in a position to press home his tactical advantage against his socialist opponents. There was, in fact, a latent conflict embodied in an Association founded upon certain central assumptions of Marxian socialism, as declared in the Rules, which nevertheless did not declare itself for Marxian socialism and which welcomed most other types of socialists to its ranks. This conflict led ultimately to the dissolution of the International.

In his polemics against the Proudhonists and Bakuninists, which dominated the theoretical life of the International, Marx made much of the supposed openness of the International. Thus, in March 1869, upon receiving a request for affiliation by the Bakunin-inspired International Alliance of Socialist Democracy, Marx replied on behalf of the International's General Council that

it is no part of the function of the General Council to make a critical study of the Alliance's programme. It is not for us to analyse whether or not it is a genuine expression of the proletarian movement. All we need to know is that it contains nothing counter to the *general tendency* of our Association, in other words, the *complete emancipation of the working class*. There is one sentence in your programme which fails this test. We read in Article 2: 'It [the Alliance] desires above all the political, economic and social equalization of classes'. (FIA,280)

It was not so much that the 'equalization of classes', as Marx pointed out, was a logical impossibility, but that it could be construed as advocating harmony between capital and labour rather than their abolition, which countered the 'general tendency' of the International's programme. Yet this 'general tendency' was of Marx's devising. As I have argued earlier, his idea of the abolition of classes was not widely understood by workers or socialists and was rejected by most of them, understood or not. The context of the International may not at first have allowed 'the old boldness of speech' to Marx, as he confided to Engels (OFI,370), but the substance of his views was preserved there. He made concessions only to form:

It was very difficult to frame the thing [the Inaugural Address and the General Rules of the Association] so that our views should appear in a form acceptable from the present standpoint of the workers' movement. (OFI,370)

Marx's great influence over the declared policy of the International is easily explained by the stature of his intellect and the clarity of his aims and of his writing. The International had not emerged from a period of sharp disputes over goals and tactics, such as the 1840s; its members were keen not to proclaim or proscribe doctrines. Onto this unsuspecting membership, and perhaps above its level of understanding, was to burst one of the great political confrontations: between Marx and Bakunin. For the International was, at the theoretical level, tacitly Marxist. Marx had boldly presented his declarations as non-problematic to the predominantly English organizers of the Association, pragmatic organizers not given to theoretical disputes and nuances. Perhaps the English were the only ones not to see that the Inaugural Address and General Rules represented a particular socialist viewpoint; they trusted Marx's judgement even through the 1872 Hague Congress, where he effectively wrecked the International.

One point should by now be apparent. The International had two aspects, or levels, which were not closely connected: theoretical and political, and trade union. At the theoretical level Marx held—continually disputed—sway. At the trade union level, in its first years, the International was generally quite successful.[20] It acted as an international liaison for trade unions, and helped to stop a number of attempts at strikebreaking by imported foreign workers. For these efforts it attracted the affiliation of some trade unions, most of them British. But the International was unable to organize the unskilled majority of British workers.[21] So those trade unions which were represented in the International, and which were protected by it, did not truly represent the industrial working class. They were a 'privileged stratum' of the English working class, as Collins and Abramsky put it.[22] And they were usually from trades, such as tailoring, clothing, shoemaking and cabinet making. 'In mining, engineering and in heavy industry generally', the International's 'strength was to remain small or non-existent'.[23] By distinguishing between the theoretical and practical levels of the International, we can see that Marx exaggerated its theoretical influence over British workers. Shortly after the International was founded, he wrote to Kugelmann:

I prefer a hundred times my agitation here through the International Association. Its influence on the English proletariat is direct and of the greatest importance. (OFI,382)

And in 1867 he assured the wary Engels that

in the next revolution, which is perhaps nearer than it appears, we (that is, you and I) will have this powerful engine in our hands. (OFI,428)

This belief was based on Marx's claim that 'I am in fact the head' of the International (OFI,385). But Marx did not seem to realize that his leadership had definite limits, and that if he made use of the General Council it also made use of him. There is no compelling reason to accept that the General Council would have become his instrument in a revolutionary situation, or that the trade unions would have become instruments of the General Council.

At the theoretical level, the history of the International was a succession of struggles between Marx and the Proudhonists, and between Marx and Bakunin and the Bakuninists. Marx assessed the dangers of both to the International and his influence over it quite differently. Against the Proudhonists, he used diplomacy; against Bakunin and his followers he was prepared to destroy the International rather than allow it to fall under their influence. The influence of Proudhon's legacy gradually declined after the first few years. Bakunin's theories, however, which were introduced into the International around 1869, attracted increasing support from the International's adherents in the non-industrialized countries of Western Europe, particularly Italy, Spain and Switzerland. Marx had, from the first, to conciliate the Proudhonists, but it was from a position of strength in the General Council that he assailed Bakunin. As Collins and Abramsky note, in the Inaugural Address Marx 'was obliged, in deference to the French followers of Proudhon, to omit all references to State centralisation as the form which socialist society would take'.[24] But deference did not prevent him from writing into the Provisional Rules:

That the economical emancipation of the working classes is therefore the great end to which every political movement ought to be subordinate as a means. (FIA,82)

And conciliation did not prevent the Proudhonists, in their French translation of the Rules, to delete 'as a means' (OFI, 64; OFI, 502).[25] Marx made no such concessions to the Bakuninists. In opposition to them he stressed the political form of the working class struggle, and the need for the working class to rule politically as a means to their full emancipation.

Marx differed from the Proudhonists and Bakuninists fundamentally over the role of politics and of the state in the emancipation of the proletariat. He maintained that political action by the working class was essential. He also posited that the International and its 'general tendency' (for which he himself was responsible), were archetypal expressions of the working class, and that the relation to the working class of those who opposed them was not genuine, was 'sectarian'. Thus Marx transformed a dispute between different types of socialism into a dispute between the working class and its legitimate representatives, strategies and aspirations on the one hand, and pretenders, on the other. As Marx put it in 1871:

The International was founded in order to replace the socialist or semisocialist sects with a real organization of the working class for struggle.... The development of the socialist sectarianism and that of the real working-class movement always stand in inverse relation to each other. (OFI,543)

Since 1846, Marx had consistently identified his theory with the 'real movement of the working class', even though in the International he was politic enough not to claim that he was a member, or even a son, of the working class.[26] But Marx's socialism was unique in its estimation of, and role for, the working class. On this basis he ingeniously presented his theory as the proper one for the International. In fact, it was as much by accident, as by intellectual stature, that Marx came to have the International in his theoretical grip. For it was only at the last moment that he was invited to its founding meeting. Marx, however, saw his influence as confirming his theory as an expression of the interests of the working class, a belief further based on the unexamined assumption that the International represented the 'real movement of the working class'.

For Marx, the Utopian Socialists had formed a particular type of sect: 'Sects are justified (historically) so long as the working classes are not yet ripe for an independent historical movement' (OFI,544). But now the time was ripe, and any group opposing the tendency of the General Council was, for him, a (historically unjustified) sect.

The sect seeks its *raison d'être* and its *point d'honneur*—not in what it has in *common* with the class movement, but in the *particular shibboleth* which distinguishes one from the other. (OFI,450-1)

Where Marx's theories, as embodied in the major documents of the International (and partly by dint of accident), 'expressed' the movement of the working class, the theories of sects 'subordinated' the movement of the working class to abstractions. Marx was consistent in his rejection of external determination, even within the working class movement, but in his position of authority in the General Council it was easy for him to appear diplomatic, even righteous.

Despite Marx's definitional campaign to exclude his opponents from the real movement of the working class, he defended the idea of political action by the working class by relying on the notion of universality. Marx defended the demand for a *legal* limitation of the workday; the demand for compulsory *state provided* education for children; and, of course, the belief that the decisive campaign of the proletariat against the ruling class would be political. Not only did he argue that it was foolish to try to by-pass the state, but that

In enforcing such laws, the working class do not fortify governmental power. On the contrary, they transform that power, now used against them, into their own agency. (FIA,89)

But above all else, Marx saw the political as the final and necessary expression of the working class. Trade unionism, he believed, was not enough. And if Marx began to appreciate the importance of trade unions during the period of the International, he also most clearly described their limitations. As he put it in 1866:

Too exclusively bent upon the local and immediate struggles with capital, the trade unions have not yet fully understood their power of acting against the system of wage slavery itself. (FIA,91)

Yet when they begin to generalize their experiences, Marx believed that trade unions gave rise to, or assisted, political movements. By their nature, he explained, trade unions are linked to 'the system of wage slavery'. He even argued, somewhat wildly, that

The trade unions by themselves are impotent—they will remain a minority. They do not have the mass of proletarians behind them, whereas the International influences these people directly.... It is the only association in which the workers have complete confidence. (OFI,141)

For Marx, the proletariat's universality would be expressed politically. Political was the form in which the universal claims of the proletariat would be made, and the form which would assist the making of revolutionary alliances. In a sense, the importance of the political lay precisely in its *form* : in the fact that politics was the arena of generality, and that to play politics meant to advance general claims, to frame one's claims with general appeal. The proletariat's inherent universality is not in question here; that claim is needed to sustain the view that the rule of the proletariat will be the end of class rule. As a political force, the proletariat would transcend its localized and diverse economic struggles, and aim 'to effect its interests in a general form—in a form which possesses universal socially coercive force' (OFI,547). The bourgeoisie as a political class existed through its control of the state; the proletariat must become a political class as the first decisive step towards communism. At the Hague Congress of the International in 1872, Marx put the International on record as supporting the establishment of working class political parties:

Against the collective power of the propertied classes the working class cannot act, as a class, except by *constituting itself into a political party, distinct from, and opposed to, all old parties formed by the propertied classes*. This constitution of the working class into a political party is indispensable in order to insure the triumph of the social revolution and its ultimate end—*the abolition of classes*. (OFI,150)

To say that the proletariat must exist politically means that it must exist nationally, and put itself forward as the representative of the general interest. This revolutionary universality is the universality of the political role, whereas intrinsic universality is universality that is of the essence of the proletariat. This essence was first seen by Marx as philosophical, but later as political (a political goal, rather than as a political role).

Marx's conception of social class distinguished him from most other socialists of his day. In 1852, in a well-known letter to Weydemeyer, Marx described his achievements thus:

no credit is due to me for discovering the existence of classes in modern society or the struggle between them.... What I did that was new was to prove: 1) that the *existence of classes* is only bound up with *particular historical phases in the development of production,* 2) that the class struggle necessarily leads to *the dictatorship of the proletariat,* 3) that this dictatorship itself only constitutes the transition to the *abolition of all classes* and to a *classless society....* (SW I,528)

The language of class had increasing currency in Europe during the 1830s and '40s, partly as a result of the historiography of the French Revolution, but classes were not seen as a special product of capitalism (and even Marx was ambiguous on this point), nor was the solution to the social problem seen as the rule of a particular class. As I argued in Chapter Three, socialists preached a universal social interest and advocated a union of classes, communists preached a particular class interest, and Marx, with his concept of the proletariat, attempted to transcend them both. Marx believed that classes had different and mutually antagonistic interests. Novel also was his belief that the rule of the proletariat would lead to the end of class rule. Although it puzzled socialists, this position depended squarely on the idea that the proletariat was the universal class. In June 1850, for example, Marx sent a statement to the Editor of the *Neue Deutsche Zeitung,* which began as follows:

Sir, In your newspaper's article of June 22 this year you reproached me for advocating the *rule and the dictatorship of the working class,* while you propose, in opposition to myself, the *abolition of class distinctions in general.* I do not understand this correction. (CW 10,387)

He went on to cite passages from the *Communist Manifesto, The Poverty of Philosophy* and an article from the *Neue Rheinische Zeitung. Politisch-ökonomische Revue* (later incorporated by Engels in *The Class Struggles in France*), each of which declared that the rule of the working class creates the conditions for the abolition of class antagonisms and classes generally. Marx's conception of the proletariat vitiated the charge that he was pandering to the selfishness, greed and envy of the working class. Even if such attitudes prevailed among the working class, its victory would put an end to all class rule.

Marx's views on the intrinsic universality of the proletariat were as little understood during the period of the First International as after. Mazzini had directed his followers 'to cut out... all hostile references to the bourgeoisie' in the debate over (Marx's) *Inaugural Address*.[27] Collins and Abramsky relate that at an anniversary dinner of the Amalgamated Society of Carpenters and Joiners in 1869, a toast was proposed to the 'Success and Prosperity' of the International. They continue:

After this, without any sense of incongruity, the branch members at the dinner unanimously approved a motion wishing 'Health and Prosperity to our Employers'. [28]

No one seems to have directly challenged Marx over his ideas on the class struggle and the abolition of classes at the time of the International, even when the opportunity presented itself, as in Marx's officially sanctioned ridicule of Bakunin's programme for the 'equalization of classes'. Marx wrote for the General Council:

It is not the logically impossible 'equalization of classes', but the historically necessary, superseding 'abolition of classes', this true secret of the proletarian movement, which forms the great aim of the International Working Men's Association. (OFI,165)

General incomprehension of the notion of the proletariat's intrinsic universality was highlighted late in the 1870s. The German Social-Democratic Workers' Party, which numbered Marx and, to Marx's chagrin, Lassalle among its theoretical guides, angered Marx and Engels by its characterization of the struggle for workers' interests. In 1879, three of its members published 'The Socialist Movement in Germany in Retrospect', which contrasted the movement of the true love of humanity with the *'one-sided struggle for the interests of the industrial workers.'*[29] Marx and Engels commented:

In [the] view of these gentlemen, then, the Social-Democratic Party is *not* to be a one-sided workers' party but a party open on all sides 'for all men filled with true love of humanity'. It is to prove this, above all, by divesting itself of rough proletarian passions and by placing itself under the leadership of educated, philanthropic bourgeois.... (FIA,369)

Their response (and Engels', in particular, for he wrote the first draft) to this challenge anticipated some of the issues of the later controversy within the SPD over Revisionism. Indeed, the major author of Revisionism, Eduard Bernstein, was one of the authors of the offending retrospective. The debate over Revisionism centred on the issue of the proper basis for the socialist movement: class struggle and workers' interests, or appeals to abstract moral standards such as *justice*. These options were outlined by Marx and Engels; but nowhere in their 1879 letter did they explicitly defend the notion of the proletariat's intrinsic universality. They argued, rather, from effect: the German position, they declared, meant that 'the working class is incapable of liberating itself by its own efforts' (FIA,370); that the German position would be acceptable even to a bourgeois democrat (FIA,372); and that it was a product of bourgeois and petty bourgeois prejudices, and not a properly proletarian outlook (FIA,373-4). Marx failed to explain what is clearly a lynchpin of his theory: that the proletariat is not simply a class with particular interests, but that its claims have a historical and logical priority over the claims of all other classes.

Marx could be highly critical of the actual proletariat when he chose to be, but he would not abandon his basic position. He had entered the International, for example, with high hopes for the English working class. Leadership was still required:

One element of success they possess—numbers; but numbers weigh only in the balance, if united by combination and led by knowledge. (FIA, 81)

England was also crucial for socialism because, as Marx argued in 1848, any social revolution on the Continent without England was 'a storm in a teacup'. England

is the only country where there are no longer any peasants.... It is the only country *where the large majority of the population consists of wage-labourers*. It is the only country where the class struggle and the organization of the working class into *trade unions* have actually reached a considerable degree of maturity and universality. (FIA,115)

Marx added that 'The English have all that is needed *materially* for social revolution' (FIA,116). But by 1870, when these lines were written, it was not just leadership which was required for an English revolution, but an anti-chauvinist tonic. (English workers were also strongly influenced by religion—Halévy has cited Methodism as reason for the lack of a nineteenth century English revolution[30]—but Marx never mentioned it.)

To say that English workers were held in thrall by an ideological conception of their superiority over Irish workers was a major departure in Marx's work. The change was signalled in some letters Marx wrote in 1869 and 1870, and it eventually found expression in his contributions to the International. He explained to Engels:

The English working class will never achieve anything before it has got rid of Ireland. The lever must be applied in Ireland. That is why the Irish question is so important for the social movement in general.... (FIA,167)

The next year, 1870, Marx wrote to Meyer and Vogt in the United States that in English industrial centres the working class was '*split* into two *hostile* camps: English proletarians and Irish proletarians' (FIA,169). The English worker, according to Marx, saw the Irish worker as a competitor for his job who would work for lower wages. The English worker believed that he belonged to a better, a ruling class, over the Irish worker:

This antagonism is artificially sustained and intensified by the press, the pulpit, the comic papers, in short, by all the means at the disposal of the ruling classes. *This antagonism* is the *secret of the impotence of the English working class,* despite its organization. (FIA,169)

If, as Marx claimed, this ideological enslavement of the English proletariat to its ruling class was the secret of preserving the bourgeoisie's power (FIA,117), he did not generalize his claim into a theory of the significance of nationalism for the working class. Nor did he explain how the working class could be influenced by ideology, where previously he had denied this. Nor did he expand upon the idea that different sections of the working class of one country might wish to preserve their privileges *vis-à-vis* one another. Although Marx often allowed that the working class was not homogeneous (giving rise to his distinction between proletarians and communists, for example), he effectively denied that different sections of the working class could have different or opposed interests. Marx's preparedness to invoke the idea of English workers' national prejudice as a reason for their failure to make a revolution seems decidedly *ad hoc,* whatever its veracity, and it is ultimately disruptive for his theory. Nevertheless, the idea that the working class is in thrall to bourgeois ideology has become a major part of post-Marx Marxism. Marx never really came to grips with Engels' perceptive observation in 1858 that 'the English proletariat is becoming more and more bourgeois'.[31] Lenin's theory of imperialism does not, as David Fernbach suggests it does, solve Marx's problem; it merely reinforces it.[32]

Marx refused to see nationalism among workers as a significant factor in the Franco-Prussian War of 1870. That war gave rise to two of his best political statements, as well as to his *The Civil War in France*, eulogizing the short-lived Paris Commune of 1871. *The Civil War in France* brought the International, and especially Marx, international notoriety. In the two addresses he wrote for the General Council (July and September 1870) on the Franco-Prussian War, Marx expected, and thought he perceived, a sort of studied neutrality on the part of German and French workers:

The very fact that while official France and Germany are rushing into a fratricidal feud, the workmen of France and Germany send each other messages of peace and goodwill, this great fact, unparalleled in the history of the past, opens a vista to a brighter future. (FIA, 176)

In his Second Address, Marx advised the French working class 'calmly and resolutely' to support the newly created republic until at least the crisis of war had passed (FIA,185). In general, he believed that war opened up opportunities and created new responsibilities for a working class. He did not see war as being waged by proletarians in uniform (a position developed within the Second International).[33] Marx thought it proper that Social Democratic deputies in the German Diet should vote against war credits and argue against the waging of war, but he did not conceive of an appeal to the working class to lay down their arms to make war impossible.

The War, however, was soon overshadowed in Marx's mind by the Paris Commune. Napoleon III had been defeated by the Prussian army at Sedan at the beginning of September 1870. Two days later, the Second Empire gave way to a republic under Louis-Adolphe Thiers, who determined to continue hostilities. The French army suffered further defeats, and the Prussians lay siege to Paris. Thiers sued for peace; he signed a preliminary peace treaty on 26 February 1871 which ceded Alsace and East Lorraine to Germany, and he agreed to a large indemnity. But when Thiers attempted to disarm the Parisian National Guard and to surrender Paris to the Prussians, Paris responded with measures for its self-defence. On 18 March 1871 Paris declared, through the Central Committee created by the National Guard, that it would not accept the authority of the Thiers government on the issue of the armistice and capitulation of Paris. It refused to hand over its arms. Thence began the Commune, an embattled city confronted by the overwhelmingly superior military forces of Thiers, who had Prussian blessing. Paris fell to Versailles troops on 28 May, and fearful reprisals began. Kamenka notes that 'before the end of 1871, it has been claimed, nearly one hundred thousand Parisians had suffered death, imprisonment, exile or transportation'.[34] The fury of the reprisals shows that the Commune was seen as something more than a desperate cry of national pride against the humiliation of defeat. It raised the spectre, if not the substance, of working class rule and socialism.

The Commune employed class language to censure 'the failures and treasons of the ruling classes' and acted explicitly on behalf of the 'proletarians of Paris'.[35] But they were Blanqui's 'proletarians' rather than Marx's, an amorphous group of 'the exploited', united by discontent rather than modern industry, and responding to specific events which outraged them rather than advocating socialism. Furthermore, this type of class language, as Rose notes,[36] was not a ubiquitous feature of Communard documents. Both the Thiers government and the International (through Marx) exploited the vaguely socialist sentiments of many of the leading Communards to turn an event in the history of France (and even more of Paris) into something of wider significance. Thiers claimed that the Commune was a plot of the International. Marx rejected the claim, but made a spirited defence of the Commune. His *The Civil War in France*, published in June 1871, exposed the characters and careers of the leading figures of the Thiers government; described some of the measures enacted by the Commune; assessed the Commune's significance as the first attempt at rule by the working class; and denounced the treatment meted out to the Parisians after its fall.

Marx accorded more significance to the Commune than perhaps its actual measures and composition would warrant, though he did so in the heat of battle, not on reconsideration afterward.[37] Although he doubted the wisdom of establishing the Commune, and even its ability to survive, he never doubted its essentially working class nature. March 18 he described as 'The glorious working men's revolution' (FIA,201); of the ruling body of the Commune, he declared: 'The majority of its members were naturally working men, or acknowledged representatives of the working class' (FIA,209); the National Guard was, for him, the armed working class. The 'true secret' of the Commune, Marx argued, was that 'It was essentially a working-class government' (FIA,212). He was aware, as he put it in the first draft of his pamphlet, that 'The principal measures taken by the Commune are taken for the salvation of the middle class' (FIA,258). But even this failed to blunt his enthusiasm. Indeed, he tended to view such expedients as a confirmation of the revolutionary universality of the Paris proletariat:

For the first time in history the petty and middling middle class has openly rallied round the workmen's revolution, and proclaimed it as the only means of their own salvation and that of France! (FIA,258)

The ability of a class to become a revolutionary universal class was, according to Marx, an ability now confined to the proletariat. The Commune

was the first revolution in which the working class was openly acknowledged as the only class capable of social initiative, even by the great bulk of the Paris middle class.... (FIA,214)

But more important than the middle class, the proletariat had the ability to win over the peasantry, that class on which the ultimate success of the French socialist revolution relied. The Commune, Marx declared, 'was perfectly right in telling the peasants that "its victory was their only hope"' (FIA,215).

Marx's writings on the Commune reaffirm the significance of the proletariat's revolutionary universality in his theory, however unreliable they are about the real place of the Commune in the history of socialism. In the Commune, Marx believed, the proletariat had for a moment become the general representative of society against its acknowledged stumbling-block, the bourgeoisie led by Thiers. Yet the Commune was more accurately an attempt by Paris to become, once again, the general representative of France.[38] At the end of the eighteenth, and during the nineteenth centuries, Paris at certain points led, or attempted to lead, France. When it did, it became truly representative of France. It could only be representative because it had its roots in the country. Paris could play its historic role because it was not proletarianized, in Marx's sense of having a large industrial base and a distinct class of industrial workers. The sociology of Paris, as Rose explains, had not changed much between 1789 and 1871; Paris was still predominantly artisanal, with emphasis on luxury trades.[39] Nevertheless, Marx used the slender evidence of Communard documents and proclamations, of the Communards' halting steps towards labour legislation, and the very firm evidence of massive post-Commune repression, to claim the Commune as a major event in the history of (his brand of) socialism. Marx was able to stress the revolutionary universality of the proletariat, and to argue that the peasant was now separated from the proletarian no longer by 'his real interest, but [by] his delusive prejudice' (FIA,257). He was also able to hint at the intrinsic universality of the proletariat in his claim that the Commune

does not represent a particular interest. It represents the liberation of 'labour', that is the fundamental and natural condition of individual and social life. (FIA,253)

But while Marx thought that the Commune was a revolution of a classical type, requiring a revolutionary universal class, the International was testimony to the idea that such a revolution may no longer be necessary, or possible. The year after the Commune, Marx himself said:

We know that heed must be paid to the institutions, customs and traditions of the various countries, and we do not deny that there are countries, such as America and England, and if I was familiar with its institutions, I might include Holland, where the workers may attain their goal by peaceful means. (FIA,324)

The International collapsed, in part, because of a tension between revolution and reform. Its founding forces, and those which gave it greatest stability, the English trade unions, had by the late 1860s become legally legitimate and widely accepted. 1867 was the last year when there was an appreciable increase in trade union affiliation to the International.[40] The organized workers could exercise their power in (English) society without the help of the International; the revolutionaries in continental Europe may have been influenced by Marx, but they were not in the main Marxists. Not one significant Communard was a Marxist, and elsewhere the influence of Bakunin continued to grow. Thus, organized workers tended towards reform, and unorganized workers were attracted to revolutionary theories alien to Marx's. The International, unable to grow in England and having admitted Bakunin's Trojan Horse, transferred its headquarters to the United States at the instigation of Marx. Marx saved the International by destroying it.[41]

* * *

George Lichtheim has described the period from 1848 to 1871 as 'The Test of Reality' for Marx's theory.[42] The important elements of that period, Lichtheim suggested, such as the 1848 Revolutions, the rise of nationalism, democracy and a labour movement, as well as the Commune, helped to mature Marx, to make him a realist, to rid him 'of his brief Jacobin-Blanquist aberration in 1850'.[43] The rise of a labour movement, rather than the proliferation of secret or conspiratorial organizations which purported to represent the proletariat, signalled to Marx—according to Lichtheim—that the old revolutionary strategy of 1789 was no longer relevant.[44] Lichtheim's conclusions about the abandonment by the mature Marx of Blanquism, vanguardism and the permanent revolution (or whether indeed Marx ever held such positions), are arguable. It is indubitable, however, that the period from 1848 to 1871 was the 'test of reality' for Marx's theory, and particularly for his concept of the proletariat. In almost every respect, Marx's concept failed the test. Ironically, Marx's theory emerged from this period strengthened, and ready to become the nominal doctrine of the Second International. The reason for this apparent success was above all the extraordinary intellectual ability of Marx. Marx responded creatively to new situations and challenges, while doggedly maintaining that new works were embellishments upon, and not departures from, a single unified theory. His theory was different from other socialist theories that fell by the wayside in its historical perspective and in its commitment to explain as well as to change. But the complexities he introduced served to undermine his conception of the proletariat. The dichotomy of today between Marxism as a radical research programme in Western universities, and Marxism as a political programme for proletarian power, has its roots in Marx's work from 1848 to 1871.

I argued in Chapter Two that Marx's concept of the proletariat had its origins in philosophy and in the histories of the French Revolution. Marx's philosophical analysis allowed for only two classes: those who felt alienation as satisfaction, affirmation, and those who felt alienation as loss, deprivation, powerlessness. These two classes were, for Marx, irreconcilable. The two-class model of bourgeois society Marx presented in the *Communist Manifesto* was abandoned in his works of contemporary historical analysis, where the petty bourgeoisie, peasantry and even fractions of classes were accorded significance. In such works, he was concerned with classes as political actors. The consequent sophistication of his class model is due to his plausibly translating political events into class terms (at which, it should be added, he excelled). His propensity for operating with political criteria of social class can be seen when he censured disreputable actions as those of the lumpenproletariat, and when the actions by Paris's 'little people' during 1848 and 1871 made them proletarians in his eyes.

However arbitrary and *ad hoc* Marx's treatment of classes may seem, we should remember that his was a theory not of class as such, but of class formation. Marx saw a dynamic society as the object of his analysis, one in which his conception of class would be realized. In this dynamic conception of the proletariat the political arena played a crucial role. Ralf Dahrendorf argues, and I think rightly, that

This may well be the most important step in Marx's theory of class formation: Classes do not constitute themselves as such until they participate in political conflicts as organized groups.[45]

This is the significance of the transition from the class *in itself* to the class *for itself*, a transition Marx conceived before 1850 as being brought about by a communist seizure of power and the proletariat thrust into the position of rulers, and after 1850 seen by him as linked more closely to the step by step advance of the opposition of labour to capital. After 1850, Marx subordinated the political or praxis-oriented approach to the developing class consciousness of the proletariat to the inexorable laws he believed controlled the destiny of the capitalist economy. In both cases, politics made the proletariat begin to think of itself as representative of the general interest. Politics became important when Marx realized that the proletariat would have to make alliances, especially with the peasantry, if it was to take power. But his stress on politics had another edge: it foreshadowed the development of Marxism after his death, which became chiefly a question of leadership and alliances.

The Revolutions of 1848 and the Paris Commune did little to confirm Marx's conception of the proletariat, but much to enhance his reputation as a theorist of class and the class struggle. Marx subtly changed his theory in the course of explaining why the proletariat could not yet come to power. What remained intact throughout this period of confrontation with reality was Marx's commitment to proletarian revolution. His unswerving faith in the proletariat from 1844 onwards, his interpretation of events to accord with it, and his grasping at the slightest pretext to reinforce it, suggests that the actual proletariat corresponded to a deep commitment made by Marx to the truly human society. Rubel argues that 'The historical mission of the proletariat is neither an economic nor a sociological concept: it is an ethical concept'.[46] Marx was convinced that the victory of the proletariat was a victory for the free, self-determining human. Perhaps he could find no other candidate for the historical role he assigned to the proletariat. Consequently, he believed that only his theory truly represented or expressed the interests of the working class, even when his own relationship to that class was tenuous. In 1865 he wrote to von Schweitzer:

you unfortunately have an official relationship to the General German Workers *Association* (which is very much to be distinguished from working *class*). (OFI,376)

But he was not so keen to reflect on the relations between the International, or himself, and the working class. Against the Proudhonists in the International, he complained that these

Parisians, who as workers in the luxury trades belonged very much to the old muck, without knowing it (OFI,423)

were not truly representative of the working class. Yet he argued that the Paris Commune, the revolt of the 'little people' of Paris, was truly representative of the working class. Where Marx believed that there was confirmation of his views, there was none to be had. The problem was that the 'real movement of the working class' to which Marx appealed in his support, and his conception of the movement of the proletariat, were never identical, and had begun to diverge sharply from at least the time of the First International.

8

The Proletariat as an Economic Class

Marx is perhaps best known as a student of classical political economy, of the political economy of Adam Smith and David Ricardo. Many consider the crowning achievement of his life's work to be *Capital*, of which Marx himself prepared only the first volume for publication (in 1867). Until 1872, when for all practical purposes he ceased major intellectual endeavour, Marx had spent the best part of his adult life engaged in the study of political economy. It was in this field, as he explained in the famous 1859 'Preface' to *A Contribution to the Critique of Political Economy*, that he believed he would find the key to the development of man and society (SW I,502–3). Marx's political economy was not so much an ethical critique of the condition of the worker under capitalism, although it contained such elements, as an investigation of the tendencies and internal tensions of capitalism. His aim was the liberation of capitalism from the constraints of capital itself, which could only occur with the intervention of a conscious working class and the subsequent subordination of economic activity to human ends.

Although Marx's political economy is a great intellectual achievement, and represents the most worked-out and coherent critique of capitalism by any socialist, it is the part of his work which has dated most quickly and fared worst from prolonged criticism. Marxists themselves soon realized that Marx's political economy needed to be clarified, or supplemented, and the theory of imperialism emerged as one supplement. Empirical evidence which suggested that Marx was wrong in certain predictions was discounted,[1] or Marx's theories were reinterpreted to accommodate the evidence. Nowadays, there are criticisms of particular predictions and theories, as well as of Marx's entire approach to political economy.[2] The labour theory of value, the cornerstone of Marx's political economy, is now often held to be 'metaphysical' in the sense of unprovable and non-falsifiable; to be impracticable as a means of accounting or planning in command economies which look to his work for inspiration and guidance; to be unable to account properly for prices of goods; to be unnecessary for his purpose; and to be irrelevant to the real questions of political economy.[3] Debate has arisen about Marx's views on the condition of workers under capitalism: whether he meant that they would be absolutely or relatively impoverished. Ernest Mandel, the (Trotskyist) Marxist economist, has argued that 'The "theory of absolute impoverishment" is not to be found in the works of Marx',[4] although I shall argue below that such a theory can be found in Marx's early political economy. Marx's theory about the tendency of the rate of profit to fall also has its modern exponents and detractors, each appealing to empirical evidence.[5] His predictions about the polarization of society into two great classes, bourgeoisie and proletariat, has proved false: peasants resisted the economic tendencies he believed would ruin them, and a new middle class arose. In some cases, of course, Marx was right and prescient, but perhaps for the wrong reasons: he was right to stress the role of economic crises in periodically disturbing capitalism; he correctly foresaw the tendency to monopoly; and he foresaw the modern divorce of ownership from control, even though, as Dahrendorf among others has argued, it disrupts his essentially legalistic view of property.[6]

While I shall examine some particular aspects of Marx's political economy, I intend to highlight their links with other parts of his works, and to concentrate on the issue whether the class which in his political economy embodies labour is recognisably the same as his 'universal class' of 1844. Marx wrote as if the economic interpretation of social classes was the starting point for any discussion of class, even though his class analysis emerged from philosophy. His only explicit discussion of the concept of class occurs in an unfinished chapter of Volume 3 of *Capital* (C III,885–6), and assumes the predominance of economic factors in the determination of class. Yet the introduction of the concept of the proletariat into Marx's work preceded, even if it was crucial in his move to the study of sociology and political economy. Marx attempted to give his concept of the proletariat an objective, economic basis to account for its speculatively-derived revolutionary role and its ability to transform society and liberate man from alienation. He believed that the development of the actual working class would produce the universal class whose characteristics he had described in 1844. It is now clear that the working class has not, in the century since Marx's death, developed in the way he outlined, and that it is unlikely ever to represent in Marx's sense all of society. But was it apparent that the proletariat as a class developed by the capitalist economy could fulfil the requirements of a universal class? Should it have been clear to Marx himself that he was operating with at least two concepts of the proletariat, concepts which did not fully overlap?

In the second Hegel critique, Marx declared that

The proletariat is coming into being in Germany only as a result of the rising *industrial* development. For it is not the *naturally arising* poor but the *artificially impoverished*, not the human masses mechanically oppressed by the gravity of society but the masses resulting from the *drastic dissolution* of society, mainly of the middle estate, that form the proletariat, although it is obvious that gradually the naturally arising poor and the Christian-Germanic serfs also join its ranks. (CW 3,186–7)

It is not clear from this statement that the proletariat is simply the industrial working class. Social groups whom Marx believed formed his universal class were united by recognising that their suffering was man-made, a result of the advance of industry. It was Engels, not Marx, who was an ethusiast for the 'industrial revolution', as Lichtheim noted, and Engels who saw the modern wage worker as its specific product.[7] While Marx settled philosophical accounts with the Young Hegelians and then with Feuerbach, Engels wrote *The Condition of the Working-Class in England*, one of many such works on the 'social question' and on the 'state of the poor' of that period.[8] Engels probably helped to convince Marx that the industrial working class had the characteristics appropriate for a proletariat, and that it was, economically, the class of the future. Marx soon linked the dynamic of class development (which he had formerly described in abstract terms) to the dynamic of industrial and general economic development.

Marx began in 1844 to read the major works of political economy in French translation. By subjecting them to the human standpoint, he believed, their limitations could be transcended.

From this period come his comments on James Mill's *Elements of Political Economy,* in which he outlined his views on alienation. In its unmediated form, he argued, economic activity was a confirmation of man's essence; under the rule of private property it was a negation of that essence. Where exchange should have confirmed the interdependence of men, within the bounds of private ownership it alienated men from each other and from themselves (CW 3,217).

To say that *man* is estranged from himself, therefore, is the same thing as saying that the *society* of this estranged man is a caricature of his *real community,* of his true species-life, that his activity therefore appears to him as torment, his own creation as an alien power, his wealth as poverty, the *essential bond* linking him with other men as an unessential bond.... (CW 3,217)

In production, according to Marx, men produced alienation; the poverty of the producer (both material and spiritual) was visible proof. This analysis gave rise to a two-class model of society, since

The estrangement of man, and in fact every relationship in which man [stands] to himself, is realised and expressed only in the relationship in which a man stands to other men. (CW 3,277)

For Marx, alienation was not just a psychological but a social problem: if my product confronted me as something alien, it must belong (in a legal sense) to some *other man* (CW 3,278–9).

The relationship of the worker to labour creates the relation of it to the capitalist (or whatever one chooses to call the master of labour). (CW 3,279)

The estranged world of man is divided fundamentally into two categories, labourers and non-labourers, whatever one may wish to call them. There was active and passive alienation. The difference between them is based on a legal title to ownership, a fact which causes difficulties for Marx's later economics.

Alongside this two-class model, derived from his analysis of alienation, Marx adopted in the 1844 Manuscripts the traditional three-class division of classical political economy. In what relation does the model of labourer and non-labourer (an activity model) stand to the model of capital, land and labour (an income model)? In a sense, Marx needs both. The first, to explain why the proletarian—now the paradigmatic estranged man, the producer—

190

struggled to abolish alienation. The second, to give the first an objective, economic basis, and to be able better to locate the proletarians as wage earners. But there exists tensions between the two models, which Marx tried to reconcile with his doctrine of 'productive labour', which draws a distinction between wage earners who are productive (in the sense of producing capital and thus alienation) and wage earners who are unproductive (those who do not supplement the power of capital). Marx also tried to bring the two models together by playing down the differences between capitalists and landowners. He saw both categories as forms of private property: landed property was 'the root of private property' (CW 3,267). But private property was a dynamic relationship, and landed property became large landed property, which 'drives the overwhelming majority of the population into the arms of industry' (CW 3,269). Industrial capital is 'the accomplished objective form of private property' (CW 3,293). Land and capital were forms or moments in the development of private property, industrial capital representing the point at which private property completes its dominion over man (CW 3,293). Marx's two-class model might thus be seen as describing the highest development of private property and the antagonism on which it was based, an ideal type which was also the final historical stage in the development of class society.

In the 1844 Manuscripts, Marx identified the proletarian as 'the man who, being without capital and rent, lives purely by labour, and by a one-sided, abstract labour' (CW 3,241). This proletarian is a wage labourer, whose suffering and lack of private property are combined in the idea that he is estranged—from his products, his activity, his species being, and from other men. The emancipation of the proletariat contains universal human emancipation because the proletariat is 'the complete loss of man' in the sense that

the whole of human servitude is involved in the relation of the worker to production, and all relations of servitude are but modifications and consequences of this relation. (CW 3,280)

Marx here translates his philosophical theses into what he saw as the reality of workers' lives. Lack of private property and universal suffering are now seen as products of the work process itself under the rule of private property. Estranged labour is the source of all human servitude and suffering. This position is certainly consistent with the idea of the proletariat as a universal class, and it makes the suffering of the proletariat more comprehensible (the work relation itself is the crucial element here, and not the atrocious working conditions to which Marx devoted much space in the Manuscripts as well as in *Capital*, even if he thought those conditions were a consequence—necessary or otherwise—of the work relation), but the claim itself is far-reaching, if not outrageous. In the second Hegel critique, the proletariat was universal in that it could represent society and humanity because it had no particular interests. In the 1844 Manuscripts, the proletariat is universal in that its oppression is the source of all oppression.

The consistency with which Marx developed and applied his concept of alienation is reflected in his later decision to treat the worker and capitalist as *personifications* of economic categories (e.g. C I,20–1). Marx believed, as he wrote in *The Holy Family*, that all under the rule of private property presented the same human self-estrangement, but while the capitalist felt strengthened in his estrangement, the worker felt destroyed in his (CW 4,36). Marx wanted to indicate that even the capitalist, no matter how powerful he felt *qua* capitalist, and no matter how comfortable he felt his existence to be, was merely acting out a role determined for him by his position in the process of the production and reproduction of capital.

The idea of capitalism as a self-acting machine, impelled by the dictates of capital, not men, and in which men were mere cogs—whatever their class position—is fundamental to Marx's mature (i.e. post-1857) political economy. It arose partly from the analysis of *capital* in his 1857–58 notebooks, known to us as the *Foundations of the Critique of Political Economy (Rough Draft)* or, simply, the *Grundrisse*. In these, a central division is posited between money and capital. Money, Marx argued, was a product of a highly developed system of exchange, the symbol of the exchange relation which becomes a power external to and independent of the producers (G,146). Simple exchange, he argued, confirmed the social character of production and of man himself, but exchange through the medium of money (expressed as exchange values of products) confronted them as something alien and autonomous. 'In exchange value, the social connection between persons is transformed into a social relation between things' (G,157). The growth of the market, for example, made man ever more interdependent, yet gave rise to the idea that people were completely independent from one another (G,161–2). Thus arose the 'standpoint of the isolated individual' (G,84). Marx promoted communism as a system where men controlled their social relations. But he contrasted money and capital for another reason. The analysis of money, of exchange under capitalism, is sufficient for Marx to demonstrate the estrangement of man from his fellows and from his products, but the analysis of capital, of the abstract relation of production between worker and capitalist, is needed by Marx to explain what drives the system on (to destruction). It is in the *Grundrisse* that the capitalist first appears explicitly as the personification of capital (e.g. G,452). Capital had certain aims *of its own*, according to Marx, aims which explain the development of capitalism. Capital, for example, has a 'universalizing tendency', which makes it strive towards the universal development of the productive forces (G,540). It creates the world market and subordinates all production to itself; it accumulates and concentrates workers; and in trying to extract the maximum wealth from human labour, it introduces ever more machinery into the production process.

The chief aim of capital ('the *production of wealth* itself' (G,541)), however, can only partly be fulfilled by capital, Marx argued. Capital is, at a certain point in its development, a barrier to its own tendencies and aims:

The barrier to *capital* is that this entire development proceeds in a contradictory way, and that the working-out of the productive forces, of general wealth etc., knowledge etc., appears in such a way that the working individual *alienates* himself.... (G,541)

Capital is fundamentally in conflict with itself, as Marx would say, because in its quest to enlarge itself it seeks to diminish and finally to exclude the necessary labour time of workers—the labour time which is a condition of existence (G,543). To put it more bluntly, capital is a human product which seeks to exclude humanity from its development: it wants to be free of man. But capital will only succeed by abolishing itself. Nevertheless, this tendency of capital results in a rationalization of the work process, the introduction of machinery and science, and the reduction of necessary labour time—conditions in which Marx believed man could appropriate his own social forces and thus abolish capital.

Capital, Marx argued, tended to reduce 'human labour, expenditure of energy, to a minimum' (G,701). This, he continued, was a condition of the emancipation of labour. The reduction of necessary labour time, he declared, 'corresponds to the artistic, scientific etc. development of the individuals in the time set free' (G,706). Capital is, 'despite itself, instrumental in creating the means of social disposable time' (G,708), although under its rule it attempts to convert this time into surplus labour. In a human society, this 'free time'—time for the full development of the individual, idle time as well as time for 'higher activity' (G,712)—will be a measure of wealth; under the rule of capital, it is wealth only if it can be converted into labour which augments capital. Capital gives this nominally free time an antithetical, alienated existence: it is a measure of alienation. The distinction between the realms of necessity and freedom, developed by Marx in Volume 3 of *Capital* (C III,820), has its origins in this *Grundrisse* discussion of 'disposable time'.

Marx's discussion of 'capital' in the *Grundrisse* supplied him with a fruitful perspective on the workings of capitalism which did not rely on the intentions of particular individuals; and it supplied a dynamic which is independent of human motivation, much as the dynamic of appearance and essence was independent. It also represents the culmination of an important change is Marx's perspective from 'man' to an alienated social relation. 'Man' or 'species-being' was the subject of the Paris Manuscripts. There, Marx argued that political economy confirmed man's alienation, but that economists were blinded to alienation because they did not see *man* as the beginning, end and purpose of production. While there were echoes of this theme in *Capital*, Marx's analysis centred on the idea that alienated social relations had their own dynamic, and that capital created the conditions for the abolition of all alienated social relations. 'Man' as such almost disappeared from Marx's explanatory schemata, except in so far as 'man' was the embodiment of particular economic categories. Marx wrote in 1867:

My standpoint, from which the evolution of the economic formation of society is viewed as a process of natural history, can less than any other make the individual responsible for relations whose creature he socially remains.... (C I,20–1)

The proletariat only appears in *Capital* as the embodiment and victim of wage labour, and its development as a revolutionary class is subordinated to the struggle between capital and wage labour. Robert Tucker argues that

self-alienated man, who was the central subject of original Marxism, disappears from view in the later version. In fact, mature Marxism is a mental world from which 'man' seems to be absent.[9]

The reason for this disappearance, and one of the central problems with Marx's theory, according to Tucker, is that Marx projects as a social drama what is properly an inner drama.[10] Tucker argues that it is wrong and inappropriate to present alienation as a struggle between classes, as Marx did from at least the time of the Paris Manuscripts. The concept of alienation, however, seems to me to be equally fruitful and overdrawn whether it is treated subjectively, as a psychological state, or objectively, as a social system. The shift, therefore, from alienated man to 'The world as Labour and Capital' (as Tucker puts it),[11] is not an absurd one for Marx to make; and it helps to explain why 'man' rarely appears in his political economy. There, man is chiefly an agent of economic forces which are his own creation, but which have come to control him. The appropriator of man's alienated productive powers would be the proletariat, or wage labour, organized and concentrated by capital, educated by capital, even—to a large extent—created by capital. The proletariat would liberate the universalizing tendencies of capital by abolishing and superseding capital. Marx thus restated an idea he had used against Stirner and other Young Hegelians: the proletarian movement was not dedicated to abstract ideals, but was an actually existing movement realizing the potential inherent in the nature of its condition. So Marx argued that the political victory of the proletariat was essential to realize the potential inherent in the economic category of capital, but which capital itself could not accomplish. In *The Civil War in France*, for example, he declared that the working class

have no ideals to realise, but to set free the elements of the new society with which old collapsing bourgeois society itself is pregnant. (SW II,224)

To the objective development of capital, self-expanding value, Marx added the development of the proletariat in order ultimately to restore the unity of subject and object. As Kolakowski notes, this unity

restores to man his true function as a conscious historical subject, by abolishing the situation in which the results of his free, conscious initiative are turned against himself.[12]

Yet in *Capital* the subjective development of the working class into a revolutionary force is largely assumed to follow from its objective condition as wage labour. The conscious intervention of the proletariat makes way for the inexorable tendencies of capital: tendencies to expansion and periodic crisis. Marx is more concerned to prove that capital cannot realize its own potential, and periodically flounders in its own 'contradictions', than to specify the role of the proletariat in abolishing capital.

In his political economy, Marx described the proletariat as a product of modern industry; it was the only class which could fulfil industry's potential. He avoided the temptation to construct an ahistorical, normative ideal against which to measure society. But Marx retained, as Avineri recognises, the view of man as *homo faber*, creating himself as he creates his product. Avineri adds:

This auto-genesis of man implies not only that man satisfies his needs through his contact with nature, but also that this act creates new needs as well as the possibilities for their satisfaction. Man's needs are thus historical, not naturalistic, and the never-ending dialectical pursuit of their creation and satisfaction constitutes historical development.[13]

In the *Communist Manifesto*, Marx described the proletariat as the 'special and essential product' of modern industry (CW 6,494), chiefly on account of the role of industry in bringing workers together and forming them into a class. In the *Grundrisse*, Marx described the proletariat as a product of capitalism in the sense of being a class of universal needs created and then frustrated by capital. But human needs would triumph.

Mandel has argued that, for Marx, the proletariat was the revolutionary agent of socialism

not so much because of the misery it suffers as because of the place it occupies in the production process and the capacity it thereby possesses to acquire a talent for organization and a cohesion in action which is incommensurable with that of any oppressed class in the past.[14]

But these are clearly not the reasons Marx at first advanced for his choice of the proletariat as the agent of a truly human society. Universality abstractly, not materially, conceived was then its central feature. Marx saw the only hope for human emancipation in the formation (or education) of a class with radical needs. As he distanced himself from the German speculative tradition, and adopted the position that 'being determines consciousness', Marx substituted (although never entirely, as revealed by some of his remarks about the role of communists) formation by industry for formation by educators. The status of radical needs in Marx's theory correspondingly declined, although it always found an echo in his denunciation of factory conditions and in his immiserization thesis (or theses). Barbalet, contrasting Marx's views of the proletariat in the second Hegel critique and in the *Communist Manifesto*, notes that 'The basis of revolutionary emancipation is... differently conceived in each work'.[15] Industry now did the critical work that Marx had earlier expected of philosophy. The fact that Marx never entirely abandoned his radical-needs model of the proletariat gives rise to that tension in his work between conceiving of the proletariat as the bearers of freedom and as the bearers of industrial rationality. In a sense, Marx could not give up the radical-needs model—however untenable it became—without compromising his commitment to freedom. Yet because he shifted the basis of his conception of the proletariat from radical needs to industry, he did not thereby select a new proletariat. Barbalet declares that

the proletariat of the *Introduction* [the second Hegel critique] bears less resemblance to the proletariat of the *Communist Manifesto* than it does to what Marx identified in the latter work as the 'lumpenproletariat'.[16]

It is tempting to make Marx's theory more coherent than it is. But Marx did not discard one model for the next; he held elements of all of them together in an exciting and fruitful tension. Marx never entirely discarded anything. This, in part, is what gave his theory its 'social traction'—its ability to mesh with nineteenth-century European society and to be so influential in it.

From the time of the Paris Manuscripts, Marx believed that man objectified himself in the process of labouring. Under capitalism, however, objectified labour was alienated from the living labourer and confronted him as an independent power. Objectification is necessary but not sufficient for alienation. That objectification appears to the worker to be dispossession is, according to Marx,

a merely *historical* necessity, a necessity for the development of the forces of production solely from a specific historic point of departure, or basis, but in no way an *absolute* necessity of production. (G,831–2)

In the Paris Manuscripts, alienated labour was private property. In the *Grundrisse*, the labourer was alienated from his product as capital: a dynamic relation of 'self-expanding value' (C II,108). Aggrandizement is capital's life-urge. Capital enriches itself by creating surplus labour (G,398), labour that is surplus to that necessary for maintaining the life and labouring capacity of workers. Capital attempts to extract more surplus value in ways which are examined in Volume I of *Capital*.[17] Marx claimed that the demands of capital are at first resisted by workers, who are content merely to eke out an existence. Free labourers were the forbears of the modern proletariat because they were free from feudal obligations and free from possessing the means of production (having been dispossessed of their land); instead of to the labour market, they often turned to beggary, vagabondage and robbery (G,507). Marx explained:

It is a matter of historic record that they tried the latter first, but were driven off this road by gallows, stocks and whippings, onto the narrow path to the labour market; owing to this fact, the [English] *governments*, e.g., of Henry VII, VIII etc. appear as... makers of the conditions for the existence of capital. (G,507)

The role of the state in forcing free labourers to become wage labourers was, Marx suggested, historically necessary because 'in its historic forms... labour always appears as repulsive, always as *external forced labour*' (G,611). But external compulsion is no longer necessary when '*the exchange of capital and labour become in fact formally free*' (G,770), because labour becomes a need for man.

Marx argued that capitalism creates surplus labour as a general need of man; capitalism changes man's nature. Yet capitalism cannot satisfy this need. The proletariat feels this need most strongly, and therefore abolishes capital. Marx put this as follows:

The great historic quality of capital is to *create* this *surplus labour*, superfluous from the standpoint of... mere subsistence; and its historic destiny is fulfilled as soon as, on one side, there has been such a development of needs that surplus labour above and beyond necessity has itself become a general need arising out of individual needs themselves —and, on the other side, when the severe discipline of capital, acting on succeeding generations, has developed general industriousness as the general property of the new species.... (G,325)

Capitalism, Marx believed, drove labour beyond its 'natural paltriness' (G,325) to create the material conditions

for the development of the rich individuality which is as all-sided in its production as in its consumption, and whose labour also therefore appears no longer as labour, but as the full development of activity itself... (G,325)

Capitalism is a historically necessary phase because not only does it create 'universal industriousness' and 'a system of general exploitation of the natural and human qualities' (G,409), but it changes the nature of labour itself. Labour 'becomes attractive work, the individual's self-realization' (G,611) in the first place because machinery has taken over much of labour drudgery (G,701), allowing free time for artistic and scientific pursuits (G,706); and in the second place because the attitude of workers to the product of labour changes when they take power. Although capital kept trying to convert free time into surplus labour (G,708), Marx saw it as having 'an essential civilizing moment' (G,287) which consisted in 'the worker's participation in the higher, even cultural satisfactions' (G,287). Despite his often one-sided presentation of the proletarian's condition, Marx sometimes admitted that the proletarian—unlike the slave—could have cultural needs, agitate for his own interests, subscribe to newspapers, attend lectures and educate his children. Thus Marx could conceive of the workers taking control of their social relations. Slavery could neither prepare slaves to take power, nor create general industriousness (G,326).

The *Grundrisse* presented the proletariat as a class of universal needs. Capital, Marx argued, gave rise to the 'universal appropriation of nature', and nature became simply a matter of utility rather than a power over man.

In accord with this tendency, capital drives beyond national barriers and prejudices as much as beyond nature worship, as well as all traditional, confined, complacent, encrusted satisfactions of present needs, and reproduction of old ways of life. It is destructive towards all of this, and constantly revolutionizes it, tearing down all the barriers which hem in the development of the forces of production, the expansion of needs, the all-sided development of production, and the exploitation and exchange of natural and mental forces. (G,410)

The universalizing tendency of capital expresses, in an alienated way, the tendency towards the universal development of man. But the barrier to universality was capital itself, its own nature (G,410). For capital was, in Marx's terms, 'a moving contradiction' (G,706): based on living labour, yet constantly attempting to abolish it. Modern economic crises, according to Marx, were the means whereby periodically 'this contradiction of capital discharges itself' (G,411).

Capital created the class of universal needs, and the material conditions to satisfy them, but became a barrier to the realization of a truly human society. The knell to capital's doom was labour's recognition of 'the products as its own, and the judgement that its separation from the conditions of its realization is improper' (G,463). Marx argued that capital must be recognized as a social relation rather than a thing: 'The capitalist produces the worker, and the worker the capitalist' (G,458). The role of conscious intervention by workers in the liberation of man was not diminished by Marx's concentration on the objective movement of capital. His study of the laws of motion of capitalism was not meant to indicate that capitalism could develop of itself into socialism, nor that capitalism would entirely collapse (whatever that might mean), but that capital finally exposed itself as the essential barrier to universality and the satisfaction of human needs.

What, then, would abolish capitalism? The answer from Marx's political economy was 'the wage earners'. Marx contrasted wage labour and capital in his works from the Paris Manuscripts to *Capital*, employing the usual categories of political economy. Wage labourers were certainly propertyless, if by property one meant the means of production. But Marx did not consider all the propertyless to be proletarians, since he excluded vagabonds and other ragamuffins in *The German Ideology*. The wage labourer also suffered, in Marx's estimation, not just in the prosaic senses that he recorded in *Capital*, the Paris Manuscripts and *Wage Labour and Capital* (1849) from work conditions, but in the sense that man's work under capital was not his self-realization but a sacrifice of his life. Not all wage labourers, however, were alienated or productive in his view. In the *Grundrisse* Marx distinguished between productive and unproductive labourers; only productive labourers (we may infer) were proletarians, for only they were alienated. Proletarians were productive in the sense that they created capital.

The distinction between productive and unproductive labourers does not correspond to Marx's earlier distinctions between proletarians and ragamuffins and between proletarians and lumpenproletarians (which was chiefly political). Its essence lies in the notion that the productive labourer sells to the capitalist his labour power (his capacity for labouring), while the unproductive labourer sells to the capitalist (or any buyer he meets in the marketplace) the products of his labour. Thus the capitalist does not confront the unproductive labourer as a capitalist, but merely as a buyer. The capitalist as capitalist buys labour power in the market and uses it to create surplus value and thus more capital; productive labour augments capital (G,272). Of unproductive labour, Marx wrote:

From whore to pope, there is a mass of such rabble. But the honest and 'working' lumpenproletariat belongs here as well; e.g., the great mob of porters etc. who render service in seaport cities etc. (G,272)

It is not what (use value) the worker produces which makes him productive, but whether he produces surplus value for the capitalist: '*Labour becomes productive only by producing its own opposite*' (G,305n). Similar points are made in *Capital*.[18] Whether or not by locating precisely the alienated labourer, the agent of social change, Marx limits severely the number of workers who can be considered proletarians is a much-debated point.[19]

All wage earners, Marx implied, suffer under the rule of capital. He often highlighted the 'crippling effects', to both body and mind, of the division of labour; in *Capital* he drew evidence for his claims from British Blue Books, reports of Government inspectors into factory conditions. Marx declared:

In its blind unrestrainable passion, its were-wolf hunger for surplus-labour, capital oversteps not only the moral, but even the merely physical maximum bounds of the working-day.... Capital cares nothing for the length of life of labour-power. All that concerns it is simply and solely the maximum of labour-power, that can be rendered fluent in a working-day. It attains this end by shortening the extent of the labourer's life.... (C I,252–3)

Capital, he concluded, is 'altogether too prodigal with its human material' (C III,86). Yet Marx's sweeping statements on this issue overstate his case. The passion of capital is not unrestrainable: it can and was restrained by state laws, as Marx admitted; and by its very nature, discussed above, it cannot do away with its human base.[20] On the one hand, Marx claimed that capital separates society into two great classes, capitalist and proletariat, the latter growing ever larger; on the other hand, he claimed that capital tended to destroy the proletariat physically as well as morally.

Marx's conception of man as a species-being included the notion that man had a universal essence which was frustrated in its expression by particularity, by external determination. Man's universal needs could be fulfilled only when the contrast between appearance and essence had reached such an intensity that the proletariat felt annihilated and would be forced to destroy particularity. Capitalism, Marx believed, developed the contrast between man's needs and his ability to fulfil them, and his existence. The proletarian was not just a product of this process, but was able to apprehend it, and to act to fulfil humanity. The labourer 'comes out of the process of production other than he entered it' (C I,285).

Marx poured economic and social content into his philosophical concepts because he believed that his philosophy was an expression of the real world. Alienation, for example, had its source in the economic organization of capitalism, and could be expressed in political economy. Hence the title of Marx's 1844 Manuscripts: the *Economico-Philosophical Manuscripts*. Poverty, Marx implied there, was a visible confirmation of alienation; because man objectified himself in his products, and because they were alienated from him, the more he produced the less he was. This thesis was the foundation for his arguments about the immiserization of the worker under capitalism. Marx claimed that the development of political economy involved the progressive realization that labour was the source of wealth. As he put it, the recognition that 'the subjective essence of private property is labour' (CW 3,290) was the result of enlightened political economy. The physiocrats, Marx explained, had already transferred the subjective essence of wealth to man, but had restricted it to a particular type of productive labour: agricultural labour. They had not yet grasped labour 'in its generality' (CW 3,292); enlightened political economy had. Now, he argued, this insight must be further developed so that alienated labour could be abolished. But classical political economy, Marx suggested from the time of the Paris Manuscripts, was limited by its persistent attempts to establish the unity of capital and labour (CW 3,312), instead of seeing them as an evolving unity of opposites. Capital, he declared, is 'objective labour as exclusion of labour' (CW 3,294).

Marx was obliged to defend some sort of immiserization thesis, based on the idea that the worker is less the more he produces. But as even Marxists acknowledge, he began to shift between two types of argument once he had seen that wages could and did increase. The first is the argument for *absolute* impoverishment: that real wages of workers decrease absolutely under capitalism. The second is the familiar argument for *relative* impoverishment: that even if the workers' wages increase, the workers' position relative to that of the capitalists and their profit is worse.[21] In 1849, Marx explained that wages could increase, and he attributed the quiescence of English workers at the time to an upturn in the economic situation. He still believed that a rise in real wages was atypical, as he did in 1867, when he published the first volume of *Capital*. Marx argued that workers were paid only enough to sustain themselves as workers and to reproduce their class. Workers were commodities, and thus they cost whatever their working capacity cost to produce. We might expect that because capitalism tends to make commodities cheaper (by the application of rational methods of production, machinery, etc.) the costs of the production and reproduction of the working class would fall, and that even if wages fell the worker could maintain and might even increase his real wages.[22] But Marx did not consider this argument. He saw falling wages as a decline in workers' living standards; and he saw rising wages as merely sustaining the worker as a commodity in a situation where commodity prices were rising.

In 1865, however, Marx took a different tack on the immiserization thesis. Having already rejected Lassalle's formulation of the 'Iron Law of Wages', which postulated a steady decline in wages (without, however, considering possible decreases in prices), he rose to the defence of trade union activities as necessary to maintain and even increase wages. *Wages, Price and Profit* was a short course in political economy delivered by Marx to members of the First International. It was written to refute the view of Weston that workers would not gain by the actions of trade unions. Weston reasoned that even if workers managed to win wage rises, the prices of products would increase by at least the same rate, leaving them no better off. In *The Poverty of Philosophy*, Marx examined and rejected socialist objections to workers' combinations (CW 6,210). Combination itself was a gain, he had argued. This was now a secondary point. The everyday struggle against capitalism, he added in 1865, was linked with the 'larger movement' for working class power, even though trade unions were limited by working within the wages system rather than trying to abolish it (SW II,75–6). But Marx insisted that trade unions were not only necessary to maintain wages: they could also gain a real increase in living standards for workers. Marx qualified the argument by saying that such gains would be neither long-lived nor significant. Capitalism, he declared, tended 'to cast down the whole working class to degradation' (SW II,69), and could only be checked by the action of organized workers. But how could trade unions preside over an increase in workers' living standards? The worker will, Marx claimed axiomatically, on average only receive the value of his labour-power (SW II,71). But the value of labour-power has two dimensions: physical and historical-social. By this innovation, Marx meant that to produce and reproduce the worker requires a certain material minimum (of food, shelter, etc.), the fulfilment of which has a historically conditioned element (the modern suburban worker will not live in a tent, even though the tent supplies his basic need for shelter), and that the worker develops needs which must be met so that his labour-power is available to augment capital. Thus Marx can explain away any wage increase, no matter how large, by claiming that the historical-social needs of labour-power have increased such that the rise in wages just meets those needs. Marx's argument that the labourer receives enough wages only to sustain and reproduce his labour-power is unassailable because it is circular. That Marx argued that the labourer develops new needs under capitalism tends also to undermine one of the central points of his political economy: that the labourer is a commodity.[23]

In Volume I of *Capital*, Marx distinguished between *necessary* and *natural* wants. A worker's natural wants vary from country to country, and consist of the minimum required to sustain his life and class. But his necessary wants are a product of historical development:

In contradistinction therefore to the case of other commodities, there enters into the determination of the value of labour-power a historical and moral element. (C I,168)

In whatever manner he chose to defend it, and however he tried to maintain it in the face of increasing living standards of workers, Marx was unshakeably committed to an immiserization thesis. But the idea on which it was based, that capital is alienated labour, does not necessarily support immiserization. Marx claimed, for example, in the Paris Manuscripts that the worker's wretchedness is in *inverse proportion* to the magnitude of his production (CW 3,270). The more value he creates, the more valueless becomes the worker; the better formed his product, the more deformed is the worker; the more civilized his object, the more barbarous becomes the worker (CW 3,273). Marx's political economy was, in part, an attempt mathematically to reformulate this thesis on alienation. In the *Grundrisse*, Marx added that

Only in the mode of production based on capital does pauperism appear as the result of labour itself, of the development of the productive force of labour. (G,604)

Yet the idea of alienated labour does not lead to an immiserization thesis. Marx's reasoning here involved a *non sequitur*. For Marx believed that man's capacity to labour was not a finite quantity, from which every day a certain amount was deducted and placed over and against him. The process of production involved only a temporary diminution of the individual labourer's capacity. The labourer over time, and the working class as a whole, was not diminished by its labour. (The fact that in a different context Marx argued that labour created new needs for man indirectly supports this assertion.) If labour is an infinite capacity of man, it cannot be diminished by its finite products, even if these products come to dominate labour. Relatively speaking, the increasing amounts of wealth created by the worker when compared with his own direct share in that wealth, or his exchange for it, make him less wealthy individually (rather than relatively poorer), but such a situation will obtain even in communist society. 'Dead' labour tends always to increase in relation to living labour—Marx's communism and the realm of freedom are based on it. Relative immiserization, and only in an individual sense, is on the one hand not very helpful in explaining worker rebelliousness, and on the other hand, a bromide. The immiserization thesis had a certain plausibility for the beginning of the nineteenth century, when wages were being forced down, but it increasingly lost relevance, and it seems in no way a necessary feature of capitalism. It was, in any case, a peripheral issue (tactically important, perhaps) in Marx's theory. The real issue for Marx was that man's products should be subordinate to his will: not that man should cease producing value surplus to his immediate requirements for life, but that he should be able to control the use to which that surplus value was put.

Having adopted the labour theory of value, Marx had to solve the following problem: how, respecting the laws of exchange, could production of exchange values solely determined by labour-time result in the exchange value of labour (i.e. the cost of wages, etc.) being less than the exchange value of labour's product? How, that is, did profit arise? Systematic theft by capitalists, and buying cheap to sell dear were full explanations precluded by the premiss that, in general, the law of exchange (of an equal for an equal) was respected under capitalism. To solve the problem, Marx made a distinction in the *Grundrisse* between labour and labour-power. The worker exchanged his labour-power (or capacity to labour) for a wage: at one level, a fair exchange. But the worker thus gave up the use value of his commodity (labour-power) to his employer. The unique feature of labour-power, according to Marx, was that its use value consisted in creating more exchange value than was necessary to produce itself. Thus the capitalist buys a commodity which creates value. The laws of exchange are formally satisfied, and the source of surplus value is reaffirmed to be labour.

This theory of surplus value was a rather neat solution to a major problem of classical political economy within its own framework. It also reversed a belief Marx had held strongly until the 1850s, that the wage relationship between worker and capitalist made capitalism transparent to analysis by the workers. In the *Manifesto*, Marx had argued that capitalism was characterized by 'naked, shameless, direct, brutal exploitation' (CW 6,487). In the *Grundrisse*, he suggested that exploitation was much more complex. Wages, in fact, disguised the relations between men:

we may understand the decisive importance of the transformation of value and price of labour-power into the form of wages, or into the value and price of labour itself. This phenomenal form, which makes the actual relation invisible, and, indeed, shows the direct opposite of that relation, forms the basis of all the juridical notions of both labourer and capitalist, of all the mystifications of the capitalistic mode of production, of all its illusions as to liberty, of all the apologetic shifts of the vulgar economists. (C I,505–6)

For this reason Marx revived the distinction between appearance and essence, arguing that it was the task of the true scientist to expose the difference between them. Far from science being, as in *The Poverty of Philosophy*, merely a question of looking before one's eyes, it became for Marx a matter of the most serious, specialized inquiry. He declared that 'all science would be superfluous if the outward appearance and the essence of things directly coincided' (C III,817). It seems curious that in the pre-1850 period, when Marx promoted the role of a communist party (in what some see as his Leninist phase),[24] he denied the existence of any specialized knowledge to which the workers could not have access; yet as a political economist after 1850, he argued that the appearance of capitalism was a systematic illusion which could only be pierced by specialized knowledge, while he supported broadly-based political organizations of workers. Leninism proper, however, involves a restricted political organization based on 'socialist consciousness' which was denied to the majority of workers.

For Marx, capitalism was a system where the innately social character of activities appeared to individuals as alien (G,157):

In the money relation... the ties of personal dependence, of distinctions of blood, education, etc. are in fact exploded, ripped up...; and individuals *seem* independent.... (G,163)

But money is a social relation, so the individual 'carries his social power, as well as his bond with society, in his pocket' (G,157). Money as a universal equivalent, however, produces a respect for equality and freedom: they are 'the idealized expressions' of capital-ist exchange, which does not countenance plunder or direct compulsion (G,245). Despite its appearance, Marx claimed, wage labour is still forced labour. Formally, the relation between worker and capitalist 'has the equality and freedom of exchange as such', but this is a deception (G,464). Marx stressed that the working class was formed, at least in England, initially on the basis of state compulsion. This coercion was lifted, he believed, because

The advance of capitalist production develops a working-class, which by education, tradition, habit, looks upon the conditions of that mode of production as self-evident laws of Nature. The organisation of the capitalist process of production, once fully developed, breaks down all resistance.... The dull compulsion of economic relations completes the subjection of the labourer to the capitalist. (C I,689)

Where earlier systems were 'simple and transparent' (C I,83), cap-italism was opaque. Thus the proletarian saw his labour-power as a commodity, its sale and purchase taking place in the sphere of the 'innate rights of man' wherein rule Freedom, Equality, Property and Bentham (C I,172). In this realm surplus value is extracted from the worker as the right of the capitalist, and as an example of equal exchange. The wage relation, for Marx, 'conceals the unrequited labour of the wage-labourer' (C I,505). The labourer's belief in his independence is maintained by the changes in employer he can make, and the 'fictio juris' of a contract, yet the worker is bound to his 'owner' by 'invisible threads' (C I,538).

In *Capital*, Marx argued that the realm of the material and social relations between men under capitalism was an 'enchanted and per-verted world' (C III,827). Even the greatest of the classical political economists remained 'more or less in the grip of the world of illusion' which, he claimed, 'their criticism had dissolved' (C III,830)—a rather idealist claim. They had been scientists and ideologists: their science had begun to destroy the illusions of cap-italism, while their adherence to a bourgeois standpoint made them fall into 'inconsistencies, half-truths and unsolved contradictions' (C III,830). This discussion of appearance and essence raises a question about Marx's conception of ideology. If ideology is the representa-tion of things as they appear to be, what is the relation between ideology and illusion or distortion? Was the representation of the world by ideologists such as the political economists distorted, or did they accurately reflect a distorted world? Marx tended toward the former explanation in *The German Ideology*, where he did not employ the distinction between appearance and essence; he tended toward the latter in *Capital*. Marx increasingly came to consider reality as complex and opaque, not simple and transparent. It was not enough to be a worker, as he had supposed in the *Communist Manifesto*, to see through capitalism; critical political economy had an essential role to play.

Marx's political economy was an attempt to translate his philosophical theses about man's subordination to his own products into an empirical and scientific analysis of material life. Marx often denoted capital as a form of alienated labour by using the term 'dead labour' in its stead. Being transformed labour-power was not the unique property of capital: it was the property of every human product. Capital, however, was dead labour that stood opposed to living labour, confronted it as its negation. Because of its power over living labour, Marx likened capital to a vampire (e.g. C I,224). Capital had an independent, objective and verifiable dynamic; it dominated man in order to augment itself. Marx wrote of its life-process:

Accumulate, accumulate! That is Moses and the prophets!... Accumulation for accumulation's sake, production for production's sake.... (C I,558)

Thus capital tended towards extensional universality (in the creation of the world market), and gave rise to the felt need for the intensional universality of the individual, a need it could not fulfil. Capitalism needed mobile labour, since workers and capital were thrown from one industry to another depending on the state of conditions for the reproduction of capital (C I,457). And while modern industry developed on the basis of an intense division of labour, it eventually 'sweeps away by technical means the manufacturing division of labour' (C I,454), which had crippled and enslaved the worker.

Modern Industry, indeed, compels society, under penalty of death, to replace the detail-worker of today, crippled by life-long repetition of one and the same trivial operation, and thus reduced to a mere fragment of a man, by the fully developed individual, fit for a variety of labours, ready to face any change of production, and to whom the different social functions he performs, are but so many modes of giving free scope to his own natural and acquired powers. (C I,458)

Marx implied that this could only occur when the working class had taken power, and thus that the worker—by freeing himself from capital's domination—was fulfilling an imperative of modern industry. In Marx's political economy, it is not always clear whether the proletariat frees production from capital in order to free itself, or frees itself in order to free production from capital. Capital tends to abolish the division of labour, according to Marx, and to create 'a system of general social metabolism, of universal relations, of all-round needs and universal capacities' (G,158). Only the proletariat, however, could realize these tendencies and liberate man. But was the proletariat the carrier of freedom, or the carrier of industrial rationalization?

Marx never claimed that capital could abolish itself: its universalizing tendencies were held in check by its own nature. Capital tends, for example, to an unlimited expansion of production, but this expansion 'comes continually into conflict with the limited purpose, the self-expansion of existing capital' (C III,250). Because of the centralizing and reproductive tendencies of capital, Marx argued, joint-stock companies had begun to form to control the large amounts of capital needed by the system. 'This is the abolition of the capitalist mode of production within the capitalist mode of production itself' (C III,438). Private industry declines, the capitalist functions as 'a mere manager, administrator of other people's capital' (C III,436), and production begins to become social production, although in a contradictory form (C III,439–40). Capital was tending towards social property. Furthermore, co-operative factories proved to Marx that necessary supervision and management could be undertaken by workers, that the capitalist was functionally redundant, and that supervision could be separated from its capitalist form (C III,387):

The co-operative factories of the labourers themselves represent within the old form the first sprouts of the new....[T]he antithesis between capital and labour is overcome within them, if at first only by way of making the associated labourers into their own capitalist.... (C III,440)

Capital created the needs and the possibilities for their fulfilment, but until capital was abolished—until the relations between men had been consciously changed, and their products brought under their control—none of these tendencies could transcend its capitalist bounds.

The abolition of this realm of inhuman abstractions required the conscious intervention of a human agency. In Marx's political economy, this agency is the human embodiment of 'labour': the working class. Two central questions arise here. The first is whether this working class is capable of appropriating and directing the productive forces. The second is whether this working class is the same class as the proletariat of Marx's earlier philosophical and political writings. It is not necessarily crucial in this respect that the term 'proletariat' rarely appears in Marx's political economy, and that Marx adopted much of the language of classical political economy as his own. If the language of social analysis was French, the language of political economy was English. In *The Poverty of Philosophy*, Marx explained for the benefit of his French audience that the 'capitalist class [is] the bourgeoisie' (CW 6,185). But is it? Marx used different criteria to define classes in different areas of his work (and sometimes even in the same area). In his political economy, the working class is variously identified as the non-owners (in a formal, legal sense) of the means of production, the wage earners, the workers, the productive workers and the exploited. All categories were based on two assumptions, or claims: that the proletariat was poverty incarnate, and that it was the majority class. Marx used law, source of income, and alienation of their product as capital, as the major means of distinguishing proletarian from capitalist. These criteria, however, produce different results—they are not compatible with each other, nor with the idea of a majority, impoverished class.

When Marx, in Volume 3 of *Capital*, came to discuss the concept of class, he did not—and probably he could not—finish it. He began (in a rather conventional way for classical political economy) by declaring that

The owners merely of labour-power, owners of capital, and land-owners, whose respective sources of income are wages, profit and ground-rent, in other words, wage-labourers, capitalists and land-owners, constitute then three big classes of modern society based on the capitalist mode of production. (C III,885)

211

What makes these constitute three great classes, Marx asks rhetorically? Is it 'the identity of revenues and sources of revenue' (C III,886)? If that were so, he explained, then physicians and officials would form separate classes, as would many others in different occupations. So, he added, would landlords be split according to the type of land they owned: vineyards, farms, forests etc. At this point the manuscript breaks off. Thus Marx at first equated ownership with sources of income, and then separated them. He introduced another criterion of social class—the quality of being a 'distinct social group' (such as physicians and officials form). Yet Marx's actual question was *not* 'What makes a social class?', but 'What makes wage-labourers, capitalists and landlords constitute the three great social classes?' (C III,886) Even if Marx had argued that there were many social classes (on whatever grounds), he might still have been able to make a case for there being only three 'great classes'. Marx's only explicit discussion of classes disappointingly conflated a number of issues.

Marx did not simply use different criteria to demarcate classes, he used the concept of class for different purposes. In classical political economy, 'class' was used as a means of classification, a tool of analysis. Marx inherited this usage, but wanted 'class' to do much more. He believed that the politico-economic determination of class—about who'se precise criteria he could not decide—had a direct parallel, in fact produced effects, in the political sphere. The more the working class developed as an economic class, the more it would become, he believed, a class *for itself*, ready to defend its interests politically. But the intrinsic link between economic and political spheres was never properly established by Marx, and while he made the reasonable point that economic crises produced social disasters for sections of the population and were often related to political disturbances, it was not the actual working class which was most active in such disturbances. As Frank Parkin has put it,

the perennial problem for Marxism... [is] how to account for the awkward discrepancies between classes defined as embodiments of productive relations and classes as active political agencies.[25]

Marx's 1847 analysis of the transformation of the class *in itself* into a class *for itself*—an ability which distinguished proletariat from peasantry—was based as much on a philosophical conception of the development of concepts as on an intuitive grasp of the union of workers into trade unions and thence into political parties.

While the class which embodied (productive) labour in Marx's political economy may have had only a tenuous relation to the proletariat of his philosophical and political works, could it nevertheless take over the functions of capital? Could it destroy the rule of capital over man? Marx believed that it could, but the evidence from his political economy is meagre. He held that co-operative factories were a sign of the future, a sign that the capitalist was functionally redundant.[26] But although Marx suggested that capital had replaced enterprise, innovation and risk in production for supervision and control, he did not directly argue that capital developed the supervisory qualities of the proletariat. In the struggle of labour against capital, labour seemed to develop only those qualities needed for opposition, not those for a new ruling class. As Sorel put it, Marx did not see that an ethic of the producers as producers was required for the proletariat. Perhaps it was because Marx considered that production would become a value for its own sake once man was freed from dire necessity and that, in Tucker's words, Marx thought of communism 'in terms of the transformation of economics into aesthetics'.[27] The proletariat would become as artists. But did the proletariat have the enterprise and initiative to destroy capitalism?

9

Conclusion

Lenin's observation that the three sources of Marxism are 'German philosophy, English political economy and French socialism'[1] has become a commonplace. Yet his perspicacity on this issue is confirmed by Marx's concept of the proletariat, which combines elements of each source, while remaining (as Lenin implicitly perceived of all three) chiefly conceptual. If we are properly to understand Marx's proletariat, we must recognize that it was largely the product of an abstract theoretical development, and that it played a vital role in the formation and elaboration of Marx's theory. It was not the product of empirical investigation. To know something substantial about the actual nineteenth-century proletariat, we would do better to look elsewhere than to Marx. This study has shown that, on the whole, Marx's proletariat remained abstract and conceptual.

Marx's proletariat was an innovation which has made a lasting impression on socialism. While most other socialists believed that socialism needed the assistance of well-meaning bourgeois, or the plots of small, secret societies, Marx held that the proletariat was the key agent in the elimination of capitalism. For most other socialists, the idea of socialism represented the reconciliation of classes; for Marx it consisted in their abolition. He saw the proletariat not simply as among the beneficiaries of socialism, but as its creator. Marx was not always clear or consistent about the means of achieving socialism, or about the relations between the proletariat and its leaders, but he maintained that a proletarian revolution would usher in a classless society. This paradoxical combination of victorious class and classless sequel was based on an abstract conception of the proletariat as the representative of all mankind, and was a touchstone of his theory.

If Marx's concept of the proletariat was a puzzle to other socialists, however, it continued a trend in French social and political

214

theorizing which began at least with Siéyès. From about the time of the French Revolution, social and political thought had become involved with the promotion of the interests of certain social groups. Social and political theory as an expression of the interests of such groups seemed to supplant those theories which appealed to reason or to the general interest. I have already pointed to the parallel between the concept of the proletariat in Marx's early works and Siéyès' Third Estate; but Saint-Simon advocated in similar terms the cause of the *industriels*. In his *Catéchisme des Industriels*, Saint-Simon asked: 'Why does the industrial class, which should occupy the first rank, find itself occupying the last? Why are those who, in effect, are first, ranked last?'[2] Saint-Simon, Siéyès and Marx were each responding to the enormous social changes taking place in their time, changes which they analysed differently, but which they thought merited recognition in other spheres. Each perceived, and wanted to redress, a sort of imbalance in the basic institutions of society. Each sought, in particular, political recognition for the class they believed had become the leading class or the class of the future. Each preserved the notion that the proper recognition of his chosen class would serve the general interest. In this respect they did not break from the past. The fruit of their theories, perhaps, is the conception now prevalent that the state is a balance sheet on which is written the changing fortunes of various sectional interests.

As a theorist, Marx was a great synthesizer. Without his abstract conception of the proletariat, however, such synthesis would hardly have been possible. As Tom Bottomore and Maximilien Rubel have argued, Marx's concept of the proletariat was a means 'to transform speculative philosophy into a critical social theory'.[3] Elsewhere, Bottomore described Marx's concept of the proletariat as the means by which 'Marx was able to bring together the two strands of his thought—positivist and Hegelian'.[4] Marx's proletariat was also the foundation for his extraordinary optimism:

This communism... is the *genuine* resolution of the conflict between man and nature and between man and man—the true resolution of the strife between existence and essence, between objectification and self-confirmation, between freedom and necessity, between the individual and the species. (CW 3,296)

His attempt to transform Hegel's speculative account of the realization of the Idea in history into the history of man's self-emancipation required, theoretically, an expression of self-alienation in its extreme form, and practically, its embodiment in a social force. Marx chose to name these heirs of history 'the proletariat', although the theoretical imperatives of their role had a logical and chronological priority over the material requirements.

Marx's project was born in speculation, not sociology, and his choice of the proletariat as the universal class may have been based on a misunderstanding or confusion. The revolutionary actions and advanced consciousness which Marx attibuted to the proletariat were his glosses on artisan unrest at advancing industrialization and the fear of loss of skill and status, or on actions of the Paris *menu peuple*, rather than expressions of opposition to capitalism by industrial workers. Events since Marx's death (and, indeed, before it) suggest that a social group with all the characteristics his theory required has not come into being. States created in Marx's name have had their origins in the coups of vanguard parties or in military conquest; advanced, industrialized countries have remained largely immune from the ideology of the proletarian revolution. Even though socialist states have done more than any other system to create a class of privation and misery, organized in large-scale industry and provided with a sort of class consciousness, a Marxian proletariat is yet to emerge. In fact, Marxism after Marx has been a series of attempts to come to terms, theoretically and practically, with the actual working class.

Is the failure of a revolutionary proletariat yet to appear inherent in Marx's concept of the proletariat? Could Marx's requirements for such a class ever be fulfilled? Marx's difficulty, I have argued, stems from the fact that he tried to reconcile three different models of the proletariat, each of which had its own problems. Marx believed that the philosophical, political and economic models of the proletariat were simply aspects of one whole, and consequently he shifted from one to another whenever disagreeable evidence in one area seemed threatening. Because of these shifts, and his use of *ad hoc* theories in particular cases, Marx's conception of the proletariat was not just unfalsifiable, but created confusion even among some of his followers. Ralph Miliband, for example, conceded that

216

In fact, it is quite *difficult* to find out precisely what Marx meant by the terms 'working class' or 'proletariat'; and later [Marxist] work has not advanced matters very far.[5]

Marx developed his concept of the proletariat in the context of a speculative approach to the dialectic of universal and particular. The proletariat, Marx concluded, was intrinsically universal in that it was the class most alienated from the human essence, and the class whose emancipation included the emancipation of all humanity. Although the philosophical construction of this universal class was primary, Marx set the limits to its social location and declared his entry into the socialist tradition by his use of the—increasingly widespread but generally ill-defined—term 'proletariat'. In the years which followed, he tried to provide an account of the proletariat and its necessary development to class consciousness and revolutionary action. Instead, however, Marx identified revolutionary groups of people (particularly the Paris *menu peuple*) with the proletariat; he identified wage labourers, and then productive labourers, with the proletariat, even though there appeared to be little link between them and revolutionary sections of the population. Marx did not properly integrate the political, economic and philosophical spheres of his conception of the proletariat, and each has an independent dynamic in his work.

The economic development of the working class from a group of competing individuals to a cohesive and assertive class, acting in and for its own interests, which Marx painted in terms of the development of trade unions, workers' political parties and communist consciousness, has its origins and its ultimate rationale in a speculative doctrine of essences: the transformation of the class *in itself* into the class *for itself*. Revolutionary actions had, despite Marx's analyses, little to do with his proletariat. Marx could also switch from one model of the proletariat to another, as we have seen him do in 1850, to save the coherence of his analysis. His optimism about revolution in Europe early in 1850 was based on his belief in the cumulative effect of revolutionary consciousness upon the proletariat, a political dynamic which was (somehow) completely undermined when Marx began to look closely at the economic recovery.

Marxists have tried to put Marx's relatively independent models of the proletariat into some sort of causal hierarchy. But while it has become popular to say that the proletariat has an objective economic determination, which ultimately 'produces' revolutionary consciousness and organization, it is by no means clear that Marx thought consistently in this way. Nor is it clear just what the economic boundaries of the proletariat are, as the debate over 'productive' and 'unproductive' labour demonstrates. I prefer to consider Marx as having different spheres of the concept 'proletariat', spheres which no doubt overlapped, but—to continue this spatial metaphor—overlapped more in the manner of a Venn diagram than concentric circles. Marx's attempt to link classes objectively defined with the outlook of individuals, through the unfortunate proposition 'existence determines consciousness', has generated a species of problems for modern sociology of the type 'class structure versus class consciousness'. And Marx himself spent most of his life as a communist explaining why events had not gone as his theory predicted; the clearest example of this was his response to the 1848 Revolutions, where he drew new class distinctions and ultimately reasserted a historical determinism. Marx kept turning practical defeats into intellectual victories, but always at the expense of the coherence of his theory. His own procedure, complemented by his creative intellect, seems to underlie the confidence displayed by many Marxists that their theory can absorb every change of circumstance without doing violence to its fundamental position.

Having stressed the speculative origins of Marx's concept of the proletariat throughout this work, in order to underline his dim appreciation of the nature of the empirical working class and his theoretical manoeuvering in response to empirical difficulties, the speculative framework of Marx's theory needs also to be examined. Here, I believe, lies one of its major weaknesses. For Marx, the proletariat was the universal class; 'universality' was a concept which he employed in all areas of his work. He took the concept of universality from German philosophy and applied it in the analysis of politics and economics. He did not examine closely the problems associated with the idea, or with his particular speculative treatment of it. As Plamenatz wrote, Marx was a man excited by ideas, whose 'German education' had 'filled and excited his mind much more than it increased his power to control and order his thoughts: these things blinded him to his defects'.[6] Marx took the concept of universality most directly from Hegel, but changed it in a very important sense. Instead of a system of particularity and universality, a system held together by mediators, Marx came in 1843 consistently to the view that true universality consisted in the abolition of particularity. He cut through the complexities of Hegel's view of social life. Marx's 'universal class', which was set the task of abolishing particularity rather than of trying to mediate universality and particularity, was thus a solution to a rather simplified problem. In a sense, Marx solved the problems of the modern world by a theoretical sleight of hand. The issue, therefore, is not whether the proletariat embodies particularity and thus cannot emancipate humanity—Marx maintained that the proletariat had material interests, not particular interests. The issue is rather whether Marx's theoretical framework—from which he derived the specifications of his 'universal class'—is adequate to comprehend the problems of the real world. I am firmly of the view that it was not.

Marx added to his thoroughgoing speculative conception of universality two central distinctions when he came to employ the concept in his political and economic works. The first was between intensional and extensional universality: universality which expressed the nature of a thing, or which described its extent. The second was between intrinsic and revolutionary universality: universality derived from the nature of a class (a property exclusive to the proletariat), and universality expressed by the successful revolutionary role of a class (which included its ability to form alliances, and was not confined to the proletariat). In the case of the proletariat, according to Marx, intrinsic universality had to be translated into revolutionary universality. This involved, among other things, presentation by the proletariat of its demands in a general form which could appeal to other parts of society as an expression of the general interest. The proletariat was society's true representative, but it had to be acknowledged as such. Politics was thus an important medium for the expression of universality, and after a brief period in which he rejected politics as enshrining the dominance of human will and as leading to unnecessary violence,

Marx embraced the political form as a means for the proletariat to realize and act upon its universality.

But Marx wrote as if the transformation from intrinsic to revolutionary universality was paralleled by the development of the extensional universality of the proletariat. Intensional and extensional universalities are logically discrete, and there is no necessary development from the former into the latter. Yet Marx conflated the two. He implied, for example, that if the proletariat were extensionally universal (on the basis of empirical analysis) they must also be intensionally universal. The proletariat as a 'world-historical class' was an expression, in politico-economic terms, of the proletariat's (extensional) universality, and had no necessary correlation with its nature. Marx erred in believing that empirical analysis could establish the nature of a thing. By treating the two dichotomies (intrinsic, revolutionary; and intensional, extensional) as similar, or parallel, Marx took empirical evidence as proof for an existential problem. That the workers were the vast majority of society—however arguable the proposition—was irrelevant to their human condition, even though it helped to accustom some of the Marxist parties of the Second International to formal democracy as a means of taking power.

Apart from these conceptual difficulties with the proletariat, there are related problems with Marx's idea of social class. Because he moved, perhaps unwittingly, from one model of the proletariat to another, Marx obscured the non-revolutionary nature of even the nineteenth century working class. But even had he admitted this, the dynamic element of his theory provided a convenient recourse: it was not what the actual proletariat believed that was important, but what it would be forced by its nature to become. Graeme Duncan has written, by way of illustration, that

The proletariat is a prime example or 'ideal type' of a class. Marx's account of it... was something more than a description of existing realities. He was anticipating a process of class development, under the pressure of specific economic forces.[7]

Duncan echoes the view of Stanislaw Ossowski, that

In the Marxist view of social classes in a capitalistic system the social class *par excellence*, the class which is nearest to the general model of a class, is the proletariat, and the Marxist model of a proletarian is that of a class-conscious factory worker.[8]

Ossowski notes, however, that the Marxist definition of a proletarian 'allows manifold deviations from the model of a proletarian';[9] and that discrepancies in Marx's use of the concept of class will be overcome by historical development.[10] But this is a curious sort of 'ideal type' which is not an abstraction of certain elements of reality (which consists of mixtures and degrees of ideal types), but is asserted to be the shape of reality to come. If the proletariat is an 'ideal type' (in Max Weber's sense) which exists to some extent in the modern working class, there is no necessity for it to become coterminous with that class. Marxists tend to misuse 'ideal type' so that it approximates a Hegelian 'essence' with its notion of becoming, i.e. of different levels of existence. Nevertheless, Duncan and Ossowski rightly point out that the proletariat is for Marx the archetypal social class; to question Marx's concept of the proletariat is to question Marx's concept of class itself. If, therefore, Marx used three different types of criteria to identify the proletariat, and not an economic definition as primary, with additional criteria in concrete situations, his concepts of the proletariat and of social class are not properly consolidated.

Marx made an early commitment to the cause of the proletariat which he upheld for the rest of his life. Yet there were important changes in the way he conceived of the development of the proletariat, and of its revolutionary role. If he saw the economic determination of the proletariat as primary, and if the creative development of the proletariat as a class *for itself* became for him the inexorable development of the proletariat by capital, then not only is the proletariat as an economic class different from the proletariat which appeared in Marx's work in 1844, but Marx's project is altered. The idea of man's self-emancipation gives way to the idea of economic progress and the proletariat as the class of economic rationality. Human emancipation is subordinated to the need for economic development, even if it is seen to be a product of that development. That Marx began to stress the impersonal laws of history and the tasks created for the proletariat by capital, rather than the self-motivation of the proletarians, suggests that he had lost faith in the positive values of the proletariat—initiative, enterprise and freedom—and had begun to rely on negative values such as security. If so, Marx had perhaps begun to recognize the quiescence of industrial workers and their limited, self-interested aims, but hoped nevertheless to achieve socialism through some cunning of history.

Many observers have felt that Marx's concept of the proletariat is inadequate for his purposes. I have tried to explain precisely why that is so. It is widely held that Marx's discussion of the proletariat in the second Hegel critique lacked a historical and sociological dimension, which were added later.[11] I have suggested further that this very 'filling' of the concept created problems for Marx's theory, and that Marx ultimately relied on a conceptual approach to the proletariat. I also maintain that the problems which befell Marx's attempts to locate the proletariat his theory required stem from, and are an expression of, a fundamental flaw in his theory: its short-cut approach to social problems.

Tucker wrote of Marx, perhaps too severely, that 'the only proletarians he knew were the ones he read about in books'.[12] It is true that Marx was no son of the working class, that he had no sustained contact with the working class of any country,[13] and that he was selective in his use of evidence about the working class (stressing some facts and impressions, ignoring others). Yet the proletariat is more than just the agency of socialism in Marx's theory; it is the element of theoretical coherence. No social group, in Marx's time or since, has displayed all the characteristics of Marx's proletariat. This fact is fatal for Marx's conception of socialism and for his theory itself. Having been one of its most distinctive features, the reliance of Marx's theory upon the proletariat has become its biggest liability.

Marx's theory is now incidental to radical social change; it has become the basis for radical research programmes kept alive in and by Western universities. It no longer has the power to convince us that the working class is the class of the future, the instrument of history. The varieties of Marxism, where they are offered as political programmes, are now chiefly concerned with questions of leadership and alliances. At the theoretical level, there has been talk recently of a 'crisis' of Marxism, caused essentially by the failure of the Western working classes, and by the long and unhappy 'detour' of Marxism through Soviet, East European and Chinese channels.

Conclusion

Western Marxist intellectuals, such as Alex Callinicos, perceive an 'opportunity to close the gap between marxist theory and working-class struggle' (through a revolutionary party),[14] yet they propose newer and ever more elaborate theories, chiefly to explain the quiescence of the working class (that is, the continuing dominance of 'bourgeois' ideas, and thus of bourgeois social relationships). For Marxists, capitalism becomes more complex and more opaque, as they become more helpless to change it. Perhaps Marx's concept of the proletariat is suited only to simpler, more hopeful times.

Notes

Author and full title are given when a work is cited for the first time in these notes. Subsequent references to it, where they do not follow directly, are covered by the author's surname and the title, or an abbreviation of the title.

1. INTRODUCTION

1   Letter to J.B. von Schweitzer, 24 January 1865, S.K. Padover (ed.), *The Letters of Karl Marx*, p. 193.
2   Alexis de Tocqueville, *The Recollections of Alexis de Tocqueville*, edited J.P. Mayer, p. 85.
3   R.N. Berki, *Socialism*, p. 56.
4   This situation was noted in 1966 by Maximilien Rubel ('Did the Proletariat Need Marx and did Marxism help the Proletariat?' in N. Lobkowicz (ed.), *Marx and the Western World*, p. 46), although it has improved since then.
5   G.A. Briefs, *The Proletariat: A Challenge to Western Civilization*, p. 269.
6   Ibid., p. 234.
7   T. McCarthy, *Marx and the Proletariat. A Study in Social Theory*, p. 49.
8   First published 1961.
9   First published 1961.
10 First published 1962.
11 First published 1968.
12 Leszek Kolakowski, *Main Currents of Marxism: Its Rise, Growth, and Dissolution*. In three volumes, but especially relevant is the first, 'The Founders'. First published in 1978.
13 Eugene Kamenka, *Marxism and Ethics*, p. 1.
14 Although first published in 1842, and anonymously reviewed in the *Rheinische Zeitung*, Stein's work went through two revised editions by 1850. It is the 1850 edition, now translated into English and edited by K. Mengelberg, with which most of the scholars who pronounce on this issue are familiar. Stein's revisions, the extent of which I am not aware, are ground for caution. Herbert Marcuse claims that the 1850 edition is significantly different from that of 1842; see his *Reason and Revolution, Hegel and the Rise of Social Theory*, p. 374.
15 S.M. Lipset, 'Whatever Happened to the Proletariat? An Historic Mission Unfulfilled', *Encounter*, June 1981, Vol. LVI, No. 6, pp. 18–34.
16 Maximilien Rubel, 'Notes sur le proletariat et sa Mission', *Marx Critique du Marxisme. Essais*, p. 193. The 1844 'Introduction' will hereafter be designated in the text as the second Hegel critique, to

distinguish it from the quite separate notes now collected as the *Contribution to the Critique of Hegel's Philosophy of Law* (1843), which I shall designate the first Hegel critique. I use 'Law' instead of 'Right' here to conform to the usage of the *Collected Works* edition, not because I think it an appropriate translation of *Recht*.

17 Shlomo Avineri, *The Social and Political Thought of Karl Marx*, pp. 56–7.

18 On the origins of this discussion, see K. Mengelberg's 'Introduction' to Lorenz von Stein, *Socialism and Communism in Contemporary France*, pp. 25–33.

19 See Jean-Jacques Rousseau, *The Social Contract*, IV, 4, and Montesquieu, *The Spirit of Laws*, chapter 27. Both presented the archaic use of the term.

20 See below, Chapter Three.

21 George Lichtheim, *Marxism, An Historical and Critical Study*, p. 42.

22 An argument developed by Kamenka, 'The Baptism of Karl Marx', *The Hibbert Journal*, Vol. LVI, 1958, pp. 340–51.

23 Cited Paul E. Corcoran, 'The Bourgeois and Other Villains', *Journal of the History of Ideas*, Vol. 38, No. 3, 1977, pp. 477–8. Corcoran's thesis is particularly interesting for those who believe that Marx was fundamentally concerned with human dignity. He argues that, historically, the term *bourgeois* has been used as a pejorative epithet by aristocratic culture to express 'the unworthiness of entrepreneurial life and urban dependency as compared with noble refinement and chivalrous self-sufficiency' (p. 478).

24 Letter to L. Kugelmann, 11 January 1868, in Padover (ed.), p. 241.

25 In 1933, Nicholas Berdyaev made a similar point: 'The distinction between "proletariat" and "*bourgeois*" unwittingly coincides with that between "good" and "evil"' (see N. Berdyaev, *The Russian Revolution. Two Essays on its Implications in Religion and Psychology*, p. 68). Berdyaev, however, believed that Marx was profoundly influenced by the religion of his forbears: 'His proletarian Communism is a secularized form of the ancient Jewish chiliasm. A Chosen Class takes the place of the chosen people' (p. 74).

26 Kamenka, *The Ethical Foundations of Marxism*, Part I.

27 Hereafter designated in the text as the Paris Manuscripts, or the 1844 Manuscripts.

28 Alex Callinicos, *Marxism and Philosophy*, chapter 2, especially pp. 26–35.

29 Alfred G. Meyer, *Marxism, The Unity of Theory and Practice*, p. 107.

30 H. Marcuse, *One-Dimensional Man*, pp. 199–200. From the vantage of the nineteen-eighties, it seems as if the Western alliance of radical students and Marxism in the 'sixties and early in the 'seventies was a temporary phenomenon, produced by exceptional circumstances. Students rebelled against industrial society; Marxism is rooted in it and in its rationality.

31 Adam B. Ulam, *The Unfinished Revolution*, p. 43.

32 Kamenka, *The Ethical Foundations of Marxism*, p. 160.

2. THE DIALECTIC OF UNIVERSAL AND PARTICULAR

1 Noted by, among others, Paul Kägi, *Genesis des historischen Materialismus*, p. 191.
2 Avineri, p. 52.
3 Marx's early political position is difficult to characterize in a word or phrase. 'Radical democrat' and 'liberal' each has its limitations (see, for example, Avineri, pp. 33–4), and I explain below in what sense I describe Marx as a liberal. The problem is that until about 1844 Marx used concepts which were *more than* political, but not yet fully social.
4 Ludwig Feuerbach, *The Essence of Christianity*, in Lawrence S. Stepelevich (ed.), *The Young Hegelians, An Anthology*, p. 139.
5 Heinrich Marx to Karl Marx, 9 December 1837, Padover (ed.), p. 509.
6 G.W.F. Hegel, *Hegel's Lectures on the History of Philosophy*, Vol. 2, translated F.S. Haldane, p. 288.
7 None of Epicurus's writings has survived, but he was extensively (and we must hope, accurately) reported by Diogenes Laertius, among others.
8 Hegel, Vol. 2, p. 289
9 Although it is not my purpose to explain the concept of 'essence', some points need to be made so that Marx's use of it is understood. Marcuse explains that *essence* is 'the one true Being', to be distinguished 'from the constantly changing multiplicity of appearances' (H. Marcuse, 'The Concept of Essence' in *Negations, Essays in Critical Social Theory*, p. 43). As Hegel used the concept, it embodied a critical and dynamic thrust because it contrasted reality with its potentiality. Charles Taylor argues that, for Hegel, essence is 'the underlying necessity which determines the unfolding of external reality' (C. Taylor, *Hegel*, p. 262). Essence underlies external reality; it does not hide behind appearances. Taylor adds: 'What is afoot here is the development of a notion of Essence as a necessity which must come to full manifestation in external reality' (p. 274). It was from Hegel that Marx drew the concept of essence that he used in the years covered by this Chapter.
10 On the Young Hegelian 'party', see William J. Brazill, *The Young Hegelians*, Chapter 2.
11 Rubel, *Karl Marx. Essai de Biographie Intellectuelle*, p. 30.
12 Auguste Cornu, *Karl Marx et Friedrich Engels, Leur vie et leur oeuvre*, Vol. 1, p. 194.
13 Karl Löwith, *From Hegel to Nietzsche*, p. 48.
14 Cornu, Vol. 1, p. 169.
15 Cited ibid., Vol. 2, p. 30.
16 Ibid., Vol. 2, p. 103.
17 Giovanni Sartori, 'Constitutionalism: A Preliminary Discussion', *American Political Science Review*, Vol. 59, 1962, pp. 853–64.
18 Bruno Bauer, 'Der christliche Staat' (1841), cited David McLellan, *The Young Hegelians and Karl Marx*, p. 66.
19 Sidney Hook, *From Hegel to Marx, Studies in the Intellectual*

Development of Karl Marx, p. 158.

20 See also *Collected Works*, Vol. 1, pp. 180 and 365.

21 For this reason, and for related reasons discussed below, I cannot agree with Jerrold Seigel (*Marx's Fate. The Shape of a Life*, p. 109) that there is a parallel in Marx's work between the proletariat and the free press. Interestingly, Seigel claims that Ruge in 1843 identified radical writers as proletarians (p. 110).

22 Michael Lowy, *La théorie de la révolution chez le jeune Marx*, p. 39.

23 S. Avineri, *Hegel's Theory of the Modern State*, p. 148.

24 H. Lubasz, 'Marx's Initial Problematic: The Problem of Poverty', *Political Studies*, Vol. 24, 1976, pp. 24–42.

25 Arnold Ruge, 'Hegel's *Philosophy of Right* and the Politics of our Times', in Stepelevich (ed.), p. 214.

26 Ibid., p. 225.

27 McLellan, p. 24.

28 Ruge, p. 230.

29 For a discussion of the so-called 'transformative method', see Avineri, *The Social and Political Thought of Karl Marx*, pp. 10–12.

30 J. O'Malley, 'Introduction', to Marx, *Critique of Hegel's 'Philosophy of Right'*, translated A. Jolin and J. O'Malley, edited J. O'Malley, p. xxxiii.

31 Feuerbach, *Provisional Theses for the Reformation of Philosophy*, in Stepelevich (ed.), p. 167.

32 In the first Hegel critique Marx does not propose a candidate for universal class, as Jack Barbalet, *Marx's Construction of Social Theory*, p. 134, claims he does. The citizens of Marx's 'true democracy' would embody universality, but Marx is not yet clear about the means of abolishing the present state of affairs. For Marx, the first Hegel critique established a new problem (how to abolish particularity entire); the second solved it to his satisfaction. In Marx, socialism conquered Rousseau.

33 Avineri, *Hegel's Theory of the Modern State*, p. 167.

34 Raymond Plant, *Hegel. An Introduction*, p. 172.

35 Although see Marx and Engels, *The Holy Family*, *Collected Works*, Vol. 4, pp. 121–2, for Marx's criticisms of the appeals of the political model of ancient times for the Jacobins.

36 Dick Howard, *The Development of the Marxian Dialectic*, p. 128.

37 The charge that Marx was anti-Semitic (which relies on Marx's acceptance of popular stereotypes of Jews, as evidenced in 'On the Jewish Question' and elsewhere, and his use—privately—of the racial origins of some of his opponents to damn and ridicule them) is discussed by Julius Carlebach, *Karl Marx and the Radical Critique of Judaism*, especially pp. 261–89, and more shrilly by Nathaniel Weyl, *Karl Marx: Racist*, especially pp. 83–96. Avineri gives some perspective to this discussion by pointing out that Marx never opposed political emancipation for Jews, as Jews. Rather, Bruno Bauer declared that Jews must renounce their religion as a condition of emancipation. See S. Avineri, 'Marx and Jewish Emancipation', *Journal of the History of Ideas*, Vol. 25, No. 3, 1964, pp. 445–50. Some have even claimed that Marx's Jewish origins significantly influenced his

revolutionary career, and that he substituted a chosen class—the proletariat—for the 'chosen people'. See Carlebach, p. 317 and R.S. Wistrich, *Revolutionary Jews from Marx to Trotsky*, as well as Chapter One, Note 25. I do not believe that there are many specifically Jewish themes in Marx's theory, although his early uncertainty over his religious identity may have had an important formative influence upon Marx; see Chapter One, Note 22.

38 In his Doctoral Dissertation, Marx argued that the Young Hegelians (the 'liberal party', the 'party of the concept') understood the inadequacies of the world which 'has to be made philosophical'. Philosophy, too, had to change. To transform the world, it had to become more worldly. Marx thus saw the Young Hegelian project as a 'turning-towards-the-outside of philosophy'. See *Collected Works*, Vol. 1, p. 86.

39 Feuerbach, *Provisional Theses*, p. 163.

40 Ibid., p. 163.

41 Ibid., pp. 163–4.

42 On the whole, history too has been unkind to Feuerbach. Where Feuerbach's influence on Marx is not depreciated, it is often deplored. Louis Althusser, for example, declared that 'All the expressions of Marx's idealist "humanism" are Feuerbachian' (L. Althusser, *For Marx*, p. 45). At the other extreme, Feuerbach has been elevated to the status of major philosopher by Marx Wartofsky, *Feuerbach*. Kamenka's *The Philosophy of Ludwig Feuerbach* seems more balanced because Kamenka makes it clear that Feuerbach gave certain ideas which are still current a particularly striking formulation, that he was crucial to Marx's intellectual development, but that he does not deserve to be ranked with the greatest philosophers of the Western heritage. Feuerbach is a major figure in the history of ideas, but not in philosophy.

43 Lichtheim, p. 38. Avineri's point about Marx's distance from Jacobinism is well taken (Avineri, *The Social and Political Thought of Karl Marx*, pp. 187–92), but Lichtheim captures here the 'instrumental' quality of the proletariat for Marx, a quality which largely disappeared from his work after the second Hegel critique.

44 See Cornu, Vol. 2, p. 68, and Zvi Rosen, *Bruno Bauer and Karl Marx. The Influence of Bruno Bauer on Marx's Thought*, p. 121.

45 See Cornu, Vol. 2, pp. 286 and 347.

46 Feuerbach, *Provisional Theses for the Reformation of Philosophy*, p. 171.

47 Nevertheless, Marx did not—as John Maguire implies he did—have a worked-out theory of class and class struggle by the time of the second Hegel critique (see John Maguire, *Marx's Paris Writings: An Analysis*, p. 37). Indeed, in that work Marx used 'class' and 'estate' synonymously.

48 I do not think it is appropriate to describe the universality of the proletariat as a 'negative universality' as Herbert Marcuse, for example, describes it (*Reason and Revolution*, p. 291). The proletariat's universality, for Marx, was grounded in its conditions of existence, which he presented in terms of the negation of man. But the

proletariat's revolutionary role and intrinsic universality consisted in its need and attempts to assert humanity. Inhuman conditions produced degraded men, but also radical needs; radical needs produced radical action and ultimately the emancipation of all men. The proletariat's universality was not negative. Rather, it represented the capacity of the proletariat to bring humans into harmony with their essence. Despite their degradation, the species-essence of man survived among the proletarians; because of their degradation, humanity could triumph through their rebellion.

49 Cornu, Vol. 2, p. 272.
50 Ibid., p. 288.
51 Avineri has properly brought to our attention 'The Hegelian Origins of Marx's Political Thought', but to say that Marx's concept of the proletariat 'is nothing else than a further development of a theme that was central to Hegel's political theory' (Avineri (ed.), *Marx's Socialism*, p. 9), is to discount the influence of Feuerbachian and Saint-Simonian elements and that of Marx's study of the French Revolution, as well as to miss the point that Marx fundamentally altered Hegel's conception of universality and the universal class.
52 Hegel, *Hegel's Philosophy of Right*, addition to paragraph 2.
53 See Judith N. Shklar, 'Hegel's "Phenomenology": an elegy for Hellas', in Z.A. Pelczynski (ed.), *Hegel's Political Philosophy, problems and perspectives*, p. 79.
54 Hegel, *The Phenomenology of Mind*, p. 237.
55 Ibid., p. 239.
56 See Richard Norman, *Hegel's Phenomenology: A Philosophical Introduction*, p. 55.
57 Lowy, p. 65.
58 Avineri, *The Social and Political Thought of Karl Marx*, p. 59.

3. SOURCES

1 Georges Gurvitch, among other Frenchmen, has stressed the influence of Saint-Simon's work over Marx (see Gurvitch, *La Vocation actuelle de la Sociologie, vers une Sociologie différentielle*, pp. 574 and 580), but Engels may have been more influenced by it than was Marx.
2 On the career and thought of Hess, and his sometimes stormy relations with Marx, see J. Weiss, *Moses Hess, Utopian Socialist*.
3 See Lowy, p. 44, who raises doubts about the extent of Marx's acquaintance with the works of the French socialists.
4 Rosen, p. 121; and Cornu, Vol. 2, p. 68.
5 Ruge, p. 235.
6 Feuerbach, *Provisional Theses*, p. 164.
7 D.G. Rohr, *The Origins of Social Liberalism in Germany*.
8 Ibid., p. 115.
9 Gustav von Struve, cited ibid., p. 117.
10 There is, of course, considerable debate on this point. My point is generally supported by George Lichtheim, *The Origins of Socialism*. An opposing view has been put by Alexander Gray, *The Socialist*

Tradition: Moses to Lenin. My account of the origins and early development of socialism has, however, been drawn from these two sources, as well as from Lichtheim, *A Short History of Socialism*, Harry Laidler, *History of Socialism*, and especially from Volumes I and II of G.D.H. Cole, *A History of Socialist Thought*.

11 John Plamenatz, *The Revolutionary Movement in France, 1815–71*, p. 170.
12 Cited E. Levasseur, *Histoire des Classes ouvrières*, Vol. 2, pp. 3–4.
13 Jacques Droz, *Europe Between Revolutions, 1815–1848*, p. 91.
14 Eduard Dolléans, *Histoire du Mouvement Ouvrier*, Vol. 1, *1830–1871*, p. 33.
15 Cited ibid., p. 46.
16 William H. Sewell Jr., *Work and Revolution in France*, p. 195.
17 Cited ibid., p. 195.
18 Cited Dolléans, p. 48.
19 Enfantin, letter of 1 August 1830, cited Lichtheim, *The Origins of Socialism*, p. 245.
20 Cited Dolléans, p. 54.
21 Cited ibid., p. 56.
22 *L'Artisan*, 22 September 1830, cited Sewell Jr., p. 197.
23 Thomas Kirkup, *A History of Socialism*, p. 41.
24 Eric J. Hobsbawm, *The Age of Revolution, 1789–1848*, p. 140.
25 Jacques Droz (ed.), *Histoire Générale du Socialisme*, Vol. 1, p. 331.
26 *Doctrine de Saint-Simon. Exposition*, p. 73.
27 Ibid., p. 87.
28 Ibid., p. 93.
29 Ibid., p. 94.
30 Ibid., p. 225.
31 Ibid., p. 240.
32 In *Le Journal des débats*, 8 December 1831, cited J. Bruhat, *Histoire du Mouvement Ouvrier Français*, Vol. 1, p. 243.
33 In *Moniteur Universel*, 22 December 1831, cited R.J. Bezucha, *The Lyon Uprising of 1834*, p. 66.
34 Bruhat, p. 219.
35 Cited E. Levasseur, p. 11.
36 Cited Leroy, p. 403.
37 Cited ibid., p. 403.
38 Jean Reynaud, 'De la Nécessité d'une Représentation speciale pour les Prolétaires', *Revue Encyclopédique*, April 1832, pp. 12–13.
39 Ibid., p. 18.
40 Ibid., p. 20.
41 Louis Blanc, *Histoire de Dix Ans, 1830–1840*, p. 31.
42 See Plamenatz, Chapter 3.
43 Frederick Engels, *The Condition of the Working Class in England, Collected Works*, Vol. 4, p. 518.
44 Plamenatz, p. 54.
45 Cited G.D.H. Cole and A.W. Filson (eds.), *British Working Class Movements. Select Documents, 1789–1875*, p. 229.
46 Auguste Blanqui, 'Rapport sur la Situation intérieure et extérieure de la France depuis la révolution de Juillet', 2 February 1832, *Textes*

Choisis, p. 85.

47 Cited E. Coornaert, *Les Compagnonnages en France*, p. 93.

48 Cited Armand Cuvillier, *Hommes et Idéologies de 1840*, p. 237.

49 R.B. Rose, '*Prolétaires* and *Prolétariat*: Evolution of a Concept, 1789–1848', *Australian Journal of French Studies*, Vol. XVIII, No. 3, 1981, especially pp. 285–8.

50 Ibid., p. 293; and P. Kessel, *Le Prolétariat français*.

51 Rose, p. 289; Kessel, pp. 16–17.

52 Charles Béranger, 'Pétition d'un Prolétaire à la Chambre des Députés', *Le Globe*, No. 34, 5 February 1831.

53 Ibid.

54 Ibid.

55 Pierre Leroux, 'Cours d'Economie Politique, par M. Jules Leroux', *Revue Encyclopédique*, October-December 1833, p. 102.

56 Ibid., p. 103.

57 Ibid., p. 106.

58 Ibid., p. 108.

59 Simonde de Sismondi, *Nouveaux Principes d'Economie Politique*, Vol. 2, p. 243. Leroy describes Sismondi as the 'Premier analyste de la notion de prolétariat'; M. Leroy, Chapter IX.

60 Sismondi, p. 177.

61 Ibid., p. 232.

62 Adolphe Blanqui, *Histoire de l'Economie Politique en Europe*, p. 351.

63 Frederick Morton Eden, *'The State of the Poor': A History of the Labouring Classes in England*, cited Cole and Filson (eds.), p. 6.

64 Cornu, Vol. 2, p. 168 lists some of the works on pauperism from the 1830s and '40s.

65 Adolphe Blanqui, pp. 428 and 429.

66 Simonde de Sismondi, *Political Economy*, p. 68.

67 Cited E. Labrousse, *Le Mouvement Ouvrier et les Théories Sociales en France*, p. 141.

68 Cited Leroy, p. 395.

69 The Third Estate, according to Siéyès, was alone among the Estates in being productive. Abbé Siéyès, *What is the Third Estate?*, pp. 53–8.

70 Fourier did not reject the role of industry in the *phalanstère*, but he did not see the future as being industrial. Instead, like much else in his system, he seemed to believe that industry had to be balanced with other types of occupations and activities. See N. Riasanovsky, *The Teaching of Charles Fourier*, pp. 196–9.

71 F. Lamennais, *De l'Esclavage Moderne*, p. 48.

72 Ibid., p. 50.

73 Ibid., pp. 51–2.

74 Ibid., pp. 120–1.

75 Cited E. Coornaert, p. 93; also included in Auguste Blanqui, *Textes Choisis*, p. 105, as perhaps written by Blanqui in 1830.

76 Cited P. Angrand, 'Notes critiques sur la formation des Idées communistes en France', Part II, *La Pensée*, 20 November 1948, p. 58.

77 Laurent, 'Parti Politique des Travailleurs', *Oeuvres de Saint-Simon et d'Enfantin*, Vol. 45/46, p. 110. No date; probably 1831.

78 Ibid., p. 111.

79 Ibid., p. 111n.
80 After the November 1831 Lyon rebellion; cited Labrousse, pp. 104–5.
81 Cited Leroy, pp. 407–8.
82 Cited Roger Garaudy, *Les Sources françaises du Socialisme scientifique,* p. 135.
83 Pecqueur is discussed by McCarthy; see especially p. 77.
84 Cited Garaudy, p. 197.
85 The increasing precision with which the term 'bourgeoisie' was used in France at this time is traced by S. Gruner, 'The Revolution of July 1830 and the Expression "Bourgeoisie"', *The Historical Journal,* Vol. 11, No. 3, 1968, pp. 462–71.
86 Sewell Jr., p. 219.
87 Blanc, p. 450.
88 Jules Leroux, *Le Prolétaire et Le Bourgeois. Dialogue sur la question des salaires,* p. 32.
89 P.-J. Proudhon, 'Lettre à l'Académie de Besançon', 3 August 1840, *Oeuvres Complètes* (1926), p. 119.
90 Ibid., p. 351.
91 Proudhon, *De la Création de l'Ordre dans l'Humanité, Oeuvres Complètes* (1927), p. 312.
92 Ibid., p. 312.
93 Ibid., pp. 408–9.
94 Ibid., pp. 408–9.
95 Ibid., p. 360.
96 Hobsbawm, p. 248.
97 Sewell Jr., Chapter 9.
98 E. Coornaert, 'La pensée ouvrière et la conscience de classe en France de 1830 à 1848', *Studi in Onore di Gino Luzzato,* Vol. 3, 1949–50, especially p. 28.
99 See Asa Briggs, 'The Language of "Class" in Early Nineteenth-Century England', in M.W. Flinn and T.C. Smout (eds.), *Essays in Social History.*
100 Hobsbawm, p. 152. Others agree: see, for example, Maurice Agulhon, *Une Ville Ouvrière au Temps du Socialisme Utopique,* p. 327.
101 Christopher Johnson, cited Bezucha, p. 114.
102 Coornaert, 'La pensée ouvrière', p. 20.
103 Sewell Jr., p. 157. Bernard H. Moss, *The Origins of the French Labour Movement 1830–1914,* however, makes a sharp distinction between artisans and skilled workers; see especially p. 13.
104 Sewell Jr., p. 161.
105 Sewell Jr., 'Social Change and the Rise of Working-Class Politics in Nineteenth-Century Marseille', *Past and Present,* No. 65, November 1974, p. 82.
106 Christopher Johnson, 'Patterns of Proletarianization: Parisian Tailors and Lodève Woolen Workers', in J.M. Merriman (ed.), *Consciousness and Class Experience in Nineteenth-Century Europe,* p. 70.
107 Moss, p. 23.
108 Bezucha, p. 54. Indeed, Leroy claims of the term proletariat that 'Une classe nouvelle naît avec le mot'; M. Leroy, p. 312.

109 *The Doctrine of Saint-Simon: An Exposition, First Year, 1828–1829,* p. 129.
110 Bezucha, p. 54.
111 Louis Chevalier, *Classes Laborieuses et Classes dangereuses à Paris,* p. 518.
112 Kessel, pp. 249–50. *Prolétaire* was sanctioned by the Académie's Dictionnaire in 1835; *prolétariat* in 1878.
113 Rose, pp. 296–7.
114 Flora Tristan, *Union Ouvrière,* p. 5.
115 Ibid., p. 27.
116 Lowy, pp. 94–6; Rubel, p. 92.
117 T.B. Bottomore, 'Socialism and the Working Class', in L. Kolakowski and S. Hampshire (eds.), *The Socialist Idea, a reappraisal,* p. 123.
118 A. Lichtenberger, *Le Socialisme et la Révolution française,* p. 291.
119 Cited C. Johnson, 'Etienne Cabet and the Problem of Class Antagonism', *International Review of Social History,* Vol. XI, 1966, p. 418n.
120 Ibid., p. 424.
121 Cited ibid., p. 422.
122 Cited ibid., p. 425.
123 Ibid., p. 435.
124 Cited A. Cuvillier, p. 461.
125 Cited M. Agulhon, p. 159.
126 G.D.H. Cole, *Socialist Thought, The Forerunners, 1789–1850,* p. 313
127 *Selected Works,* Vol. I, p. 103.
128 Rose, p. 294.
129 Coornaert, 'La pensée ouvrière', p. 29.
130 Ibid., p. 29.
131 Lamennais, pp. 122–3.
132 Augustin Thierry, *Considérations sur l'Histoire de France, Oeuvres de Thierry,* Vol. IV, p. 93.
133 Avineri has also made this point; see *The Social and Political Thought of Karl Marx,* p. 57.
134 Lowy, p. 71.
135 Rubel, *Karl Marx. Essai de Biographie Intellectuelle,* p. 92.
136 Cornu, Vol. 2, p. 251.
137 Ibid., p. 251.
138 G.W.F. Hegel, *Philosophy of Right,* translated T.M. Knox, paragraph 244.
139 Ibid., addition to paragraph 244.
140 Cited E. Sagarra, *A Social History of Germany,* 1648–1914, p. 395.
141 Cited Rohr, p. 123.
142 Sagarra, p. 227.
143 Lorenz von Stein, *The History of the Social Movement in France, 1789–1850,* translated and edited K. Mengelberg, p. 256.

144 Ibid., p. 259.
145 Ibid., p. 262.
146 Ibid., pp. 88–9.
147 See the discussion of Stein in Chapter One.
148 Baron von Bibra, chamberlain and high bailiff of the Duchy of Sachsen-Meiningen, 1845, cited Jurgen Kuczynski, *The Rise of the Working Class*, translated C.T.A. Roy, p. 83.
149 Ibid., pp. 83 and 85.
150 Friedrich List, Preface to *Das nationale System der politischen Oekonomie*, 1843, cited Rohr, p. 105.
151 Cited ibid., p. 107.
152 Anonymous, *Über den vierten Stand und die socialen Reformen*, Magdeburg, 1844, cited Kuczynski, p. 73.
153 Cited ibid., p. 81.
154 Cited ibid., p. 81.
155 Theodor Mundt, *Die Geschichte der Gesellschaft in ihren neueren Entwicklungen und Problemen*, Berlin, 1844, cited ibid., pp. 85–6.
156 Cited ibid., pp. 85–6.
157 Bezucha, p. vii.
158 Hobsbawm, p. 45.

4. MARX'S PROLETARIAT CHALLENGED

1 Cited *Collected Works*, Vol. 3, p. 189.
2 Cited ibid., p. 200.
3 Kamenka, *The Ethical Foundations of Marxism*, p. 44. In his first Hegel critique, Marx contrasted universality 'as an *external* multiplicity or totality of the individuals' to universality as an 'essential, spiritual, actual quality of the individual' (*Collected Works*, Vol. 3, p. 117).
4 A point already made by M. Rubel, 'Socialism and the Commune' in E. Kamenka (ed.), *Paradigm for Revolution?*, p. 46.
5 Engels to Marx, 22 February 1845, cited *Collected Works*, Vol. 4, p. 697, n. 91.
6 See D.W. Lovell, *From Marx to Lenin. An Evaluation of Marx's Responsibility for Soviet Authoritarianism*, p. 36.
7 A better translation is 'non-responsibility'.
8 The Paris Manuscripts have been widely discussed in the last twenty-five years. The following account of Marx's use of the concept of alienation and his transformation of it from a critical philosophical to a critical sociological category draws upon the fuller analyses of Avineri, *The Social and Political Thought of Karl Marx*, especially pp. 96–123; Tucker, especially pp. 123–61; Kamenka, *The Ethical Foundations*, especially pp. 70–86; McLellan, *Karl Marx*, pp. 104–28; Bertell Ollman, *Alienation. Marx's Conception of Man in Capitalist Society*; and John Maguire, *Marx's Paris Manuscripts*.
9 In his 'On the Jewish Question', Marx argued that money was the foundation of alienation. See *Collected Works*, Vol. 3, p. 170.
10 Tucker, p. 148.
11 Gerald A. Cohen discusses this point in his 'Bourgeois and

Proletarians', in Avineri (ed.), *Marx's Socialism*, and argues that 'It is because the capitalist has lost all perception of and contact with his essence that he tolerates his alienation. But the worker daily glimpses his essence at a distance from him and experiences his humanity in a distorted form, so that he hopes and desires to live in a nonalienated world' (pp. 104–5).

12 Zvi Rosen, p. 102, cites B. Bauer as declaring: 'When the plight reaches its peak, the solution is near', and comments that this is 'a formula typical of his conception'. Marx inherited it. See also Agnes Heller, *The Theory of Need in Marx*, p. 48.

13 Cited *Collected Works*, Vol. 4, p. 52.

14 Cited ibid., p. 82.

15 Cited ibid., p. 81.

16 Kamenka, *The Ethical Foundations*, p. 68.

17 Marx, however, made earlier references to the *popular* will as providing the content of universality. In his article on 'The Divorce Bill' in December 1842, Marx argued that the certainty that a marriage was morally dead could be achieved 'only... if the law is the conscious expression of the popular will, and therefore originates with it and is created by it', *Collected Works*, Vol. 1, p. 309. With this Rousseauan theme Marx mixes natural law theory, combining them both in the central figure of the *legislator*: 'The legislator, however, should regard himself as a naturalist. He does not *make* the laws, he does not invent them, he only formulates them' (ibid., p. 308).

5. A PROLETARIAN ETHIC?

1 H.P. Adams, *Karl Marx in his Earlier Writings*, p. 128 claims, rather too strongly I think, that 'Nobody, not even Dickens, ever made so sensational an attack on social abuses by means of a work of fiction as did Sue in his prodigious romance *The Mysteries of Paris*'.

2 Kamenka, *The Ethical Foundations*, p. 35.

3 Cited Collected Works, Vol. 4, p. 70.

4 I enclose bourgeois in quotation marks because Marx does not use the expression *bourgeois morality* in *The Holy Family*. The expression *'petty-bourgeois respectability'*, however, occurs once; ibid., p. 164.

5 Cited ibid., p. 163.

6 Cited ibid., p. 169.

7 Cited ibid., p. 171.

8 Cited ibid., p. 173.

9 Cited ibid., p. 173.

10 Cited ibid., p. 173.

11 The idea that prostitution was a product of force of circumstances was defended earlier by the Saint-Simonians; see, for example, F.E. and F.P. Manuel, p. 618.

12 For a discussion of Marx's development from an advocate of the idea of a rational law to the advocate of the abolition of law, see Kamenka, *The Ethical Foundations*, pp. 32–6.

13 See Agnes Heller, *The Theory of Need in Marx*, especially Chapter II.

14 See Heller, pp. 86–7 and 125–30; Kamenka, *Marxism and Ethics*, especially pp. 13–14.

15 In recent times, this literature has grown quickly, as can be seen from the latest Supplementary Volume to the *Canadian Journal of Philosophy*, on *Marx and Morality*, although Maximilien Rubel and Eugene Kamenka have stressed the ethical nature of Marx's thought for many years. The debate is occasioned and stimulated by the paradox that Marx declared himself opposed to morality, yet filled his work with moral judgements. Recently Steven Lukes ('Marxism, Morality and Justice', in G.H.R. Parkinson (ed.), *Marx and Marxisms*, pp. 177–206) has attempted, very ably, to explain this paradox. He distinguishes between a narrower and a broader sense of morality. In the narrower sense, morality is part of *Recht*—of rules which inevitably treat individuals unequally because they subject unequal individuals to the same standard. This morality assists in allocating resources when they are scarce (i.e. in class society). Morality in the broader sense is appropriate in a society of abundance. Thus to promote (narrower) morality is to try to reconcile classes, to 'delay the revolutionary change that will make possible a form of social life that has no need of morality' (p.203) in that sense. Lukes does not consider whether the society of abundance constitutes an 'external standard'—a higher moral standpoint—by which class society ought ultimately to be judged (like Marx, he seems to believe in inexorable material progress, which makes the question irrelevant); nor does he consider the problem of abundance that Marx's theory must confront: how can people's needs be met if they continually expand? Bertell Ollman has also considered the paradox of Marx on morality. He distinguishes between approval and disapproval on the one hand, and value judgements—or 'deductions from absolute principles' (*Alienation*, p. 42)—on the other. Only the latter, he maintains, is part of an ethic. He argues that since Marx does not judge capitalism from an 'outside' standard (p. 132), he is not a moralist. Ollman, I believe, is making an important point. In Marx's view, 'critique' is not morality as an external standard, but is immanent in history. Marx accepted a logic of essences: that appearance moved unceasingly to become one with its essence. The idea of Marx's 'logico-ethical' standpoint, analyzed by Kamenka, seems to be the best way to express this point. In a sense, however, Marx conflated logic and ethics, for the question of an 'external' standard does not have much meaning in the context of Marx's concept of essence; the various 'moments' of an essence are *both* inside and outside.

The trouble with many of the recent contributions to this debate is that they attempt not just to understand Marx's views, but also to preserve one form of Marxism or another. Able theorists engage in theoretical gymnastics in order to preserve what they see as orthodoxy. In an otherwise scholarly work, for example, Ollman is concerned to deny that Marx 'operated from fixed principles' and that his work embodied an ethic, since 'attributing an ethic to Marxism inevitably serves the ends of the bourgeoisie' (p. 50). That Marx denied morality any independent role in the struggle for socialism and in the truly human society is consistent with his refusal to appreciate the complexities of

social life, and with his determination to cut through problems which
were fundamental in shaping Hegel's political philosophy. For Hegel,
the state was an ethical community; morality was one of the means by
which particularity and universality were mediated. Marx, as I explained
in Chapter Two, had no need of 'mediators'.

16 Kamenka, *The Ethical Foundations*, p. 70.
17 Rubel, *Karl Marx, Essai*, p. 114.
18 Ibid., p. 100.
19 Anthony Skillen, 'Workers' Interests and the Proletarian Ethic;
    Conflicting Strains in Marxian Anti-Moralism', Kai Nielson (ed.),
    Marx and Morality, Supplementary Volume No. VII to the *Canadian
    Journal of Philosophy*, 1981, p. 157.
20 On the view that Kantian ethics were the 'natural completion of
    Marxism', see S. Lukes, pp. 186–7.
21 Skillen, p. 158.
22 Ibid., p. 161.
23 Ibid., p. 156.
24 Georges Sorel, *Reflections on Violence*, p. 237.
25 Skillen, p. 169.
26 Cited *Collected Works*, Vol. 4, p. 192.

6. A PROLETARIAN IDEOLOGY?

1   I do not intend to discuss fully Marx's concept of ideology in this brief
    Chapter. Any such discussion would have to examine at least three
    major aspects. First, at what level of abstraction are pitched the ideas
    which Marx took to be ideological, and how comprehensive are they?
    The term 'consciousness', which Marx used frequently in this
    connection (although not as a synonym for 'ideology'), seems too broad
    to be helpful. And Marx's formulation 'social existence determines
    consciousness' is fraught with difficulties: none of its terms was ever
    properly or convincingly defined by Marx. Marx used 'ideology' to refer
    to different ideas and different systems of ideas; when he brought
    together religion, philosophy, morality, law, etc. under the heading
    'ideology', it was not clear how they were uniformly ideological, or
    which aspects of them were ideological —for, of course, they represent
    very different things. As John Plamenatz argued, Marx and Engels
    'established a tradition of careless use' of the term 'ideology' (J.
    Plamenatz, *Ideology*, p. 20). Second, what is the truth and falsity of
    ideologies: which elements are true, and which false; in what sense are
    they 'false'? (See R.N. Berki, 'The Marxian Concept of Bourgeois
    Ideology: Some Aspects and Perspectives', in R. Benewick, R.N.
    Berki, B. Parekh, *Knowledge and Belief in Politics. The Problem of
    Ideology*, p. 89.) Marx did not seem to think that ideology was entirely
    false. Nor did he believe that all error was ideological (see Jorge Larrain,
    The Concept of Ideology, p. 51, and Bhikhu Parekh, *Marx's Theory of
    Ideology*, p. 48). The third aspect concerns the social functions of an
    ideology, where not truth but social utility is involved. Is Marx's
    concept of ideology akin to Sorel's concept of myth, or

Pareto's concept of derivations? We might broaden this aspect by considering whether certain ideas or beliefs fill a human need. Marx used differing combinations of these three aspects to condemn an idea, a theory, a belief or an attitude as 'ideological'. Is a true theory (say) ideological because it can be used to support the rule of the dominant class; is a false theory which threatens that rule ideological; can a science be ideological because of the social uses to which it is put? Marx, I believe, would have had difficulty in answering consistently questions such as these. He wanted to maintain a distinction between science and ideology, but even in the field of political economy he found it difficult. Science was clearly the result of the activities (and perhaps included those activities) of specialized scientists, and was thus a product of the division of labour, liable to one-sidedness. Yet, for Marx, although the results of science could be used by the ruling class, science dealt with independently verifiable facts (not unnaturally, he did not differentiate between the natural and social sciences), and by its nature did not entertain the illusion that it created the world it examined. Nevertheless, Marx perceived a tendency among political economists to regard present-day (transient) relations as eternal laws or categories (e.g., *Collected Works*, Vol. 6, p. 162). Proudhon was the chief culprit in 1847.

In contrast to Proudhon's, 'Ricardo's theory of values is the scientific interpretation of actual economic life' (ibid., p. 124). Ricardo exposed the mysteries of the bourgeoisie (ibid., p. 125). His language may be cynical, wrote Marx, but 'The cynicism is in the facts and not in the words which express the facts' (ibid., p. 125). Marx added that political economists such as Ricardo 'are the scientific representatives of the bourgeois class' (ibid., p. 177). In later works, Marx distinguished between scientists and apologists or vulgarisers, a distinction based in part, it seems, on the different form which their work takes and the audience for which it is intended. Marx , as I suggest in Chapter Eight, may have changed his view of the nature of reality between the 1840s and the 1860s, and with it his view of science. The scientist in 1847 had merely to open his eyes: 'the cynicism is in the facts'; twenty years later science had to uncover the in-built illusions of capitalism, to go beyond the world of appearance. Ideology, according to Larrain, only remains at the level of appearance (J. Larrain, p. 59).

I am concerned in this Chapter, however, partly with the role that the concept of ideology played in the development of Marx's theory, and how it can add to our understanding of the 'universality' of the proletariat. I suggest below that one way to comprehend the unity of what Marx called 'ideologies' is to consider them as one-sided thought. This is also one way to approach the question of ideology as error, involving as it does such matters as perspective, and not simple true-false dichotomies.

2   See Marx's attack on Proudhon in his *The Poverty of Philosophy* (in *Collected Works*, Vol. 6, pp. 105–212); for Marx's confrontation with Weitling on 30 March 1846, during which Marx exclaimed: 'Ignorance has never yet helped anybody!', see Boris Nicolaievsky and Otto Maenchen-Helfen, *Karl Marx: Man and Fighter*, pp. 124–8.

3   Stirner's work appeared early in 1845, but Engels read it in proof form at the end of 1844. He thought, at first, that communists could build upon Stirner's ideas, but was soon persuaded otherwise by Marx. See N. Lobkowicz, 'Karl Marx and Max Stirner', in F.J. Adelmann, S.J. (ed.), *Demythologizing Marxism. A Series of Studies on Marxism*, pp. 69–70.

4   Max Stirner, *The Ego and His Own*, p. 122.

5   Ibid., p. 43.

6   It is ironic, however, that 'ideology'— which Destutt de Tracy believed would supplant metaphysics with a scientific study of ideas and their origins—denoted for Marx the systematic obfuscation of social reality.

7   Notable among them is Antonio Gramsci, with his conception of *hegemony*. Alan Swingewood, *Marx and Modern Social Theory*, for example, has argued that 'Any study of class consciousness must indeed begin from an awareness which a dominant class ideology exercises over the subordinate strata' (p. 133). Georg Lukács had earlier noted 'the insidious effects of bourgeois ideology on the thought of the proletariat' (*History and Class Consciousness*, p. 24).

8   Marx might have adduced in support of this view the fact that most such Marxists are isolated from the 'reality' of social relations in universities, communist party hierarchies and prisons.

9   A point also made by Louis Dupré, *The Philosophical Foundations of Marxism*, p. 149.

10   I do not find this line of thought particularly convincing. Although in primitive societies there may be no professional ideologists, there seem, nevertheless, to be ideologies: religions, rules, beliefs about society, ceremonies, etc. —all of which have their share of truth and falsity, and their social functions. Marx seems to have employed in this area two distinctions which he did not properly clarify or separate: the distinction between literate and non-literate societies, and that between professional and non-professional activities.

11   Cited *Collected Works*, Vol. 5, p. 260.

12   Martin Seliger, *The Marxist Conception of Ideology, A Critical Essay*, pp. 1–3.

13   Karl Mannheim, *Ideology and Utopia, An Introduction to the Sociology of Knowledge*, especially pp. 237ff.

14   I describe Marx's 'sociology of knowledge' as an integral part of his argument about ideology, but not as the entire content of that argument. Seliger, by contrast, argues that in Marx's work there is an 'unreconciled coexistence' (p. 31) of the views that dependence of thought on socio-economic conditions issues in distortion and that distortion is not a necessary corollary of this dependence. Although Marx may, at times, have spoken as if the socio-economic dependence of all thought issues in distortion, it is not consistent with the major thrust of his argument about the origin of ideology. It is interesting that the two theorists who have made most of the sociology of knowledge, Karl Marx and Karl Mannheim, have each in his own way sought an escape from the relativism and limitations which seem inherent in the doctrine: Marx, with his 'universal class'; and Mannheim with his 'socially unattached intelligentsia' (see Mannheim,

pp. 136–46). According to Feuer, however, Marx's theory is ideological precisely because it contains the three ingredients of an ideology, including 'a historically determined decision as to a chosen class of the time' (Lewis S. Feuer, *Ideology and the Ideologists*, p. 1).

15 As used by Marx, this term is an insult. He added in 1877 that 'The workers themselves, when... they give up work and become *professional literary men*, always breed "theoretical" mischief and are always ready to join muddleheads from the allegedly "learned" caste' (Marx to F.A. Sorge, 19 October 1877, in Marx and Engels, *Selected Correspondence*, pp. 309–10).

16 I cannot agree with Parekh that 'Marx saw himself as a "free agent of thought"' (Parekh, p. 184) who could not remain the theorist of the proletariat because he found its 'point of view' to be 'partial, inadequate and somewhat partisan' (ibid., p. 183). Marx was nothing if not partisan. Although Marx had later to confront an empirical proletariat with a prejudiced and limited standpoint, he did not believe that these characteristics were of the essence. (As I suggest in the text, he may have considered the errors of the proletariat to be different in kind from the errors of the bourgeoisie.) Furthermore, the expression 'free agent of thought' is used only once by Marx, in the first draft of what became *The Civil War in France*, to describe men of science *under socialism*. Marx argued there that the Paris middle class had looked to the working class to emancipate them from 'priest rule, convert science from an instrument of class rule into a popular force, [and] convert the men of science themselves... into free agents of thought' (Marx, *The First International and After*, p. 259). I do not believe that Marx would have applied this label to himself.

17 The idea of the cash-nexus was probably derived by Marx from Thomas Carlyle (*Past and Present*, in *Selected Writings*, p. 277) via Engels, who was familiar with Carlyle's work (see *Collected Works*, Vol. 3, pp. 444–68).

18 In 1873, Engels took a different view of the demands of modern machinery, in his 'On Authority': 'The automatic machinery of a big factory is much more despotic than the small capitalists who employ workers ever have been. At least with regard to the hours of work one may write upon the portals of these factories: *Lasciate ogni autonomia, voi che entrate!* ' (Leave, ye that enter in, all autonomy behind!) (*Selected Works*, Vol. 2, p. 377).

19 Marx's views on the relations between proletarians and communists will be examined in the next chapter.

20 My discussion of Marx's early view of the proletariat's immunity to ideology and its ability to apprehend the universal standpoint is akin, in some ways, to Lukács' argument that the proletariat is 'epistemologically privileged'—as Parekh has put it (Parekh, p. 181) —because it can view society as a totality (see, for example, the essay on 'Class Consciousness' in *History and Class Consciousness*, pp. 46–81). But Lukács' discussion remains for the most part at the level of consciousness, and his explanation of why the bourgeoisie cannot apprehend society as a totality is not convincing. And as Lichtheim has pointed out, since for Lukács the actual proletariat remains subject to

ideological confusion (see above, Note 7), and thus requires the leadership of a revolutionary party, Lukács has provided a 'philosophical rationale of Leninism' (G. Lichtheim, 'The Concept of Ideology', *History and Theory*, Vol. IV, No. 2, 1965, p. 190).

7. THE PROLETARIAT AS A POLITICAL CLASS

1   My evidence for this claim is chiefly circumstantial. In the *Communist Manifesto*, Marx wrote that 'The immediate aim of the Communists is the... formation of the proletariat into a class' (*Collected Works*, Vol. 6, p. 498). Since, for Marx, a class was politically constituted—as I document below—the proletarian class was a product of a revolution rather than its prerequisite: the alteration of men on a mass scale, Marx argued in *The German Ideology*, takes place in revolution (ibid., Vol. 5, pp. 60–1).

2   Berki argues that at certain stages, for example, when the bourgeoisie is a universal class, its thought is more than simply ideology, because it genuinely represents for a time the universal standpoint (Berki, 'The Marxian Concept of Bourgeois Ideology', pp. 99–101). This may help to explain the pervasiveness of 'bourgeois ideology', and perhaps even the transformation of class ideologies into political ideologies.

3   See also Engels, 'The Prussian Constitution', *Collected Works*, Vol. 6, p. 71; Engels, 'The Communists and Karl Heinzen', ibid., p. 299; and Engels, 'The Civil War in Switzerland', ibid., p. 368.

4   See the account in Alan Gilbert's *Marx's Politics: Communists and Citizens*, pp. 191–2.

5   It was dated June 1, but it actually came out a day earlier.

6   See, for example, Lenin, *The Revolutionary-Democratic Dictatorship of the Proletariat and the Peasantry* (April 1905), V.I. Lenin, *Collected Works*, Vol. 8, and *Two Tactics of Social-Democracy in the Democratic Revolution* (July 1905), *Collected Works*, Vol. 9.

7   The concepts of 'minimalism' and 'maximalism' are discussed by Israel Getzler in the contexts of Germany in 1848 and Russia in 1917 in I. Getzler, 'Marxist Revolutionaries and the Dilemma of Power' in A. and J. Rabinowitch (eds.), *Revolution and Politics in Russia, Essays in Memory of B.I. Nicolaevsky*, pp. 81–112.

8   Engels was a little more cautious, especially about Germany; see *Collected Works*, Vol. 10, p. 238.

9   Marx's tactics in Germany during 1848 are discussed by O. Hammen, *The Red '48ers*, and by Kamenka, '"The Party of the Proletariat": Marx and Engels in the Revolution of 1848', in E. Kamenka and F.B. Smith (eds.), *Intellectuals and Revolution. Socialism and the Experience of 1848*, pp. 76–93. Marx dissolved the central committee of the Communist League after arriving in Cologne. Gottschalk, who led the Cologne Workers' Association, refused to accept Marx's authority; Marx thus centred his activity on the Democratic Association and on the *Neue Rheinische Zeitung*. The workers' movement did not move in the direction Marx hoped it would. Hammen reports that workers 'did indeed combine, organize, protest and even hold congresses. But they

tended to coalesce along guild lines. Many workers were more interested in regaining old guild privileges and in recapturing an imagined golden age that had passed away than in revolutionizing the world in response to a strange vision of a better future' (p. 217).

10 See Louis Blanc, for example, cited in Chapter Three, Note 41; and R.B. Rose, 'Louis Blanc: The Collapse of a Hero' in Kamenka and Smith (eds.), pp. 34–5.

11 See, for example, Marx 'The Prussian Counter-revolution and the Prussian Judiciary', *Collected Works*, Vol. 8, p. 197; and Marx, *The Class Struggles in France, Collected Works*, Vol. 10, p. 47.

12 See, for example, David Felix, *Marx as Politician*, especially Chapters 4 and 5.

13 Stirner, cited Marx and Engels, *The German Ideology*, p. 202.

14 See the collection of articles in *Theory and Society*, Vol. 12, No. 4, July 1983, pp. 449–532, especially R.J. Bezucha, 'The French Revolution of 1848 and the Social History of Work', pp. 469–84.

15 Saint-Simon had also believed that industry was a source of cohesion. He argued that all members of industry 'are united by the general interests of production, by the needs that they all have for security in work and freedom of trade'; cited E. Kamenka and M. Krygier (eds.), *Bureaucracy, The Career of a Concept*, p. 39.

16 R.C. Tucker, *The Marxian Revolutionary Idea*, p. 17.

17 Marx believed that the next crisis would come in 1852 (see *Collected Works*, Vol. 10, p. 502). Later, Engels declared that 'with a fully employed and well-paid working class, no agitation, much less a revolution, can be got up' (*Collected Works*, Vol. 11, p. 214).

18 Marx to J. Weydemeyer, 19 December 1849, Padover (ed.), p. 52.

19 The International was bound to no particular socialist theory; various currents formed it, and co-existed (uneasily) within it. See Lichtheim, *A Short History of Socialism*, pp. 172–3.

20 See H. Collins and C. Abramsky, *Karl Marx and the British Labour Movement. Years of the First International*, pp. 59–78.

21 Ibid., pp. 288–9.

22 Ibid., p. 48.

23 Ibid., p. 70.

24 Ibid., p. 54.

25 Ibid., p. 101.

26 The Proudhonists unsuccessfully attempted to restrict membership of the International to manual workers, and Marx spared them further aggravation by declining English entreaties to stand for the presidency of the General Council in September 1866. See Marx, *On the First International*, p. 421.

27 Mazzini, cited Collins and Abramsky, p. 103.

28 Ibid., p. 94.

29 Cited Marx, *The First International and After*, p. 368.

30 For Elie Halévy, the popularity of Methodism helped to explain the extraordinary stability of English society through a period of revolution and instability on the Continent; see E. Halévy, *England in 1815* (Volume I of *A History of the English People in the Nineteenth Century*), especially Part III, Chapter I.

31 Engels, cited Collins and Abramsky, p. 98.
32 David Fernbach, 'Introduction' to Marx, *The First International and After*, p. 29.
33 On the attitudes of the First and Second Internationals to the problem of war, see Julius Braunthal, *History of the International, 1864–1914*, pp. 320–56.
34 Kamenka, 'Preface', to Kamenka (ed.), *Paradigm for Revolution? The Paris Commune 1871–1971*, p. vi.
35 Cited Marx, *The First International and After*, p. 206.
36 R.B. Rose, 'The Paris Commune: The last episode of the French Revolution or the first dictatorship of the proletariat?', Kamenka (ed.), *Paradigm for Revolution?*, p. 19.
37 See Marx to D. Nieuwenhuis, 22 February 1881, Marx and Engels, *Selected Correspondence*, p. 318.
38 In 1851, Auguste Comte implied that the workers of Paris could not be considered typical of Frenchmen: 'hitherto it is only in France, or rather in Paris that they [workmen] have shown themselves in their true light, as men emancipated from chimerical beliefs, and careless of the empty prestige of social position' (A. Comte, *System of Positive Polity*, Vol. I, p. 103).
39 Rose, 'The Paris Commune', pp. 19–21.
40 Collins and Abramsky, p. 290.
41 Cf. A. Masters, *Bakunin, the father of anarchism*, p. 236.
42 Lichtheim, p. 63.
43 Ibid., p. 125.
44 Ibid., p. 126.
45 Ralf Dahrendorf, *Class and Class Conflict in Industrial Society*, p. 25.
46 Rubel, 'Socialism and the Commune', in Kamenka (ed.), *Paradigm for Revolution?*, p. 44.

8. THE PROLETARIAT AS AN ECONOMIC CLASS

1 Georg Lukács, for example, wrote: 'Let us assume for the sake of argument that recent research had disproved once and for all every one of Marx's individual theses. Even if this were to be proved, every serious "orthodox" Marxist would still be able to accept all such modern findings without reservation and hence dismiss all of Marx's theses *in toto*—without having to renounce his orthodoxy for a single moment.... [O]rthodoxy refers exclusively to *method*', 'What is Orthodox Marxism?', *History and Class Consciousness*, p. 1.
2 Able Marxists nowadays acknowledge areas of continuing difficulty in Marx's economics, especially those related to the labour theory of value. See, for example, the discussions by Terrell Carver, *Marx's Social Theory*, Chapter 6, and by Ernest Mandel, 'Economics', in D. McLellan (ed.), *Marx: the First Hundred Years*, pp. 220–34.
3 Some of these criticisms are longstanding. The attack on Marx's economics was begun in earnest by Böhm-Bawerk (*Karl Marx and the Close of His System*) soon after the publication in 1894 of *Capital* III. See also Joan Robinson, *Economic Philosophy*, Chapter 2, for the

view that the labour theory of value is metaphysical.

4   Ernest Mandel, *Marxist Economic Theory*, p. 150.

5   Mandel, for example, supports it on p. 166; Kolakowski rejects it: *Main Currents of Marxism*, Vol. 1, p. 298.

6   Dahrendorf, pp. 21–2 and 136–41.

7   Lichtheim, pp. 58–9. Although Marx expressed a debt to Engels' 'Outlines of a Critique of Political Economy', published in the *Deutsch-französische Jahrbücher* (see, for example, *Collected Works*, Vol. 3, p. 232), and his work amplifies some of the issues raised there, it was not the potential of the productive worker which animated Engels, but the potential of industry; and the merchant, not the capitalist, was Engels' main target. Engels declared: 'This political economy or science of enrichment born of the merchants' mutual envy and greed, bears on its brow the mark of the most detestable selfishness' (ibid., p. 418).

8   See Chapter Three, Note 87. As early as May 1843, Engels had identified 'proletarians' as 'working men'; see his 'Letters from London', *Collected Works*, Vol. 3, p. 379.

9   Tucker, *Philosophy and Myth*, p. 165.

10 Ibid., p. 221.

11 Ibid., p. 203. Daniel Bell, among others, has made much the same point; see D. Bell, 'The Debate on Alienation', in L. Labedz (ed.), *Revisionism, Essays on the History of Marxist Ideas*, p. 202. Kamenka adds that Marx's 'totalism' 'forces him—since his new underlying reality is to be society and no longer Man—to minimise any specific human characteristics and to treat man as no more than a reflection or product of social relations' (*The Ethical Foundations*, p. 131); thus historical materialism becomes a form of economic reductionism, and man himself is effectively diminished in stature.

12 Kolakowski, Vol. 1, p. 321.

13 Avineri, *The Social and Political Thought of Karl Marx*, p. 73. See also p. 79, where Avineri argues that for Marx 'History is not only the story of the satisfaction of human needs but also the story of their emergence and development'.

14 E. Mandel, *The Formation of the Economic Thought of Karl Marx*, p. 23.

15 Barbalet, p. 136. Marx, it should be noted, never identified the proletariat with poverty pure and simple, even though in *The Holy Family* he declared that 'Proletariat and wealth are opposites' (*Collected Works*, Vol. 4, p. 35). He linked its poverty with modern industry (see ibid., Vol. 3, p. 195), and specifically dissociated proletarians from the 'ragamuffins' who had existed 'in every epoch' (ibid., Vol. 5, p. 202).

16 Barbalet, p. 137.

17 Marx, *Capital*, Vol. 1, especially Part V.

18 See ibid., p. 477.

19 Ralph Miliband, for example, argues that the notion of 'productive labour' extends the definition of the proletariat beyond factory workers to include writers and other 'mental' labourers; see *Marxism and Politics*, pp. 23–4.

20 Marx described the English Factory Acts as 'compulsion from society'

against the capitalist: *Capital*, Vol. 1, p. 257.

21 Graeme Duncan claims that Marx's immiserization thesis has four possible meanings which are not mutually exclusive, depending on whether an increase in misery is absolute or relative, and on whether it refers to material living standards, or includes psychological and other considerations; G. Duncan, *Marx and Mill*, p. 115.

22 R.M. Hartwell has argued that the real wages of English workers rose during the period from the 1790s to the 1840s because the price of important consumer goods fell; see R.M. Hartwell, 'The Rising Standard of Living in England, 1800–1850', *The Economic History Review*, second series, XIII, No. 3, 1961, pp. 397–416, especially pp. 404–12.

23 Marx also weakened his ethical case against capitalism when he argued, from the time of the *Grundrisse* onwards, that the labourer was not a commodity, but his labour-power was.

24 Alan Gilbert, *Marx's Politics*, treats Marx as a Leninist.

25 Frank Parkin, *Marxism and Class Theory, A Bourgeois Critique*, p. 25.

26 Marx never properly considered the capitalist function of investment, or capitalism as a system of trial and error. In his model, capital was only a success story. Thus he never addressed the question how investment would be determined under the rule of the producers. This criticism was made determinedly by Ludwig von Mises, *Socialism, an Economic and Sociological Analysis*, especially pp. 186–91.

27 Tucker, *Philosophy and Myth*, p. 199.

9. CONCLUSION

1 Lenin, *The Three Sources and Three Component Parts of Marxism*, *Selected Works*, Vol. I, p. 44. See also Lenin, *Karl Marx*, ibid., p. 19.

2 Cited Ionescu (ed.), p. 182.

3 T.B. Bottomore and M. Rubel, 'Marx's Sociology and Social Philosophy', K. Marx, *Selected Writings in Sociology and Social Philosophy*, p. 42.

4 T.B. Bottomore, *Marxist Sociology*, p. 11.

5 R. Miliband, *Marxism and Politics*, p. 22.

6 J. Plamenatz, *German Marxism, Russian Communism*, p. 35.

7 G. Duncan, *Marx and Mill*, p. 123.

8 S. Ossowski, *Class Structure in the Social Consciousness*, p. 143.

9 Ibid., p. 143.

10 Ibid., p. 73.

11 See Rosen, p. 236; Rubel, *Karl Marx, Essai de Biographie Intellectuelle*, p. 100; and Rubel, 'Notes sur le prolétariat et sa Mission', *Marx Critique du Marxisme*, p. 194.

12 R.C. Tucker, *Philosophy and Myth in Karl Marx*, p. 114.

13 In 1880, Marx drew up an '*enquête ouvrière*', a questionnaire for the French socialist party, but whether or not it was used it added nothing to his knowledge of the actual working class. See M. Rubel and M. Manale, *Marx Without Myth*, p. 317.

14 A. Callinicos, *Is There a Future for Marxism?*, p. 225.

Bibliography of Works Cited

ADAMS, H.P., *Karl Marx in his earlier writings*, Frank Cass, London, 1965 (first edition 1940).

ADELMAN, F. J. (ed.), *Demythologizing Marxism, A Series of Studies on Marxism*, Martinus Nijhoff, The Hague, 1969.

AGULHON, M., *Une Ville ouvrière au Temps du Socialisme utopique, Toulon de 1815 à 1851*, Mouton, Paris, 1970.

ALTHUSSER, L., *For Marx*, translated B. Brewster, NLB, London, 1969.

ANGRAND, P., 'Notes critiques sur la formation des idées communistes en France', *La Pensée*, No. 19, pp. 38-46, and No. 20, pp. 57-67, 1948.

ARON, R., *The Opium of the Intellectuals*, translated T. Kilmartin, Secker and Warburg, London, 1957.

AVINERI, S., *The Social and Political Thought of Karl Marx*, CUP, Cambridge, 1968.

AVINERI, S., *Hegel's Theory of the Modern State*, CUP, Cambridge, 1972.

AVINERI, S. (ed.), *Marx's Socialism*, Lieber-Atherton, NY, 1973.

AVINERI, S., 'Marx and Jewish Emancipation', *Journal of the History of Ideas*, Vol. 25, No. 3, 1964, pp. 445-50.

BARBALET, J.M., *Marx's Construction of Social Theory*, Routledge and Kegan Paul, London, 1983.

BENEWICK, R., BERKI, R. N., and PAREKH, B., *Knowledge and Belief in Politics, The Problem of Ideology*, Allen and Unwin, London, 1973.

BÉRANGER, C., `Pétition d'un Prolétaire à la Chambre des Députés', *Le Globe* (Journal de la doctrine de Saint-Simon), No. 34, 5 February 1831.

BERDYAEV, N., *The Russian Revolution. Two Essays on its Implications in Religion and Psychology*, translated D.B., Sheed and Ward, London and NY, 1933.

BERKI, R. N., *Socialism*, Dent, London, 1975.

BEZUCHA, R.J., *The Lyon Uprising of 1834, Social and Political Conflict in the Early July Monarchy*, Harvard University Press, Massachusetts, 1974.

BEZUCHA, R.J., 'The French Revolution of 1848 and the Social History of Work', *Theory and Society*, Vol. 12, No. 4, July 1983, pp. 469-84.

BLANC, L., *Histoire de Dix Ans, 1830-1840*, Librairie Germer Bailliere, Paris, twelfth edition, 1877 (Vol. 3), 1880 (Vol. 5).

BLANQUI, A., *Histoire de l'Économie Politique en Europe, depuis les anciens jusqu'à nos jours*, Librairie Guillaumin, Paris, 1882 (fifth edition; first edition 1837).

BLANQUI, A., *Textes Choisis*, Editions sociales, Paris, 1971.

BOHM-BAWERK, E. Von, *Karl Marx and the Close of His System*, edited P.M. Sweezy, Kelley, Clifton, 1975 (reprint of 1949 edition).

Bibliography

BOTTOMORE T.B., *Marxist Sociology*, Macmillan, London, 1975.

BRAUNTHAL J., *A History of the International 1864-1914*, translated H. Collins and K. Mitchell, Nelson, London, 1966.

BRAZILL, W.J., *The Young Hegelians*, Yale University Press, New Haven, 1970.

BRIEFS, G.A., *The Proletariat. A Challenge to Western Civilization*, McGraw-Hill, NY and London, 1937.

BRUHAT, J., *Histoire du Mouvement ouvrier français, Vol. 1, Des Origines a la Révolte des Canuts*, Editions sociales, Paris, 1952.

CALLINICOS, A., *Is there a future for Marxism?*, Macmillan, London, 1982.

CALLINICOS, A., *Marxism and Philosophy*, OUP, Oxford, 1983.

CARLEBACH, J., *Karl Marx and the Radical Critique of Judaism*, Routledge and Kegan Paul, London, 1978.

CARLYLE, T., *Selected Writings*, edited A. Shelston, Penguin, Harmondsworth, 1971.

CARVER, T., *Marx's Social Theory*, OUP, Oxford, 1982.

CHEVALIER, L., *Classes laborieuses et Classes dangereuses à Paris pendant la premiére moitié du XIXe siècle*, Librairie Plon, Paris, 1958.

COLE, G.D.H., *A History of Socialist Thought*, Vols. I and II, Macmillan, London, 1953 and 1954.

COLE, G.D.H., and FILSON, A.W. (eds.), *British Working Class Movements. Select Documents, 1789-1875*, Macmillan, London, 1951.

COLLINS, H. and ABRAMSKY, C., *Karl Marx and the British Labour Movement, Years of the First International*, Macmillan, London, 1965.

COMTE A., *A System of Positive Polity*, Vol. 1, translated J.H. Bridges, Burt Franklin, NY, reprint of 1875 edition.

COORNAERT, E., *Les Compagnonnages en France, du Moyen Age à Nos Jours*, Les Editions ouvrières, Paris, 1966.

COORNAERT, E., 'La pensée ouvrière et la conscience de classe en France de 1830 à 1848', *Studi in Onore di Gino Luzzato*, Milano, Vol. 3, 1949-50, pp. 12-33.

CORCORAN, P. E., 'The Bourgeois and Other Villains', *Journal of the History of Ideas*, Vol. 38, No. 3, 1977, pp. 477-85.

CORNU, A., *Karl Marx and Friedrich Engels. Leur vie et leur oeuvre*, PUF, Paris, Vol. I, 1955; Vol. II, 1958.

CUVILLIER, A., *Hommes et Idéologies de 1840*, Marcel Rivière, Paris, 1956.

DAHRENDORF, R., *Class and Class Conflict in Industrial Society*, Routledge and Kegan Paul, London, 1959.

DOCTRINE de Saint-Simon, Exposition, Marcel Rivière, Paris, 1924 (first edition 1829).

THE DOCTRINE of Saint-Simon: An Exposition, First Year 1828-1829, translated G.G. Iggers, Beacon Press, Boston, 1958.

DOLLÉANS, E., *Histoire du Mouvement ouvrier*, Vol. I, Librairie Armand Colin, Paris, 1948 (fourth edition; first edition 1936).

DROZ, J., *Europe Between Revolutions, 1815-1848*, Fontana, Glasgow, 1967.

DROZ, J. (ed.), *Histoire Générale du Socialisme, Tome I: Des Origines à 1875*, PUF, Paris, 1972.

DUNCAN, G., *Marx and Mill: two views of social conflict and social harmony*, CUP, Cambridge, 1973.

DUPRE, L., *The Philosophical Foundations of Marxism*, Harcourt, Brace and World, Inc., NY, 1966.

FELIX, D., *Marx as Politician*, Southern Illinois University Press, Carbondale, 1983.

FEUER, L. S., *Ideology and the Ideologists*, Blackwell, Oxford, 1975.

FLINN, M.W. and SMOUT, T. C. (eds.), *Essays in Social History*, Clarendon Press, Oxford, 1974.

GARAUDY, R., *Les sources françaises du Socialisme scientifique*, Hier et Aujourd'hui, Paris, 1949.

GILBERT, A., *Marx's Politics: Communists and Citizens*, Martin Robertson, Oxford, 1981.

GRAY, A., *The Socialist Tradition: Moses to Lenin*, Harper and Row, NY, 1968 (first edition 1946).

GRUNER, S., 'The Revolution of July 1830 and the Expression "Bourgeoisie"', *The Historical Journal*, Vol. 11, No. 3, 1968, pp. 462-71.

GURVITCH, G., *La Vocation actuelle de la Sociologie vers une Sociologie différentielle*, PUF, Paris, 1950.

HALÉVY, E., *England in 1815*, translated E. I. Watkin and D. A. Barker, Ernest Benn Ltd., London, 1949 (second, revised, edition).

HAMMEN, O. J., *The Red '48ers. Karl Marx and Friedrich Engels*, Charles Scribner's Sons, NY, 1969.

HARTWELL, R.M., 'The Rising Standard of Living in England, 1800-1850', *The Economic History Review*, second series, Vol. XIII, No. 3, 1961, pp. 397-416.

HEGEL, G.W.F., *Hegel's Lectures on the History of Philosophy*, Volumes I and II, translated E. S. Haldane, Routledge and Kegan Paul, London, 1892.

HEGEL, G.W.F., *The Phenomenology of Mind*, translated J.B. Baillie, Allen and Unwin, London, 1931 (second edition).

HEGEL, G.W.F., *Hegel's Philosophy of Right*, translated T.M. Knox, Clarendon Press, Oxford, 1952.

HELLER, A., *The theory of need in Marx*, Allison and Busby, London, 1976.

HOBSBAWM, E. J., *The Age of Revolution, 1789-1848*, Mentor, NY, 1962.

HOOK, S., *From Hegel to Marx. Studies in the Intellectual Development of Karl Marx*, Gollancz, London, 1936.

HOWARD, D., *The Development of the Marxian Dialectic*, Southern Illinois University Press, Carbondale and Edwardsville, 1972.

JOHNSON, C.H., 'Etienne Cabet and the Problem of Class Antagonism', *International Review of Social History*, Vol. XI, 1966, pp. 403-43.

KÄGI, P., *Genesis des historischen Materialismus: Karl Marx und die Dynamik der Gesellschaft*, Europa Verlag, Wien, 1965.

KAMENKA, E., *The Ethical Foundations of Marxism*, Routledge and Kegan Paul, London, 1962.

KAMENKA, E., *Marxism and Ethics*, Macmillan, London, 1969.

KAMENKA, E., *The Philosophy of Ludwig Feuerbach*, Routledge and Kegan Paul, London, 1970.

KAMENKA, E. (ed.), *Paradigm for Revolution? The Paris Commune 1871-1971*, ANU Press, Canberra, 1972.

KAMENKA, E. and KRYGIER, M. (eds.), *Bureaucracy, The Career of a Concept*, Edward Arnold, London, 1979.

KAMENKA, E. and SMITH, F.B. (eds.), *Intellectuals and Revolution, Socialism and the Experience of 1848*, Edward Arnold, London, 1979.

KAMENKA, E., 'The Baptism of Karl Marx', *The Hibbert Journal*, Vol. LVI, 1958, pp. 340-51.

KESSEL, P., *Le Prolétariat français. Avant Marx. 1789-1830-1848. Les Révolutions escamotées*, Plon, Paris, 1968.

KIRKUP, T., *A History of Socialism*, Black, London, 1913 (fifth edition, revised by E.R. Pease).

KOLAKOWSKI, L., *Main Currents of Marxism. Its rise, growth and dissolution*, translated P.S. Falla, Clarendon Press, Oxford, 1978.

KOLAKOWSKI, L. and HAMPSHIRE, S. (eds.), *The Socialist Idea, a reappraisal*, Weidenfeld and Nicolson, London, 1974.

KUCZYNSKI, J., *The Rise of the Working Class*, translated C. T.A. Roy, Weidenfeld and Nicolson, London, 1973.

LABEDZ, L. (ed.), *Revisionism, Essays on the History of Marxist Ideas*, Allen and Unwin, London, 1962.

LABROUSSE, E., *Le Mouvement ouvrier et les Théories sociales en France de 1815 à 1848*, Centre de Documentation Universitaire, Paris, 1961.

LAIDLER, H., *History of Socialism, A Comparative Survey of Socialism, Communism, Trade Unionism, Cooperation, Utopianism, and other Systems of Reform and Reconstruction*, Cromwell, NY, 1968.

LAMENNAIS, F., *De l'Ésclavage Moderne*, Pagnerre, Paris, 1840 (fourth edition).

LARRAIN, J., *The Concept of Ideology*, Hutchinson, London, 1979.

LENIN, V.I., *Collected Works*, Vols. 8 and 9, Progress, Moscow, 1977.

LENIN, V.I., *Selected Works* (in three volumes), Vol. I, Progress, Moscow, 1975.

LEROUX, J., *Le Prolétaire et le Bourgeois. Dialogue sur la question des salaires*, Michel Fossone, Paris, 1840.

LEROUX, P., 'Cours d'économie politique, fait a l'Athénée de Marseille, par M. Jules Leroux', *Revue Encyclopédique*, October-December 1833, pp. 94-117.

LEROY, M., *Histoire des Idées sociales en France, de Babeuf à Tocqueville*, nrf, Paris, 1950 (fifth edition).

LEROY, M., *Le Socialisme des Producteurs, Henri de Saint-Simon*, Marcel Rivière, Paris, 1924.

LEVASSEUR, E., *Histoire des Classes ouvrieres et de l'Industrie en France de 1789 à 1870*, A. Rousseau, Paris, 1903-1904 (second edition in two volumes).

LICHTENBERGER, A., *Le Socialisme et la Révolution française, Étude sur les Idées socialistes en France de 1789 à 1796*, Slatkine Reprints, Genève, 1970 (reprint of 1899 edition).

LICHTHEIM, G., *Marxism: An Historical and Critical Study*, Routledge and Kegan Paul, London, 1971 (second edition; first edition 1961).

LICHTHEIM, G., *The Origins of Socialism*, Praeger, NY, 1969.

LICHTHEIM, G., *A Short History of Socialism*, Fontana, Glasgow, 1975 (first edition 1970).

LICHTHEIM, G., 'The Concept of Ideology', *History and Theory*, Vol. IV, No. 2, 1965, pp. 164-95.

LIPSET, S.M., 'Whatever Happened to the Proletariat? An Historic Mission Unfulfilled', *Encounter*, Vol. LVI, No. 6, June 1981, pp. 18-34.

LOBKOWICZ, N. (ed.), *Marx and the Western World*, University of Notre Dame Press, Notre Dame, 1967.

LOVELL, D.W., *From Marx to Lenin. An Evaluation of Marx's Responsibility for Soviet Authoritarianism*, CUP, Cambridge, 1984.

LÖWITH, K., *From Hegel to Nietzsche, the revolution in nineteenth-century thought*, translated D.E. Green, Constable, London, 1965.

LOWY, M., *La théorie de la révolution chez le jeune Marx*, Maspero, Paris, 1970.

LUBASZ, H., 'Marx's Initial Problematic: The Problem of Poverty', *Political Studies*, Vol. 24, 1976, pp. 24-42.

LUKACS, G., *History and Class Consciousness. Studies in Marxist Dialectics*, translated R. Livingstone, MIT Press, Massachusetts, 1971.

McCARTHY, T., *Marx and the Proletariat. A Study in Social Theory*, Greenwood Press, Connecticut, 1978.

McLELLAN, D., *The Young Hegelians and Karl Marx*, Macmillan, London, 1969.

McLELLAN, D., *Karl Marx: His Life and Thought*, Macmillan, London, 1973.

McLELLAN, D. (ed.), *Marx: the First Hundred Years*, Fontana, Great Britain, 1983.

MAGUIRE, J., *Marx's Paris Writings: an Analysis*, Gill and Macmillan, Dublin, 1972.

MANDEL, E., *Marxist Economic Theory*, translated B. Pearce, Merlin, London, 1968.

MANDEL, E., *The Formation of the Economic Thought of Karl Marx, 1843 to 'Capital'*, translated B. Pearce, Monthly Review Press, NY and London, 1971.

MANHEIM, K., *Ideology and Utopia, An Introduction to the Sociology of Knowledge*, translated L. Wirth and E. Shils, Routledge and Kegan Paul, London, 1936.

MARCUSE, H., *Reason and Revolution, Hegel and the Rise of Social Theory*, Routledge and Kegan Paul, London, 1955 (second edition; first edition 1941).

Bibliography

MARCUSE, H., *One Dimensional Man*, Sphere, London, 1968 (first edition 1964).

MARCUSE, H., *Negations. Essays in Critical Social Theory*, translated J. J. Shapiro, Allen Lane, London, 1968.

MARX, K., *Critique of Hegel's 'Philosophy of Right'*, edited J. O'Malley, translated A. Jolin and J. O'Malley, CUP, Cambridge, 1970.

MARX, K., *Selected Writings in Sociology and Social Philosophy*, edited T. B. Bottomore and M. Rubel, translated T. B. Bottomore, Penguin, Harmondsworth, 1963 (second edition; first edition 1956).

MARX, K., *The Letters of Karl Marx*, edited and translated S.K. Padover, Prentice-Hall, New Jersey, 1979.

MARX, K., *The First International and After*, edited D. Fernbach, Penguin, Harmondsworth, 1974.

MARX, K., *On the First International*, edited and translated S. K. Padover, McGraw-Hill, NY, 1973.

MARX, K., *Grundrisse, Foundations of the Critique of Political Economy (Rough Draft)*, translated M. Nicolaus, Allen Lane, London, 1973.

MARX, K., *Capital. A Critique of Political Economy*, Vols. I-III, Progress, Moscow, 1954-59.

MARX, K. and ENGELS, F., *Selected Works* (in three volumes), Progress, Moscow, 1976.

MARX, K. and ENGELS, F., *Selected Correspondence*, FLPH, Moscow, 1956.

MARX, K. and ENGELS, F., *Collected Works*, Lawrence and Wishart and Progress, London and Moscow, 1975.

MASTERS A., *Bakunin, the father of anarchism*, Sedgwick and Jackson, London, 1974.

MERRIMAN, J.M. (ed.), *Consciousness and Class Experience in Nineteenth-Century Europe*, Holmes and Meier, NY, 1979.

MEYER, A. G., *Marxism, The Unity of Theory and Practice: a Critical Essay*, Harvard University Press, Massachusetts, 1954.

MILIBAND, R., *Marxism and Politics*, OUP. Oxford, 1977.

MONTESQUIEU, C. L. de S., *The Spirit of Laws*, translated T. Nugent, Hafner, NY, 1949.

MOSS, B. H., *The Origins of the French Labour Movement 1830-1914. The Socialism of Skilled Workers*, University of California Press, Berkeley, 1976.

NICOLAIEVSKY, B. and MAENCHEN-HELFEN, O., *Karl Marx: Man and Fighter*, translated G. David and E. Mosbacher, Penguin, Harmondsworth, 1976.

NIELSON, K. (ed.), *Marx and Morality*, Supplementary Volume to *The Canadian Journal of Philosophy*, 1981.

NORMAN, R., *Hegel's Phenomenology: A Philosophical Introduction*, Humanities Press, New Jersey, 1976.

OLLMAN, B., *Alienation. Marx's Conception of Man in Capitalist Society*, CUP, Cambridge, 1976 (second edition; first edition 1971).

OSSOWSKI, S., *Class Structure in the Social Consciousness*, translated S. Patterson, Routledge and Kegan Paul, London, 1963.

PAREKH, B., *Marx's Theory of Ideology*, Croom Helm, London, 1982.

PARKIN, F., *Marxism and Class Theory. A Bourgeois Critique*, Tavistock, London, 1979.

PARKINSON, G.H.R. (ed.), *Marx and Marxisms*, CUP, Cambridge, 1982.

PELCZYNSKI, Z. A. (ed.), *Hegel's Political Philosophy, problems and perspectives. A collection of new essays*, CUP, Cambridge, 1971.

PLAMENATZ, J., *The Revolutionary Movement in France, 1815-71*, Longmans, Green and Co., London, 1952.

PLAMENATZ, J., *German Marxism and Russian Communism*, Longman, London, 1954.

PLAMENATZ, J., *Ideology*, Macmillan, London, 1971.

PLANT, R., *Hegel. An Introduction*, Blackwell, Oxford, 1983 (second edition; first edition 1972).

PROUDHON, P-J., *Oeuvres complètes de P-J. Proudhon*, (sous la direction de C. Bougle et H. Moysset), Riviere, Paris, 1926-27.

RABINOWITCH, A. and J. (eds.), *Revolution and Politics in Russia, Essays in Memory of B.I. Nicolaevsky*, Indiana University Press, Bloomington, 1972.

REYNAUD, J., 'De la Nécessité d'une Représentation spéciale pour les Prolétaires', *Revue Encyclopédique*, April 1832, pp. 5-20.

RIASANOVSKY, N.V., *The Teaching of Charles Fourier*, University of California Press, Berkeley, 1969.

ROBINSON, J., *Economic Philosophy*, Penguin, Harmondsworth, 1964.

ROHR, D.G., *The Origins of Social Liberalism in Germany*, University of Chicago Press, Chicago, 1963.

ROSE, R.B., 'Prolétaires and Prolétariat: Evolution of a Concept, 1789-1848', *Australian Journal of French Studies*, Vol. XVIII, No. 3, 1981, pp. 282-99.

ROSEN, Z., *Bruno Bauer and Karl Marx. The influence of Bruno Bauer on Marx's Thought*, Martinus Nijhoff, The Hague, 1977.

ROUSSEAU, J.J., *The Social Contract and Discourses*, translated G. D. H. Cole, Dent, London, 1916.

RUBEL, M., *Karl Marx. Essai de Biographie intellectuelle*, Rivière, Paris, 1957.

RUBEL, M., *Marx Critique du Marxisme. Essais*, Payot, Paris,1974.

RUBEL, M. and MANALE, M., *Marx Without Myth. A Chronological Study of his Life and Work*, Blackwell, Oxford, 1975.

SAGARRA, E., *A Social History of Germany 1648-1914*, Methuen, London, 1977.

SAINT-SIMON, H., *Oeuvres de Saint-Simon et d'Enfantin*, Zeller, Aalen, 1963-64.

SARTORI, G., 'Constitutionalism: A Preliminary Discussion', *American Political Science Review*, Vol. 59, 1962, pp.853-64.

SEIGEL, J., *Marx's Fate. The Shape of a Life*, Princeton University Press, New Jersey, 1978.

SELIGER, M., *The Marxist Conception of Ideology. A Critical Essay*, CUP, Cambridge, 1977.

SEWELL, W.H. Jr., *Work and Revolution in France. The language of labor from the old regime to 1848*, CUP,Cambridge, 1980.

SEWELL, W.H. Jr., 'Social Change and the Rise of Working-Class Politics in Nineteenth-Century Marseille', *Past and Present*, No. 65, November 1974, pp. 75-109.

SIÉYES, E.J., *What is the Third Estate?*, edited S.E.Finer, translated M. Blondel, Pall Mall, London, 1963.

SIMONDE de SISMONDI, J.C.L., *Nouveaux Principes d'économie politique; ou, De la richesse dans ses rapports avec la population*, Edition Jeheber, Geneva, 1951–53 (third edition).

SIMONDE de SISMONDI, J.C.L., *Political Economy*, Kelley, NY, 1966.

SOREL, G., *Reflections on Violence*, translated T.E. Hulme and J. Roth, Collier, NY, 1961.

STEIN, L. Von, *The History of the Social Movement in France, 1789-1850*, edited and translated K. Mengelberg, Bedminster, New Jersey, 1964.

STEPELEVICH, L.S. (ed.), *The Young Hegelians, An Anthology*, CUP, Cambridge, 1973.

STIRNER, M., *The Ego and His Own*, edited J. J. Martin, translated S.T. Byington, Libertarian Book Club, NY, 1963.

SWINGEWOOD, A., *Marx and Modern Social Theory*, Macmillan, London, 1975.

TAYLOR, C., *Hegel*, CUP, Cambridge, 1975.

THIERRY, A., *Oeuvres de Thierry*, Vol. IV, Furne, Paris, 1864.

TOCQUEVILLE, A. de, *The Recollections of Alexis de Tocqueville*, edited J.P. Mayer, translated A. Teixeira de Mattos, Harvill, London, 1948.

TRISTAN, F., *Union Ouvrière*, Editions d'Histoire Sociale, Paris, 1967 (reprint of 1844 edition).

TUCKER, R.C., *Philosophy and Myth in Karl Marx*, CUP, Cambridge, 1972 (second edition; first edition 1961).

TUCKER, R.C., *The Marxian Revolutionary Idea*, Norton, NY, 1969.

ULAM, A.B., *The Unfinished Revolution. An Essay on the Sources of Influence of Marxism and Communism*, Random House, NY, 1960.

VON MISES, L., *Socialism, An Economic and Sociological Analysis*, translated J. Kahane, Liberty Classics, Indianapolis (follows second English edition of 1969).

WARTOFSKY, M., *Feuerbach*, CUP, Cambridge, 1977.

WEISS, J., *Moses Hess. Utopian Socialist*, Wayne State University Press, Detroit, 1960.

WEYL, N., *Karl Marx: Racist*, Arlington House, NY, 1979.

WISTRICH, R.S., *Revolutionary Jews, from Marx to Trotsky*, Harrap, London, 1976.

Index